HOUNDS
IN THE
MORNING

HOUNDS IN THE MORNING

SUNDRY SPORTS OF MERRY ENGLAND

Selections from
THE SPORTING
MAGAZINE
1792–1836

EDITED BY

Carl B. Cone

THE UNIVERSITY PRESS OF KENTUCKY

Library of Congress Cataloging in Publication Data

Main entry under title:
Hounds in the morning.

  Bibliography: p.
  1. Sports—England—History—19th century—Addresses, essays, lectures. I. Cone, Carl B.
II. Sporting magazine.
GV605.H68   796'.0942   81-51017
ISBN 978-0-8131-5179-3   AACR2

Copyright © 1981 by The University Press of Kentucky

Scholarly publisher for the Commonwealth,
serving Berea College, Centre College of Kentucky,
Eastern Kentucky University, The Filson Club,
Georgetown College, Kentucky Historical Society,
Kentucky State University, Morehead State University,
Murray State University, Northern Kentucky University,
Transylvania University, University of Kentucky,
University of Louisville, and Western Kentucky University.

Editorial and Sales Offices: Lexington, Kentucky 40506

For Regan

Contents

INTRODUCTION 1

Part I. THE SPORTING SCENE
Sporting Intelligence 29

Part II. THE EQUESTRIAN SPORTS
Riding to Hounds 53 • On the Letters of Nimrod 59 • Nim South's Southern Tour 60 • Fox-Hunting 71 • Sporting Trifles 83 • His Majesty's Stag-Hounds 84 • Lord Derby's Stag-Hounds 87 • A Brief Review of the Racing Season of 1828 88 • Eclipse 93 • Guy Stakes at Warwick 95

Part III. A MISCELLANY OF SPORTS
Pedestrianism 99, 103 • The Game at Golf 104 • Skating 108 • Fish and Fishing 109 • Billiards – The Dutch Baron 113 • Pistol and Rifle Shooting 115 • Archery 119 • Royal Kentish Bowmen 120 • A Town Besieged in Time of Peace 121 • The Laws of Cricket 124 • Amazonian Cricket Match 127 • On Throwing the Cricket Ball 129 • Cricket 131

Part IV. THE BLOODY SPORTS
Billy, the Rat-Killer 137 • Bull-Baiting at Bristol 138 • Vindication of Cocking 142 • Fight between Crib and Molineux 144 • A Fresh Challenge 151 • The [Second] Battle between Crib and Molineux 152 • Sparring 158 • Pugilism – between Owen and Mendoza 158 • Wrestling 163 • Shooting Parties 164 • Shooting 165 • Dreadful Accident on Chester Race Course 166 • Sporting Accidents 169 • On Due Discrimination between Barbarous and Fair Sporting 171 • On Mr. Martin's Bill for Animal Protection 174

Part V. THE MARGINS OF SPORTS
May in London 181 • Horse-Dealing in London 182 • Poachers 191 • A Specimen of Some Modern Gamekeepers 193

Part VI. THE PASSING OF YOUTH
Death of the Dowager Marchioness of Salisbury 197

CONCLUSION 201

Sources of Selections 206

A Note on the Illustrations 208

Notes 212

THE Sporting Magazine

OR

MONTHLY CALENDAR

of the

TRANSACTIONS OF

THE TURF, THE CHACE,

And every other Diversion

Interesting to

The Man of Pleasure and Enterprize.

VOLUME THE FIRST.

LONDON.

Printed for the PROPRIETORS, and Sold by J. WHEBLE;
N.º 18, Warwick Square, Warwick Lane, near S.ᵗ Paul's.
MDCCXCIII.

Introduction

During the first half of the nineteenth century, indubitably, and thereafter for a period of arguable length, England was the world's leading sporting nation. This book is concerned with English sports of the period up to about 1835 when, for reasons explained here and in the conclusion, important changes affecting sports manifested themselves in English life. I call this period the youth of modern sports. During these years many sports that were spontaneous, ritualistic, or traditional local activities or recreations—some that King James I referred to approvingly in 1618 in his famous "Declaration of Sports," or that Joseph Strutt described in *Sports and Pastimes of the People of England* (1801)—either had ceased to exist or were dying away as England's rural preindustrial society changed into an urban industrial society. The major sports also changed, taking on a national character under new and clearer agreed definitions (that is, rules) administered by accepted private governing bodies of sportsmen whose authority extended throughout the nation.

In the period of concern here, English national sports became not only well organized as compared with earlier times but better organized than those of any other nation, foreshadowing the high degree of organization and centralized control, both national and international, that we know today. Under conditions of the last century, the sporting life, so to speak, passed from youth into the full maturity of almost excessive regulation.

Governments today play roles in sports that would have been inconceivable to sportsmen of the early nineteenth century. With state subsidies, regulatory agencies, and governmental sponsorship—displayed most vividly in the Olympic Games—sports today function in a milieu of public supervision that English gentlemen and players of a century and a half ago would not have tolerated. They lived in an atmosphere of laissez-faire. They were self-sufficient people imbued with the prevailing doctrine of self-help, and thought themselves quite capable of regulating their own affairs, whether in domestic economy or in sports. Only to protect or promote the sporting life they loved were the upper classes ready to use the legislative authority of Parliament, as in the case of the game laws enacted to protect their shooting or hunting interests. Even this was a form of self-help, for the beneficiaries of the game laws were the very men who controlled Parliament or, as justices of the peace, were responsible for enforcing the game laws.

Contrariwise, some magistrates might choose *not* to enforce certain laws, such as those prohibiting boxing, but again to protect the interests of gentleman sportsmen. In September 1811, for example, when the boxing champion Tom Cribb defended his title against the formidable black challenger Tom Molyneux, the fight was held at a site in Leicestershire close to the borders of the counties of Lincoln and Rutland. If the Leicestershire magistrates should intervene, the pugilists and spectators would simply move across the county line. But the magistrates preferred prudence, for many of the spectators were noblemen and gentlemen who had come from all over England for the celebrated match.

Apart from protection, the members of the English sporting world, if they thought of it at all, had no desire for government to concern itself with the regulation of sporting activities. That was their own business as promoters, participants, and spectators, and they thought themselves quite capable of managing their sporting lives. The ethos of the times upheld their freedom to organize and discipline their sports. This they did voluntarily, and better and more fully than it was done in any other nation. In some instances they did it by their own well-defined rules, enforced by their own chosen governing bodies with recognized authority to command nationwide obedience. In other instances they did it by empirically developed codes of etiquette that were self-enforcing. The codes commanded observance because they embodied the traditions of gentlemen which gentlemen imposed upon themselves and which they were honor-bound to obey at the risk of forfeiting the respect of other gentlemen. Thoroughbred racing, ruled by the originally self-constituted and them self-perpetuating Jockey Club, or cricket, governed by the Marylebone Cricket Club, which merely assumed the authority and maintained it unchallenged, were examples of the first kind of self-government. Fox hunting and shooting were examples of the second.

The advanced state of English sports in this period was explained by contemporaries as a consequence of the superiority of England and Englishmen. They had, after all, won Trafalgar and triumphed over Napoleon. The Duke of Wellington is supposed to have said that Waterloo was won on the playing fields of Eton. If he did, he should have added the boxing rings and playing grounds of England. The statement perfectly fit the mood of the nation. The sporting part of the population could see themselves displaying in their sports—fox hunting, boxing, steeple-chasing and others—the courage and manliness they and their compatriots demonstrated in war. Sports, in their mileu, had a nobler justification than mere entertainment and wholesome recreation. Their diversity became fused into a great national endeavor in which English superiority showed itself to the world in sports as much as in war, on the high seas, in the art of government, or in manufacturing and trade.

The leading sports writers of the very early nineteenth century, Pierce Egan and Jonathan (or John) Badcock,[1] were proud patriots (not quite chauvinists) who preached the virtues of sport, especially pugilism, as a source and inspiration for British courage. This virtue belonged to all Englishmen, regardless of class or rank, but most noticeably to the upper and lower classes. It was considered the mark of an Englishman, for example, that he knew the art of self-defense with his bare fists. Sword play was for effete continentals. University and public school scholars were eager to learn boxing as a part of the preparation for life, and this was considered a proper accomplishment for an Englishman. When Lord Barrymore quarreled with a perfumer at Brighton, according to Egan, the perfumer, "being an Englishman," stood up to the noble lord and gave better than he took in fisticuffs. Badcock tells the same story, showing no surprise at the perfumer's prowess, for pugilism came naturally to freeborn Englishmen.[2] In June 1814, when the emperor of Russia, the king of Prussia, and General Blucher visited England, among the entertainments provided for them and their entourages was a sparring exhibition by leading boxers, offered by Lord Lowther in his home in Pall Mall.[3] The European dignitaries were deeply impressed with this display of the peculiarly English sport; General Blucher seemed especially interested in the physique of the English champion, Tom Cribb.

In certain respects, sports were a social equalizer, but the statement needs immediate qualification. Professional boxers came invariably from the working class, and a few attained some social recognition from those above them. The one-time champion John Jackson kept rooms in Bond Street where, until he retired into private life in 1824, he presided as a kind of boxing impresario, teaching boxing to young gentlemen and arranging and supervising matches. Most boxers went from the ring into the tavern business, and their pubs were sporting centers.[4] The Castle Tavern in Holborn was a gathering place for the Fancy (the fight crowd), presided over in succession for nearly the first half of the century by leading boxers Bob Gregson, Tom Belcher, and finally Tom Spring. Tom Cribb, champion from 1809 to 1822, returned in triumph to London after beating Tom Molyneux in their second bout in 1811, and was welcomed in the metropolis as though he were a Caesar or an Alexander returning from the wars. Never fighting again, he lived respectably thereafter as a tavern keeper, and then a baker and confectioner. The most outstanding career of an ex-boxer was that of John Gully, champion in 1808, who quit the ring after only three matches, acquired coal lands, grew rich, developed a successful racing stable, and sat in the House of Commons from 1832 to 1837.

Gully proved the rule. Class distinctions between boxers and their patrons or between fight fans of different stations in life were not at all weakened by the shared interest in boxing or the shoulder rubbing among spectators at a fight. The upper-class spectators gathered between the ring proper and an outer ring, beyond which stood or sat the lower orders, rural or urban. If Jackson was called Gentleman John, he bore only a courtesy title, like the later American pugilist "Gentleman Jim" Corbett.

So it was in other sports. The barriers between classes remained firm. Professional jockeys might win fame and plaudits and even live well but they were not thought of as gentlemen. Common people played cricket, even with or against gentlemen, but the social distinctions remained clear. An athlete might be recognized and applauded for his prowess but his social orbit was restricted. If occasionally his fame earned him some privileges, he was not among or of the privileged classes. Sports had no mission to be a levelling influence, and men did not engage in them as a means of ascending the social ladder. English society did not aspire to egalitarianism.

Because Englishmen defined and organized their indigenous sports earlier than other peoples, in the late eighteenth and early nineteenth centuries, English sports were early available to whatever foreign markets desired to import them. At the same time, Englishmen were moving out into an expanding worldwide empire and taking with them the sports they had grown up with at home and at the schools and universities they had attended. Notable among these organized sports were Thoroughbred racing, fox hunting, and cricket. After the midnineteenth century, while the empire was continuing to expand and these sports with it, two late-developing sports also submitted to firm rules and, once organized, went out into the empire and the foreign markets. These were two forms of the old game of football, now distinguished and disciplined as rugby and soccer. Why soccer more than rugby appealed to non-English peoples is not the concern here, but the fact is that in time it became the most nearly universal of all team sports. It is a nice argument whether or not basketball challenges it today for leadership. Differences in national character may explain all of this. When European countries established colonies, so the saying went, the

Germans at once laid out parade grounds, the French built sidewalk cafes, and the English marked off cricket grounds and race courses.

England could not claim similar patrimonial authority over cruel sports such as boxing, cock fighting, dog fighting, bear baiting, or bull baiting, for in one manner or another these had developed in many countries. Boxing, however, in its modern revival in the early eighteenth century was identified with England. Not until after the middle of the nineteenth century did the championship of England cease to be tantamount to the championship of the world. But even after boxing leadership passed to the United States, the Marquis of Queensberry rules, "made in England" in the 1860s and 1870s, governed the sport. England also produced a particular breed of dog for certain of these sports—the bull dog. That animal was not only marvelously adapted to the uses to which it was put, but had the exceptional virtues of embodying what Englishmen of that self-confident age liked to think of as their unique, manly national character. The bloody sports were immensely popular in England among all classes.

Another popular sport, neither a field sport nor a bloody one, could not by its very nature be claimed as exclusively English. No country could be thought of as the native home of pedestrianism, simply because human beings wherever they live normally have two legs and like to test how fast and how far they can walk or run, either against time or against other persons. But in England, as a national, competitive sport, pedestrianism was more formally developed than elsewhere. It was an individual sport, for the most part. The age of track and field as team sports was yet to come.

The most prestigious sports until well into the nineteenth century were equestrian. In one way or another—in racing, fox hunting, coursing, or coaching—the horse was of pivotal importance. The title of Nimrod's great book *The Chace, The Turf, and The Road* (1837) just about covered the ground.[5] This was an equestrian age and anything involving the horse in trials of speed or endurance or jumping ability attracted interest. Almost everyone knew something about horses, just as today almost everyone knows something about automobiles. Anyone of any importance, and many of no importance, rode or drove horses for purposes of transport and travel, for sport, and for business. The cavalry was the most glamorous of the military services. Fox hunting, stag hunting, Thoroughbred racing, and steeple-chasing were thought to represent best the red-blooded (and blue-blooded) Englishman in the most heroic of recreations and the most striking of postures. A man on horseback cuts a figure that is nobler than a man on foot, as sculptors have known since ancient times.

The sporting writers who became prominent as Egan and Badcock

6 Hounds in the Morning

passed their prime—Nimrod, Nim South, the Druid, Craven—were primarily interested in equestrianism, and notably fox hunting. They discussed equestrian sports at a high level of sophistication and expert knowledge. The magazines for which they wrote, partly because they wrote for them, emphasized equestrianism. That part of the sporting public which bought and read these magazines was deeply engaged with equestrian sports and desired to read about them. The sporting magazines and sporting art of the time may have distorted the importance of equestrian sports, but probably not by much. There are no statistics to back up the statement (and none to refute it), but the literature creates an impression that the horse population in this period, like the human population, was greater than ever before in English history. Unlike the human population, however, it did not continue to grow.

Perhaps England's most illustrious contribution to modern sports was the development of the Thoroughbred horse, with its unique combination of speed, endurance, and high spirit. Along with the development of the breed came a new pattern of racing and an extensive literature, much of it in the form of breeding and racing records. This sport was the achievement of English noblemen and gentlemen, the landed classes which dominated public life in England in the eighteenth and nineteenth centuries. It is not historically accurate to call Thoroughbred racing the sport of kings, even taking into consideration the contributions of Charles II in the seventeenth century.

All modern Thoroughbreds descend in the male line from the mid-eighteenth century English stallions Eclipse, King Herod, and Matchem. Those three traced back to Arabian, Turkish, and Barbary stallions brought to England about half a century earlier to breed with native stock. By the end of the eighteenth century the breed had stabilized so far as to call for an official registry of pedigrees, the General Stud Book, a kind of Burke's Peerage of breeding which established the genealogical criteria of the Thoroughbred. Early in the eighteenth century appeared the first racing calendar, showing that race meetings were being regularly constituted and results recorded. In 1772 James Weatherby began publication of a racing calendar with which Weatherbys are still associated. About 1750 the elite of racing founded the Jockey Club. Its rules for racing at Newmarket gradually won acceptance throughout England, and the Jockey Club became the recognized interpreter of the rules and adjudicator of disputes. The publication in 1797 of its rules for racing gave uniformity to the sport and strongly influenced the conduct of racing in all parts of the world to which the Thoroughbred horse was exported.

The field sports of shooting and fox hunting were also

eighteenth-century definitions. Refinements of etiquette and protocol were essentially completed about the time England was fighting for her life against Napoleon. When peace came, these sports entered into a golden age which lasted over half a century. Agricultural depression and later two twentieth-century world wars, with all the social and economic changes they produced, did not destroy these two sports but did reduce them in relative popularity and extent of participation from their earlier prominence.

Prior to the development in the eighteenth century of a lighter and more reliable sporting gun, rabbits, hares, and game birds were usually hunted by netting or hawking. With the new gun, a flintlock muzzle loader, the sport assumed a new form. The breech loading gun, which gradually replaced the muzzle loader in the nineteenth century, did not change the basic character of the sport except that gentlemen did not need (though they might still desire) attendants to load for them. It was in the era of the flintlock that shooting as a sport for gentlemen and aristocrats and their guests took shape under the aegis of the landowners. Their houses in the country and their staffs of servants provided for the parties of house guests and day guests who had to learn the elaborate rituals of shooting to enjoy the wholesale slaughter of the *grande battue*. Poor shots and careless hunters caused frequent accidents and thus were not delightful guests on shooting parties. But what did one do with the great Duke of Wellington, the first subject in the kingdom? If the soldiers in his army on the Peninsular campaigns or at Waterloo had been as unhandy with guns as he (see p. 170), Napoleon might have remained emperor a few years longer.

Laws passed by Parliament catered to the needs and pleasures of the landed shooters because the landed interest, before the Industrial Revolution got well under way, was accepted by everyone as the nation's greatest interest. It controlled the House of Lords and the House of Commons. Even before the modernization of field shooting, in 1671 Parliament enacted the first and basic modern law to regulate the taking of game. A long and detailed statute, it restricted the taking of game, by whatever method, to owners of land worth at least £100 income a year. The law also forbade the sale of game, thus unintentionally encouraging an active black market much patronized by innkeepers and by dealers who found eager customers among the wealthy, especially in London.

This statute, followed by some two score kindred ones making adjustments to the basic law in the next century and a half, produced chronic tensions between privileged and unprivileged in the countryside. Tensions may be too mild a word—in many instances it was war on a small scale as poachers, often operating in gangs, shot it out with gamekeepers. Because poachers were of the lower classes and gamekeepers acted in the interest of the upper classes, this conflict had the appearance of class warfare. If she had lived in this period, Lady Chatterley would have had to worry about her lover becoming a victim of ambush or a gang shootout. The punishment for poaching was harsh and, as with other parts of the criminal law, jurors, appalled by their power, sometimes refused to convict. Many respectable rural people, small holders and tenants, also detested the game laws, which protected the rabbits and hares that ate their crops, and which widened the gulf between the rural classes. It took half a century to modify the laws, beginning in 1827 with the prohibition of spring guns, the fearsome devices employed to check poachers. An act of 1831 gave the owners of land, even those below the formerly magic figure of £100 annual value, the right to take game on their own property. The act also faced up to reality and human ingenuity by legalizing the sale of game, and made shooting licenses available to all who cared to purchase them, though, of course, landowners still decided who could shoot on their property. The Ground Game Act of 1880 permitted tenants and small occupiers to shoot game to protect their crops. Nevertheless, shooting as a sport retained its exclusive character. Smolderings of chronic rural discontent in the nineteenth century were fueled by the game laws and all they implied about privilege.

Fox hunting remains even now the English sport par excellence. The rules and ritual as they are known today were defined and refined in the last half of the eighteenth century and the early part of the nineteenth. It was in this period that England was divided into "countries" with clearly understood territorial boundaries for each hunt and pack. Subscriptions for the upkeep of the hunt became the norm, though a few men, for one or another reason, kept up packs at their own expense—up to £6,000 a year. With sixty-nine packs formally recognized in 1812 and ninety-one in 1835, with as many as a hundred or more hunters following and many attendants serving a hunt, an approximate number of participants in fox hunting may be estimated.

Discriminating hunters distinguished among the various hunts, judging them by the men who belonged, the packs, or the character of the land forming the hunting country. The Quorn hunt, with its capital at Melton Mowbray, Leicestershire, ranked at the top, and Hugo Meynell of Quorndon Hall was esteemed as the greatest hunter of his or perhaps any era. Near the lower end of the hierarchy of hunting was the Cumberland country on the Scottish border, yet ironically it is a Cumberland hunter whose name is most widely remembered today.

Many who have heard and sung "John Peel" may wonder if Peel was merely a character from folklore. No, he lived and breathed (1776–1854) and avidly hunted foxes most of his life. Although obscure and only locally known in his own day, his fame lives on in the song written by his friend John Woodcock Graves, to the tune of an old border rant, "Bonnie Annie":

> D'ye ken John Peel with his coat so gray?
> D'ye ken John Peel at the break of day?
> D'ye ken John Peel when he's far, far away,
> With his hounds and his horn in the morning?

The verses are said to have so affected Peel when he first heard them that he shed tears, and Graves exclaimed, "By Jove, Peel, you'll be sung when we're both run to earth!"[6] And so it has been. Neither *The Sporting Magazine*, the *Gentleman's Magazine*, nor the London *Times* published an obituary of Peel, yet his name went round the world with Scottish regiments in Her Majesty's Service in the late Victorian empire. Something of his spirit lives in every fox hunter, and indeed in every sportsman.

Fox hunting had important social impacts. It was not nearly so exclusive or elitist as mythology makes it out to be, though conformance to the code of etiquette was expected of all participants in a hunt, or whatever degree or station in life, from the nobility, gentry, and clergy down to the urban middle-class hunters. R. S. Surtees' portrayal of the scene around Croydon, London, where cockney hunters gathered on a Saturday morning, anticipated the scene around the first tee of a big-city public golf course on a summer Sunday morning in our times. If John Jorrocks, Master of Fox Hounds at Handley Cross, was a fictional character, the portrait was true to life in that, assuming the time and the money, anyone not particularly obnoxious could join a subscription hunt. Townsmen of the middle class journeyed out from the cities to join the country fox hunters, aristocrats and gentlemen. Fox and stag hunting brought town and country together and gave a common pride to the people of a hunting district. It also joined people of all classes in the rural areas in a common endeavor. Except for some individual participants, fox hunting was not an occasional diversion. Packs hunted their districts systematically, frequently, and thoroughly throughout the hunting season. Reynard the Fox as the object of all this attention, and Diana as the sponsoring goddess helped repair the damage the game laws did to the harmony and spirit of rural society.

Because of their role in fox hunting, great attention was paid to the breeding of hounds, as speed was more and more desired, especially

after experience taught that breeding for speed did not adversely affect the hound's "nose." Concomitantly, the need for fast horses became urgent, and Thoroughbred bloodlines entered into the breeding of hunters. At the same time, changes were occurring in the pattern of land distribution. The enclosure of once open fields made the countryside an irregular checkerboard of fields fenced by hedges, and horsemen had to choose according to the abilities of their horses and their own courage or foolhardiness whether to jump the fences, crash through them, or look for gates. Fox hunting became a faster and more dangerous sport, with hounds and horses tearing across the country, taking fences in one way or another.

Like fox hunters, travelers went at a faster pace in keeping with the temper of the times. Contemporaries remarked upon the peculiar propensity for speed among Englishmen. On the improved roads in the great age of coaching—the first half of the nineteenth century—the urge to speed possessed men, and traveling became more hazardous even though roads were better. Writers discussed the merits and deficiencies of various styles of coach building in terms of safety and efficiency, just as motoring writers today discuss automobiles. It was as though coaching interests were trying to delay the inevitable triumph of the faster railroads. Coaching as a sport and a business reached its height just when the railroad threatened to destroy it, just as a century

later the zenith of the railroad age overlapped the beginnings of the age of automobiles and trucks.

From the new character of fox hunting, steeplechasing, with its military ancestry, became more sharply defined. There also evolved a pattern of flat racing in warm weather and obstacle racing in cool weather. Fox hunting was a cold-weather sport, too, with the off months used for regrouping and refreshing for the next season.

The grandeur of the equestrian sports and the elitism of shooting, supported by statute, distinguished them from sports that appeared humbler. But when studied more closely these other sports—pedestrianism, golf, skating, tennis, football, cricket and others—were simply slower or later to develop and become refined, and were practiced by the common people, sometimes in company with the upper classes.

The sporting press treated pedestrianism—walking or running feats—as worthy of generous notice, but sports such as bowls, croquet, tennis, racquet, and golf attracted little attention. When Jem Belcher lost an eye playing racquet in 1803, the event was noticed only because Jem was pugilistic champion. He lost the title two years later to Henry Pearce, the "Game Chicken," and fight fans attributed the loss to his handicap. Bowls and croquet were merely quiet pastimes for people of all ages playing on village greens or private lawns. Golf, played by only a few persons, was always identified as a Scottish game and, like tennis, had a kind of foreign character unappealing to red-blooded Englishmen of that time. Not until almost the last quarter of the century did golf and tennis win attention and emerge from the idiosyncratic, unorganized stage. Angling, by contrast, was a universal sport but with its own history in England. It was an ancient, honorable, and popular sport and achieved a high degree of sophistication perhaps earlier than any other indulged in by Englishmen of this period.

All of these sports steadily became more popular as the nineteenth century progressed, and engaged larger numbers of people as participants and spectators. All sooner or later became more highly organized and supervised by voluntary, private governing bodies, which also presided over national and eventually internationsl competitions. But up to 1835 they remained in their formative stages, and few foresaw their potential for organized and popular competitions before large crowds of spectators.

The place of boxing in the hierarchy of sports is harder to define. It became well organized in the eighteenth century and acquired an unusual social status, being patronized by royalty, aristocracy, and gentlemen. In 1743 John Broughton, himself a champion, lifted boxing above free-for alls and brawls by drawing up rules that governed the sport until modified in 1838 by the London Prize Ring rules. Both sets of rules permitted tactics such as grappling, and did not provide for padded gloves in formal matches. It was forty years before the Marquis of Queensberry rules made those changes. So boxing in the youthful era of sports had its rules and a semblance of private, volunteer organizations, but the use of bare knuckles made it a bloody sport. The Fancy—the dandies or swells or Corinthians, the sons of George III and their cronies, the nobles and gentlemen who followed sports, and especially boxing—loved to see blood flow. This age in England, for all of its gentility, was a cruel one. It punished convicted criminals brutally; it delighted in public executions; it worked the laboring class—men, women, and children—very hard, especially in the factories and mines and docks. This same spirit carried over into the sporting world. Boxers battered one another into pulp; courageous cocks spurred one another into gory, quivering, expiring little mounds of bloodied feathers; dogs chewed at dogs or at defiant bulls or at scurrying rats, while noblemen, gentlemen, shopkeepers, and working men laid bets on the combatants. Cock fighting was a favorite traditional diversion from horses and women at race meetings.

Yet there was something that ennobled boxing. The courage of men who battered one another into bleeding, exhausted, gruesome hulks was both sad and grand, in the way that gladiators in ancient

14 Hounds in the Morning

Rome or cocks in the pits of England were sad and awesome. They faced their destiny—death or mutilation—almost as though it was an unavoidable fate. Jeremy Bentham's Society for Mutual Improvement, after debating the subject in April 1820, decided that it was better for magistrates to yield to public taste than to try to enforce the laws prohibiting boxing.[7] In their view boxing, even though illegal, represented the unique virtues of Englishmen: courage and manliness, generosity toward conquered foes, pride in one's honor and the honor of England, and readiness to defend it. To Pierce Egan, the most widely read sports writer of the first quarter of the nineteenth century, boxing was "truly national," an interest interwoven with the wellbeing of England.[8] The sport was England's sport, and when occasionally a foreigner intruded into it, the English boxer had the honor of England uphold. Tom Molyneux, the black American, was the most formidable challenge to English supremacy in this period. Twice he fought the champion, Tom Cribb, in 1810 and 1811; Cribb barely won the first bout but took the second decisively. The accounts of these fights reveal the currents of racial prejudice and xenophobia that swirled around them.[9]

Ordinarily, questions of race and nationality hardly entered into the sporting scene. Englishmen might sneer at the backward state of French horse racing, but foreigners found no bars to participation in English sports. Only in boxing might this sentiment be felt clearly, and that was because it was a contest between two men in public view. The largest group of fighters not native to England were the Irish, and they never complained about discrimination. English boxing was an entry for them into a better life. Of the two well-known Americans who fought in London in the Regency period, both were black and one was a serious contender for the championship. Bill Richmond, a good boxer, also well regarded personally, lived with perfect freedom in London, where he enjoyed a status as a tavern keeper that he never could have attained in America at that time.

Molyneux was a special case. An ex-slave and an untutored boxer on arrival in England, he sought out Richmond, who gave him support, taught him boxing, and helped him secure matches. He made something of a name for himself and finally gained two matches with Cribb. He was a threat to England's boxing supremacy, and doubly so because he was a black. Precisely because he was a strong threat, Englishmen lost their equanimity. Both of the matches with Cribb were surrounded and infused with muted racism and zenophobia in the press and among the spectators, but happily not demonstrably between the boxers. Yet Cribb could not be unaware that the hopes of England and the white race rested with him, and to lose to Molyneux would be something more than a personal defeat.

Yet if Molyneux encountered these prejudices when he met Cribb, he lived and moved freely about England, Scotland, and Ireland. He created some of his own problems by his ostentatious, flashy manner of conducting himself, and English women embraced him too generously for his own good. His loose life hastened his end, and he died in Dublin in 1818 at about the age of thirty-four.

The Cribb-Molyneux fights, taken together, constituted a unique sporting event in the period under consideration here. Nationalism and racism were absent in the other sports because English supremacy was never at stake, and where social problems existed, they were of a different order.

Despite the great popularity of the bloody sports, as the nineteenth century wore on, a growing number of poeple were repelled by them. England's conscience was urging relaxation of the severity of the criminal law and improvement of working conditions for the laboring classes, and generally aspired to make England a more humane nation. The Evangelicals within the established church and the Methodists were becoming increasingly influential in directing that conscience toward religious and humane ends. Their fervent piety combined with the work ethic of the growing middle class to impart to society a moral tone associated with what is known as the Victorian ethos. This was strong even before Victoria came to the throne in 1837; indeed, it was evident before Victoria was born. Humanitarian sentiments were closely related, and if sometimes they were officious and even misguided, they were well intentioned. These sentiments, which disapproved of pugilism as cruelty of man to man, also abhorred cruelty of man to animals, as when horses were pushed too fast, too far, or too hard, or when men set animals against one another in the ring or the pit. The nobility, the gentry, and the lower orders who patronized bloody sports were all targets of humanitarian attacks in and out of Parliament. Other sports that merited the label, such as hunting or fishing, have never fallen under such widespread opprobrium for cruelty except where there has been a question of endangered species.

Notable among humanitarians was Richard "Humanity" Martin (1754-1834), a founder in 1824 of the Royal Society for the Prevention of Cruelty to Animals. Two years earlier, though not a member of Parliament, he had promoted a statute entitled "An Act to prevent the cruel and improper treatment" of horses, mules, cattle, and sheep, "and other Cattle." The fictional Mr. Jorrocks complained that "Humanity is all the h'order of the day—folks protect other people's donkeys and let their own relations starve." An 1835 statute declared that cock fighting, dog fighting, bull baiting, and badger and bear baiting create "nuisances and annoyances to the neighbourhood—and tend to demoralize" persons who frequent the places where they are conducted. So the act provided for fines against convicted "keepers" of such premises, that is, all persons who helped in some way to conduct such contests.

By their nature, sports have always been more or less rough, and liability to injury has always accompanied them. It is simply that some are rougher than others with injuries a greater risk. But that element has been considered one of the virtues of sport, for sports have been thought to develop character and foster courage and fortitude. Injury or death is always a possibility, but the possibility should not be exaggerated to the point where the sport becomes unjustifiable. And so Pierce Egan wrote of pugilism as a manly sport, and Nimrod thought of fox-hunting in the same way. They frequently used military synonyms and extended the qualities encouraged by sports to the battlefields, where British soldiers exemplified the same manly virtues, to the greater glory of Britain.

Perhaps a distinction should be made between bloody sports and rough sports. It was only after the mid-nineteenth century that the rough mass spectator sports such as we know today came into vogue. Rugby and soccer were two later refinements of what before that time was merely an unorganized, sporadic village or school sport known as football. It was not played on such a scale as to attract attention to the accidents that accompanied its roughness. Later, as football in its two major variations became more sophisticated and professionalized, injuries were more frequent. In our own times, there is some justification for calling them cruel sports, to signify that the numerous injuries, while not necessarily bloody, are often serious and are sometimes caused intentionally, as in American football.

Just as Englishmen for centuries fought with the weapons nature gave them and refined brawling into the science of pugilism, they almost as naturally played games with balls by kicking them or striking them with sticks or clubs from one goal to another. In early disorganized and spontaneous form in England, the men of entire villages would engage against others over hill and dale from one village to another, across the boundaries of intervening parishes. These were often melees so likely to produce riots and mayhem that statutes as far back as the fourteenth century aimed to check them in the interest of public order. It was characteristic of the eighteenth century, with its passion for order and regularity, to attempt to give some uniformity to these recreations of the village greens or the playing fields of the public schools. Voluntary, private effort was equal to the task. In 1787 the newly formed Cricket Club of St. Mary-le-Bone issued rules which were accounted superior to existing understandings. Six years later it revised them and they were published in the new *Sporting Magazine* in June 1793, just a few months after England entered the war against France and in the year when Lord's Cricket Ground opened at its original location. Like the Jockey Club, the Marylebone Cricket Club assumed jurisdiction over its sport and no one disputed its claim. To this day it rules the cricket world, which consists mainly of those countries still or formerly parts of the British Empire and Commonwealth.

Football, like cricket, was a natural village or school sport, but the rules developed sowly in the absence of any authoritative governing body. Generally, however, football acquired a loose pattern, so that in 1823 when, at Rugby, William Webb Ellis carried the ball instead of kicking it, he breached a widely accepted prohibition. Ellis's formative role in the history of football may be similar to that of Abner Doubleday in American baseball, that is, a bit exaggerated. For a generation after Ellis two schools of thought differed over the proprieties of football. The debate ended in gentlemanly fashion when each school devised rules for its game. The London Football Association in 1863 legislated for the kickers, and in 1871 the Rugby Football Union for the carriers. Rugby and soccer went on from there to become international team sports attracting masses of spectators.

For the spectators, the excitement of a sports event was not only in the prowess of the participants, displayed for their own satisfaction and for the admiration of spectators. There was always the ultimate question: Who will win? Human nature compels the sports fan to want to predict the winner, and just as strongly compels support of a prediction with a wager. Likewise the participant, or the owner of a participant, has to demonstrate faith, and how better than by betting? To the pedestrian, for example, the prospect of winning a bet that he could walk an agreed distance in a specified time was a powerful incentive to making the effort. No one suspected any conflict of interest if the athlete bet on himself. Carried to the extreme, the bet becomes more important than the contest, and to those who go to such an extreme, betting becomes an end in itself, even a way of life. Sports offered opportunities for the life of a gambler, and the sporting scene was for bettors what honey is to flies.

In the history of betting, the early nineteenth century constitutes an important chapter. It was an age of betting; stories of impulsive and fantastic wagers, and not only in sports, abound. The development of sports simply multiplied opportunities for wagering. When cocks or dogs or boxers fought or horses ran, people bet on the outcome, not only for the pleasure of making the right choice or the satisfaction in getting back at someone, but also to make money.

In early nineteenth-century England, as since in every time and place, there were people who lived for sports and flourished in the world of sports. Some of them operated in full view, others skulked on the margins in the dark fringes. Without sports, their lives would have been empty; without these people, the picture of the sporting scene would be incomplete, as any reader of Damon Runyon will know. Living "by their wits," they found the wagering, gaming parts of sports exciting, and when the law might intervene to challenge their zeal and enterprise, the challenge added gusto to the sporting life.

On the margins of sports also were those who operated, not as bettors, though they might be called gamblers, but who gambled on their ability, by shady practice, to outwit others. They might be engaged in an established and quite legitimate enterprise, but they brought into it sharp practice or shady dealing. An entire commercial sector—horse dealing—flourished in this equestrian age, and earned a character that has descended to our times. Though not yet an abandoned trade, it has been largely superseded. Today's used car dealer is the descendant of the horse dealer of earlier times. No discussion of the sporting world of the early nineteenth century would be complete if it did not take account of those who operated on the margins of sports, especially the horse dealers.

Another group of persons, these quite legitimate, also came to make their living from sports—the sporting press. With sports so diversified and the sporting public growing larger in the late eighteenth century, it is not surprising that the English press took an increased interest in them. Enterprising entrepreneurs and eager writers developed the new literary specialty of sports journalism. *The Sporting Magazine*, a monthly founded in 1792, and the *Weekly Dispatch*, a Sunday newspaper begun in 1801, attracted a wide and influential readership among people of all ranks in life. Thus, the noblemen and gentlemen who governed England and the press which published sporting news tied the sporting life intimately to the public life of the nation. Even the more staid press, the London *Times* or *Blackwood's Magazine*, began to take notice of sporting events and personalities. By the 1830s it was not at all unusual or shocking for the church and state periodical *The Quarterly Review* to publish sporting pieces.

Among sporting journalists, writers of real talent emerged who wrote both for the sporting press and as literary personages in their own right. Even literary persons not identified with sports could write about them and retain their literary reputations. Thus the essayist William Hazlitt (1778-1839) wrote a famous account of a boxing match. His "The Fight" appeared in the respectable literary periodical *The New Monthly Magazine* in February 1822 over the pseudonym "Phantestes."[10] Though a novice and out of his field, Hazlitt produced a classic sporting piece. Similarly, Thomas Holcroft (1745-1809), the dramatist and author, had worked as a stable boy for Richard, first Earl Grosvenor, and told of his early life in his *Memoirs* (1816). The leading sports writer of the first quarter of the nineteenth century, Pierce Egan, wrote *Life in London* (1821), not about sports as such but largely about the sporting crowd of high and low station. It was a best-seller, widely imitated, and for a while Egan rivalled Sir Walter Scott in popularity. Egan was primarily concerned with sports in the metropolis, and boxing, then in its golden age, was the sport he knew best.

Sporting journalism thus attained literary respectability within a generation after John Wheble in 1792 ventured to introduce the first exclusively sporting periodical, *The Sporting Magazine*,[11] into a society which, he rightly calculated, was ready and eager to receive such a publication. Its success encouraged the appearance of rival sporting magazines. Francis Charles Lawley, an authority on the matter, was correct in saying that *The Sporting Magazine* was the "undoubted prelude" to later well known sporting journals.[12] A natural, even necessary condition of the growth of sporting journalism was its acceptance as a profession. Lawley himself flourished, later in the century, in a tradition of well regarded sports journalism that began in the period of the youth of sports, just a few years before Lawley was born.

Among the gentlemen of the press, Wheble was one of the most enterprising. Born in 1746, he was a London bookseller-publisher who had a varied and successful career in journalism.[13] In October 1792 he brought out the first issue of his new publication in association with a bookseller named Harris. Their venture, *The Sporting Magazine,* bore the subtitle "Monthly Calendar of the Transactions of the Turf, the Chace and every other diversion Interesting to the Man of Pleasure and Enterprize." It was the first magazine "expressly calculated for the Sportsman."[14]

The magazine was a kind of miscellany with no ax to grind. It printed unsigned articles; communications from readers who signed with Latin or other fictitious names; reports of every kind of sport; "Sporting Intelligence," a summary of the preceding month's activities in the field or the pit, on the road or the race course, or on the boxing stage; and, as a regular feature, a racing calendar. In the first number,

Mr. John Wheble

in no particular order of importance, the magazine discussed the origins of horses and horse racing in England, notable pedestrian performances, the history of boxing, two recent boxing contests, the founding of a veterinary college in St. Pancras, the origin of cocking, and a duel. It also printed letters on hunting moose in Cape Breton Island and on "Domestic Hunting," that is, fortune hunting. Succeeding numbers followed this pattern, so that for its first thirty years the magazine had no particular character other than that of an eclectic miscellany. Wheble, already semiretired at Willesden Green, died in 1820, opening the way for changes when his nephews, the Pittman brothers, acquired the magazine. Their greatest inspiration was to employ a writer to contribute regularly to the magazine he had formerly called a "cockney concern." This was Charles James Apperley, who wrote as Nimrod. If not the first sports writer, he was the first gentleman sports writer and became one of the best of that or any time. His chief interests were horses and hunting, especially fox hunting. Perhaps among modern sports writers, John Oaksey of the London *Sunday Telegraph* comes closest to matching Nimrod for writing ability and knowledge of his specialty, the turf, gained from participation and from close attendance upon it.

The editors' announcement of the engagement of Nimrod appeared in *The Sporting Magazine* of January 1822: "Our present Number contains the first of a Series of interesting Letters ... written by a Practical Sportsman, an eye witness of the scenes described." Nimrod introduced himself as though he were an occasional reader rather than a contributor enjoying a salary and expense account: "I have sent you a few remarks, founded on my personal observation" about what is going on in the hunting districts. He would begin, he said, with the premier fox hunting county, Leicestershire, and "if acceptable" would write later of hunting in other counties.[15]

Apperley/Nimrod was a gentleman, born in 1778 into an established Denbighshire family.[16] At the age of eleven he entered Rugby, where he absorbed the sound classical education which so liberally displayed itself in his writings on sports. According to Mr. Jorrocks, he hiccuped Greek and spoke Latin "like a native." On leaving Rugby he served in the cavalry in Ireland during the dangerous, melancholy aftermath of the 1798 uprisings. After this service he married a "dowerless" young lady, a marriage, as readers of Jane Austen will understand, viewed by contemporaries as a financially imprudent one for a young man of his station in life, a gentleman and a second son. He tried to support his family by doing what he knew best, training and selling hunters. His earnings from writing for provincial newspapers supplemented his income and stimulated his literary ambition.

Hard-pressed for money, in 1821 he introduced himself to the new proprietors of *The Sporting Magazine.* Though something of a snob, he had no compunctions about engaging as a sporting writer, especially at an annual salary of £ 1,500 and expenses. He always went first class on his hunting tours, but his employers paid the bills cheerfully because he was so valuable to the magazine. In fact, what he laid out for himself was a new kind of career that would enable him to live well, consort with important people, engage in his favorite sport, and write for publication as a kind of arbiter of fox hunting. He could not foresee that in doing all these things he would in certain circles become one of the most important men in England. He took the name Nimrod after the "mighty hunter" of Scripture who was also "a mighty one in the earth" (Gen. 10:8-9). Few sports writers have approached him in power and influence.

His rival, Surtees, portrayed him as a prig and a kind of dandy, yet Nimrod was said to have a "sunny" disposition. In any case he was the star of the media for a decade after the mid-1820s. This was at the time when boxing was declining and the media star of the preceding two decades, Pierce Egan, whose writing was identified with pugilism, was losing his audience. Speaking in journalistic terms, the age of Egan gave way to the age of Nimrod and Surtees, an era that lasted a little more than a decade.

To say that Nimrod dominated this era is no exaggeration. People crowded around to get his attention as though he carried a microphone and commanded a television camera. His judgment on things pertaining to fox hunting was as important to fox-hunting men as the judgment of a metropolitan drama critic to theatre people. The important thing was that he knew what he was writing about and was also a fine horseman. He was both feared and welcomed as a guest of hunting men and at hunts. It was at the less highly regarded hunts that he was most feared.

One indication of Nimrod's place in the sporting life of his time is the fictional caricature of him produced by his principal rival in sports writing, R. S. Surtees, who signed himself Nim South. In his writings about fox hunting, Surtees created one of the great comic characters of English literature, the grocer fox hunter John Jorrocks, whose money and zealous devotion to the sport elevated him to such a position that he could designate himself M.F.H. A "Master of Fox Hounds" was a man of status, and the cockney tea merchant was able to invite the great "Pomponius Ego" (Nimrod) to inspect the Handley Cross pack and take part in a hunt. Surtees indulged in hyperbole only slightly when he represented Pomponius Ego as a writer whose authority on the printed page could make or ruin the reputation of a fox-hunting man, a pack of fox hounds, or a horse. The passage is worth quoting.

Jorrocks informs his huntsman James Pigg of the impending visit. "You must get all on the square; the great Pomponius Hego is a-coming', and we shall be all down in black and white." Puzzled, the Scotsman Pigg thinks Ego may be a "skeulmaister." No, says the indignant Jorrocks, he is "a master of 'unting—not an M.F.H., like me, but a man wot makes hobserwations on M.F.H.s, their packs, their 'osses, their 'untsmen—their everything, in fact." Pigg remains puzzled. "What's he de that for?" "Vy, that the world at large may know what he thinks on 'em, to be sure. He prints all he sees, hears, or thinks in a book." "Ye dinna say se!"

Jorrocks projects the dire possibilities. "If by any unlucky chance he blames an 'untsman, or condemns a pack, it's all dickey with them for ever; for no livin' man dare contradict him, and every one swears by wot he says." Pigg is properly impressed. "You must exert your hutmost powers," says Jorrocks, "for dash my vig, if we fail, I, even I,—

John Jorrocks himself, will go perfectly mad with rage and wexation."

Pigg allows that he is properly warned of this man who knows all about "hunds and huntin'." Yes, says Jorrocks, "at least he writes about them; and no one disputes print. O dear! oh dear! I almost fear that I've made a mess o' myself, by axin' of him to come. I question if the world would not have been as 'appy without the mighty Hego. Hoil, butter, sugar, soap, all that sort o' thing is werry pleasant; but then—oh, 'orror! the idea of being rubbed the wrong way by Hego! Death itself would be better!" Jorrocks becomes pensive. "Here, for five-and-thirty years, have I been a hardent follower of the chase— . . . and now, when greatness has been thrust upon me—when I shines forth an M.F.H. . . . I may be dashed t' oblivion! Oh, Pigg!—hambition is a frightful, a dreadful thing!"[17]

Nimrod's connection with *The Sporting Magazine* lasted just under a decade and ended over a salary dispute. The issue of February 1830 carried his last contribution, with no hint to readers that he would write no more for the magazine. The relationship was mutually beneficial while it lasted. Nimrod's pieces gave class and character to *The Sporting Magazine*, which knew its greatest days when he wrote for it, and the magazine gave Nimrod a vehicle which carried him a good distance along the road to fame. His later pieces on fox hunting, racing, and coaching appeared in the prestigious literary periodical *The Quarterly Review* in 1832 and 1833, and with slight revision were published as a book, *The Chace, the Turf, and the Road* (1837), that became a classic.

A replacement for Nimrod on *The Sporting Magazine* made his appearance in the issue of June 1830. He was another fox-hunting writer, who signed himself Nim South. He was in reality Robert Smith Surtees, then twenty-seven, born to a north country landed family with a fox-hunting tradition.[18] His father, grandfather, and great-grandfather were masters of hounds. Surtees came to London in 1825 to study law, but fox hunting was his passion and he gave more attention to it than to the law. He traveled to France in 1829 and on his return engaged to write for *The Sporting Magazine*. The editor probably did not envisage Surtees' becoming another great writer; but it was expected that he would follow Nimrod's example of going on hunting tours and writing of them. The editors were probably relieved to learn that Surtees had none of Nimrod's taste for living in grand and expensive style. His writing style was also different—less pretentious, more down to earth, and inconoclastically humorous. His contributions to the magazine consisted of a series about fox hunting in the South of England which appeared in monthly installments throughout the remainder of 1830. His last piece for the magazine appeared in January 1831. Refused a share in the magazine, Surtees left to start his own, *The New Sporting Magazine*, in association with the publisher Rudolph Ackerman. He remained as editor of that periodical for five years and then returned to the family estate in the county of Durham, where until 1864 he lived quietly, out of the limelight, as a novelist and a fox-hunting landowner. He was one of the greatest of sporting writers.

If it is true that his great comic character, John Jorrocks, appeared early in the career of Surtees' new magazine, the August 1830 issue of *The Sporting Magazine* (see pp. 67–71, below) presented his adumbration of Mr. Jorrocks in the person of an unnamed "Cockneyshire" fox hunter whom Nim South introduced to hounds and stag hunting at Mr. Tattersall's farm west of London just beyond Hounslow.

Nimrod's career after leaving *The Sporting Magazine* was less happy than Surtees'. Without a salary he had to live much more modestly than he had been accustomed to. With bitterness, he did what many Englishmen of that period did when in his circumstances or worse ones—he moved to Calais, where living was cheaper. His pride would not let him live in nearby Boulogne, where Englishmen taking refuge from creditors tended to congregate. Nimrod remained in touch with events and persons in England and paid occasional visits there. In Calais he wrote some of his best works, including the three long articles for *The Quarterly Review*. He finally returned to England, where he died within a year, in 1843.

Even after Nimrod and Surtees left it, *The Sporting Magazine* maintained so high a reputation that it could withstand the competition its success inspired. Occasionally other famous writers, such as Henry Hall Dixon, wrote for it. The profession of sporting writer achieved status in these years, but *The Sporting Magazine* was gradually losing its preeminence, having to share leadership with *The New Sporting Magazine* and *The Sporting Review*. As time passed, other changes occurred. Volume 112 (July–December 1848) was the last under the old title; thereafter the periodical was called *The New Sporting Magazine*, suggesting some kind of behind-the-scenes agreement. Finally, volume 126 (July–December 1855) bore on the title page "*The New Sporting Magazine* united with *The Sportsman, The Sporting Review* & *The Sporting Magazine*." This title carried to the end in 1870. Along the way, there was no discussion of changes of editors or proprietors, nor any suggestion of financial difficulties or other internal problems. The reasons for the changes and then the demise in 1870 remain obscure.

This book is made up of articles from *The Sporting Magazine*, dating from its beginning in 1792 until 1836—the period when organized sport was in its youth. Quite properly it gives a prominent place to the writings of Nimrod and Surtees, even though this weights the collection towards fox hunting. So far as is known, neither Pierce Egan nor Jonathan Badcock wrote for *The Sporting Magazine*. Yet occasionally articles in the magazine are so much like articles written by Egan that it is apparent that someone was copying, a nice question of provenance that remains to be solved.

Like *The Sporting Magazine* as a whole, this collection of articles illustrates the variety, vigor, and joyous exuberance of the youth of the sporting life. There is much other evidence to support the view that this period was distinctive and remarkable in sporting history for its spirit, and not merely because it saw the beginning of sport in the modern meaning. Whether sporting enthusiasts made a living from sports, or lived sports, or participated for money or only for the sheer joy of it, professionals and amateurs in this period had much in common. They were filled with *joie de vivre*, and displayed it without self-consciousness. It was not quite the innocence of naiveté but there was little sense of guilt in their indiscretions or excesses of exuberance. Noticeably absent was the oppressive heaviness and surly seriousness weighing upon modern sports, amateur or professional. Sports and the sporting life of this time were gay, in the unperverted sense of that word.

In his book *Life in London,* Pierce Egan included a poem of the same name, which was set to music. The song captured the spirit of the poem and the book, with its recurring refrain, "Dancing singing full of glee, O London London town for me." Egan, of course, was a Londoner, writing about the life he knew among the Fancy. But there was light-hearted enjoyment of sports throughout England—on the race courses, in the villages and the fields, in provincial towns, in the inns, the ale houses, the manors, and the great houses of England. Though a generation of war ended with the defeat of Napoleon in 1815, though the postwar period presented difficult problems of adjustment, though discontent with the traditional constitutional and political system was widespread and threatening, the sporting life of England flourished throughout the period. It was the time of the exhilarating youth of sports.

∽ *Part I* ∽

The Sporting Scene

Sporting Intelligence

HUNTING

ROYAL HUNT—on Friday, March 29, a fine deer was uncarted at Langley Broom, for the day's diversion. The day was very fine, and the field numerous. The deer at first took towards Iver, then to the left through the inclosures between Stoke and Stowe, where he crossed the Bath road near Salt Hill, and ran with great speed down to the right of Darvy, towards the Thames, which he crossed. The sportsmen went by Maidenhead Bridge and Bray, and renewed the chase in the woods situate by St. Leonard's Hill and Hinckfield Plain, at which place the deer passed, near the residences of Lord Harcourt and Squire Daw, taking to the left towards Cranbourne, into Windsor Great Park, which he crossed, and went over Winkfield Green, down Cooper's Hill, to the left of Egham, where he crossed the Thames near Staines, through the fields and meadows to the left of Colnbrook. This fine deer was taken after a long chase, within half a mile of the place from which he started in the morning. Many of the Windsor sportsmen gave up the chase near Winkfield Plain, and returned to Windsor, not expecting the deer would cross the Thames a second time.

On Easter Monday, the GRAND ROYAL HUNT took place, as usual. It was very numerously attended by all ranks and descriptions of persons, who travelled in vehicles of various kinds, as well as several hundred pedestrians. The Royal huntsmen, sportsmen, and hounds, crossed from Windsor to Eton in the ferryboat, and proceeded to Farnham Common, where several hundred sportsmen awaited their arrival. At half-past ten o'clock a remarkably fine deer was turned out of the cart for the day's diversion.

Monday, March 25, the BERKELEY HOUNDS threw off at Shortwood, and whilst running through Hilcote Woods, the groom of J. Aspinall, Esq. attempting to leap his beautiful chesnut horse over a wall and ditch, the animal cleared the former, but slipping in the latter, fell and broke his back. The poor horse died on the spot.

The DEVON FOX-HUNTERS' CLUB had some capital runs lately among the beautiful hills and dales of the North of Devon. Earl Fortescue, the Hon. N. Fellowes, Sir John Rogers, Mr. Lucas, Mr. Templer, Mr. Buck, Mr. Whyte, Mr. Furze, and numerous others, were in the field.

April 2, 1822—About ten days since, the SOMERSETSHIRE SUBSCRIPTION FOX-HOUNDS (hunted by Mr. Reed) found a fox, at half-past ten, in Coombe Sydenham Brake, and ran him an hour and a half without a check, carrying him beautifully through Oakhampton Wood, and back over Brandon Hill: here they met with a long check, and getting so far behind their game, old reynard, after leading them a dance until five o'clock, bid them good bye until next October. They hunt this day, for the last time this season, at Orchard Portman Wood, near Taunton.

The ROXBY HOUNDS, Yorkshire, met Wednesday, April 3 (a bye day), at Roseberry, and found a dog [male] fox, which they killed in fine style, after running not more than three miles. At the moment they were breaking up this fox, they were hallooed to another, which, after a run of ten miles, without a check, was likewise killed; but the pleasure of this chase was somewhat destroyed to the sportsmen, when they found it to be a bitch fox, with no less than eight young ones in her,—a number seldom, if ever, heard of. They found again, and, after a severe run of six miles, killed, in gallant style, their third fox—horses, hounds, and sportsmen, alike ready to retire to rest. It was the best scenting-day these hounds have had this season.

Newport, Isle of Wight, March 29.—On Wednesday, being the last day of hunting, the HOUNDS belonging to William Thatcher, Esq. of Wackland, in this island, threw off in the finest style on St. George's Down, and had many excellent runs, which afforded the most agreeable sport to a highly-respectable and numerous assemblage of horsemen present, who afterwards partook of a splendid dinner at the Green Dragon.

Friday, March 29, a bag fox was turned out [from a bag] before the staunch pack of HARRIERS belonging to——Sanderson, Esq. of Tunbridge Wells, at Camp Hill, in the parish of Maresfield. He took away to Greenwood Gate, by Fisher's Gate, Crowborough Chapel, and over Ashdown Forest; then wound along by Jervis brook, the Grey Burchetts, Grove Hurst, and Mr. Olive's farm at New House, over Five Ash Down, and through the views of Buxted-place Park, the seat of the Hon. C. C. Jenkinson; and, after a gallant chase of two hours and twenty minutes, he was run into a wood near Framfield-place, the residence of A. Donovan, Esq. Our informant, an old sportsman, states that he never recollects a better chase. The riding about Ash Down Forest and Crowborough Warren, was particularly dangerous and bad, and the sportsmen had many "hair breadth 'scapes" in that neighbourhood.

Monday, April 8, General Fitzroy's BEAGLES (Norfolk) terminated the season, by having an excellent day's sport at Litcham, and the neighbourhood, after which about forty of the principal gentlemen of the hunt sat down to a dinner provided for the occasion, at the Bull Inn,

Litcham, the Hon. General Fitzroy in the chair.... The evening passed off with the greatest conviviality and good humour, and, enlivened by the urbanity of the Hon. Chairman, the festive meeting was prolonged to a late or rather an early hour.

CURIOUS FOX CHASE.—On the morning of Friday se'nnight, it being reported that a fox had been seen in the neighbourhood of Landrake, several gentlemen farmers of that parish proceeded to the spot with Mr. Nettle's hounds. After a long search, the loud *Tally ho!* put all on the *qui vive*. The eager sportsmen instantly set off with the dogs, in full cry, and succeeded in coming up with their victim after half an hour's chase. Mr. S. was the Nimrod of the day, and being foremost, seized the brush [tail], which he bore off in triumph! The other horsemen were soon up, and, to their great astonishment, discovered the animal, gasping at the point of death, to be only a brown cur or half terrier dog!! The burst of laughter that followed may be easily conceived.—*Plymouth Chron. April 8.*

HUNT MEETINGS

MEYNELL HUNT DINNER AND BALL.—The Derby Race-course presented a scene of much animation and gaiety. As the weather was fair, a considerable concourse of people assembled to share in the sport prepared for them by the Gentlemen of the Meynell Hunt Club. The severe coldness of the day was unfavourable to the full enjoyment of the beautiful scenery surrounding the Siddals, and the pleasures of the race. The interior of the spacious stand was, however, crowded with lively and fashionable company, and on no previous occasion was the great accommodation of this building more completely experienced. After the sports of the turf were ended, a very large party, Members of the Club, and their friends, sat down to an excellent dinner at the King's Head, and spent some hours in cheerful festivity. Charles Arkwright and John Beaumont, Esqrs. were appointed the Stewards for the next spring meeting.—The ball in the evening, given by the Gentlemen of the Meynell Hunt Club, was on this, as on every former occasion, conducted with a spirit and liberality worthy of the Members. A very large company had been invited; they comprised almost all the rank and beauty, and elegance and fashion, of the county and neighbourhood. They were received with great courtesy by the stewards, the Hon. Edward Curzon and G. R. Hulbert, Esq. About half-past ten dancing commenced, the ball being opened by the Hon. Edward Curzon and the bride of Samuel Ellis Bristowe, Esq. Dancing was continued with unabated spirit till near two o'clock, when a most excellent supper was served up, to which all present, in number three hundred and sixty-six, sat down. Soon after this refreshment, some of the company withdrew, but the dancing was recommenced and sustained with great animation till the dawn of day. We do not remember on any occasion to have seen among so large a number of guests an appearance of greater enjoyment. The preparations which had been made for their accommodation, all with the most unsparing generosity, the kind attentions of the Members of the Club, the affability of those most eminently distinguished for rank and station, conspired to throw over the whole an ease, a grace, and a charm, which were irresistible.— Among this brilliant party were his Grace the [sixth] Duke of Devonshire, who, as usual, was the soul of urbanity and genuine politeness, for his courtesy is that of the heart no less than of manner; the Earl of Chesterfield, Lord Vernon and family, Lady Scarsdale and family, Lord Kirkwall; the Honourables Henry and Thomas Cavendish, Sir Henry Fitzherbert, Sir George and Lady Sitwell, Sir Trevor Wheler and the Misses Wheler, Sir Charles and Lady Colville, Mr. Smith Wright and the Dowager Lady Sitwell, Mr. W. Coke, jun. M.P. Mr. Watts Russell, M.P. &c. &c. &c.

PONTEFRACT HUNT MEETING was numerously and fashionably attended, and the races were well contested. The fineness of the day contributed much to enliven the scene. About seventy gentlemen sat down at the ordinary, provided by Mr. Tute, and the wines, dessert, &c. did him great credit. The Hon. Mr. Petre (to whom the country is indebted for the establishment of these races) presided, and the afternoon was spent in the greatest conviviality. The ball at the New Assembly Room was attended by nearly two hundred ladies and gentlemen from the town and neighbourhood; the excellent York Quadrille Band attended; waltzing, quadrilles, and country dances, were kept up with great spirit until four o'clock in the morning; and the refreshments provided by Mr. Arton, of the Star Inn, were highly creditable. The following morning about five hundred gentlemen assembled at the Park to meet the Badsworth fox-hounds. This pack, under the management of the Hon. E. Petre, has had very brilliant sport, having killed thirty-six brace of foxes during the season.

CROXTON PARK RACES.—We have seldom witnessed better sport, or a greater assemblage of equipages and spectators at Croxton Park, than on the 3d inst. The weather was very favourable, and the course in excellent order.

At CROMWELL HUNT RACES, over Meredith Downs, the Hunters' Plate of 50 £. for all ages, was won by Mr. P. Villier's b. h. [bay horse] Chance, beating seven others: a fine race, and 2 to 1 agst the winner.—The Cromwell Stakes of 15 gs. each was won by Mr. Parker's c. [colt] by Gohanna: 6 to 4 on the winner.

SNARESBROOK HUNT RACES, ESSEX.—The Hunters' Cup, with 15 gs. added, was won by Mr. R. Gould's Modena, beating Capt. Hall's Bounder, Mr. Bouverie's Goldfinder, and four others.—The Half-bred Stakes, a sweepstakes of 15 gs. was won by Mr. Aubree's Ringworm.—The Farmers' Stakes of 5 gs. each, with ten added, was won by Mr. Jordan's Turk. It was a ludicrous wind-up race, rode by the owners, carrying 12st [1 stone = 14 lb.]. Of seven which started, four only came in the first heat to save their distance. The Down was very numerously attended.

At BEADNELL MEETING, Northumberland, April 11, a Hunters' Stakes of 50 £. gentlemen riders, three mile heats, was won easy, at two heats, by Mr. Fawcus's b. h. Dr. Blemish, by Apollo, aged, 12 st. rode by the owner, beating Mr. G. Smith's b. h. Chieftain, by Orville, aged, 12 st. and Mr. Wrigglesworth's b. m. [bay mare] Coquet-side, by Langton, 5 yrs old, 11 st. 10 lb.

The BERKELEY HUNT DINNER at the Plough Hotel, Cheltenham, on Monday, March 25, was far more numerously attended than ever remembered. The leader of the hunt, Col. Berkeley, was prevented by indisposition from meeting his brother sportsmen.

The MOSTYN HUNT RACES, on Wednesday last, were most numerously attended. The weather being so remarkably favourable, tempted many persons to witness the sport, who dare not in general face a March wind on Cottisford Heath. The first race, for a sweepstakes of 10 gs. each, was won by Mr. Faulkner's bay horse by Pioneer. The second, for a sweepstakes of 5 gs. each, was won by Mr. Day's Swindon. The Farmer's Cup was won by Mr. Deakin's bay horse. The running was not considered by any means good. One of the light-fingered gentry was detected in an attempt to ease a person's pocket of its contents, and dealt with most summarily, being taken to a pond near the course, and most completely ducked. A sweep volunteered to give him ablution, and was well rewarded for his exertions, which he deserved; for it is a query whether he or the pickpocket was most ducked, for they both looked like drowned rats. The pickpocket would in all probability have fallen a victim to the fury of the mob but for the humane interposition of Lord Nugent; for, after treating him as above stated, they began to beat him with sticks, and some who were mounted endeavoured to make their horses kick him, when he was rescued from further violence by the exertions of his Lordship.

SURREY HUNT RACES, at Epsom, April 17.—The races by the Surrey Hunts have, until this year, produced a fine day's sport. The fineness of the morning attracted much company, but great disappointment followed. Three horses only started for the Farmers' Plate of 50 £.

Mr. Maydewell's b. m. 6 yrs old, 11 st. 11 lb. 1   1
Mr. Gray's br. m. [brown mare] 5 yrs, 11 st. 3 lb. 2   2
Mr. Holman's Dancing Master dis. [distanced] Won in a canter. No betting. Sweepstakes of 20 gs. each.—Two-mile heats.
Mr. Knighton's ch. h. [chestnut horse] Friar Bacon. 1   1
Mr. Field's ch. h. Lounger 2   2
Mr. White's br. h. Dominichino 3   3
A good race. Five to 4 on the winner.

RACING.—RACES TO COME

Irvine .... *May* 1	Knutsford 30
Chester 6	Newcastle
Newmarket 6	(Staffordshire) .... *August* 6
York 13	Nottingham 6
Epsom 22	Burton 22
Manchester 29	Warwick .... *September* 3
Ascot Health .... *June* 4	Lichfield 10
Guildford 12	Aberdeen, &c. 10
Bibury 18	Doncaster 16
Newmarket .... *July* 8	Leicester 18
Cheltenham 17	Newmarket 30
Winchester 24	

An occupier of the OLD RACE GROUND at Brighton having prohibited the use of it, the Race Committee have provided another ground. A doubt thence arose whether the subscribers to the three sweepstakes already made for the first and second days of these races in 1822, and the first day of 1824, were bound to run their horses on the New Ground—the Jockey Club, to whom it was referred, have decided in the negative, and the sweepstakes are consequently void.

A correspondent writes us:—"It is supposed by those who are *down to a thing or two*, that POSTHUMA is the best mare that has run at Newmarket for many years." . . .

A match took place at Waltham, near Grimsby, on the 9th April, between W. Dawson, Esq.'s bay horse, Radamanthus, and Mr. Sanderson's (farrier) bay mare, Fanny, which was won by the former. Mr. Sanderson not being satisfied, made a second match, in which Radamanthus won in grand style. Both horses were ridden by gentlemen belonging to the Brocklesby Hunt.—Another match then took place between Mr. Thomas Robinson's (of Ashby) bay horse, Joseph, and Mr. Richard Surfleet's (of Waltham) bay mare, Kate, which was won easily by the former.

The annual EASTER PLATE was run for on Barham Downs, Kent, on Tuesday, April 9, and won by Mr. Easton's br. h. Creeper, beating two others.

LEITH.—Saturday, April 13, a match for twenty-five guineas a-side was run for, over Leith Sands, between a chesnut horse, Sandy o'er the Lee, and a bay horse, Young Harmless, both the property of a gentleman of that place. The chesnut was rode by the owner, and Harmless by Mr. Thomas King, horse dealer. Betting six to four on the chesnut at starting. Harmless took the lead for two hundred yards, when the chesnut passed, and was winning, till the stirrup leather gave way within three hundred yards of home, by which the rider lost his seat. It was a well-contested race, both horses making play from the starting. Considerable bets were pending.

An elegant and commodious stand, upon a permanent scale, is about to be erected on Ascot Heath, for the accommodation of his Majesty.

KELSO RACE COURSE.—The [fifth] Duke of Roxburghe has spared no expence in preparing the new course over the Berry Moss, at Kelso, for the meeting of the Caledonian Hunt, which is fixed for October next. The work of drawing, paring, and turfing the grounds, has gone on with unexampled rapidity; a number of carts, in addition to those of his Grace, have been employed, belonging to the farmers and gentry in the neighbourhood. Too much praise cannot be given to the Duke for his munificence and zeal in this work. Kelso races have long been celebrated, but the want of stabling near to the old course was often injurious to the horses, and the proximity of Berry Moss to the town will in future remedy this inconvenience.

RACES AT JAMAICA.—A correspondent has transmitted us a detailed account of the races in this island, during the year 1821, which we fear, if inserted, would not interest our readers generally....

We are sorry to have to announce to our numerous sporting readers, the death of that justly celebrated racer and stallion Ebor (the winner of the St. Leger Stakes at Doncaster, in 1817), which took place on the 4th instant, at the Rand Grange, near Bedale, of an inflammation in the bowels. This is the second severe loss which Mr. Peirse has sustained in his stud by the same disorder; the other, a bay colt, by Amadis, out of a Sister to Rosette, of which we stated the particulars in our Magazine for January last....

COVERING STALLIONS

We regret having, through accident, omitted giving the following among our list of covering stallions for 1822, inserted in last Number:—WILDBOY, 15 years old, by Sir Peter, out of Rosalind, by Volunteer (Son of Eclipse), out of Eyebright, Sister to Conductor, by Match'em—Snap, etc. at Oakfield House, near Hay, South Wales, at three guineas and five shillings. Wildboy is considered to be the best-bred son of Sir Peter living.

COCKING

This amusement, which has become nearly obsolete in many parts of the kingdom, is still kept up at Newcastle-on-Tyne, with great spirit. Every day during Easter week was fully occupied by this diversion, at Messrs. Best and Salter's pit, Turk's Head, Biggmarket; and many large sums of money were lost and won on the occasion. On Monday, twenty-six cocks fought, the united weight of which was 94 lb. 14 oz. and the sums fought for were 50 £. 24 gs. and 6 gs. On Tuesday, twenty-six cocks fought for 50 £. 24 gs. and 6 gs.; the weight of the cocks being 99 lb. 12 oz. On Wednesday, thirty-six cocks, weighing 146 lb. 4 oz. fought for two 50 £. and 12 gs. On Thursday, thirty-four cocks, weighing 144 lb. 8 oz. fought for two 50 £. and 6 gs. On Friday, twenty-four cocks weighing 106 lb. 8 oz. fought for 50 £. and 24 gs. And on Saturday, forty-two cocks, weighing 196 lb. 8 oz. fought for two 50 £. 24 gs. and 6 gs. The attendance was very great; and the whole may be considered as an extraordinary occurrence in the annals of cockfighting; for it will be perceived that in one week, cocks, weighing *seven hundred weight, four pounds, and six ounces,* fought (independent of bets) for sums amounting to no less than 601 £. 4 s.

The three double days' play of cocks, at the White Swan Inn, Norwich, for ten guineas a battle, and two hundred guineas the odd, between Norwich and Northampton, was, after three days' good fighting, on Monday, Tuesday, and Wednesday, the 15th, 16th, and 17th April, declared a drawn main [a match of several bouts].

A grand MAIN OF COCKS took place this month at the Royal Pit, Westminster, between a sporting Baronet, and a Merchant of the City. Three double days' play for six guineas a battle, and one hundred guineas the odds. Nash and Hall, feeders:—

NASH	HALL
Monday 6	Monday 4
Tuesday 8	Tuesday 4
Wednesday 4	Wednesday 8
18	16

One main battle drawn, both having refused to fight in the law. The fighting altogether was the worst we ever saw at this pit. Nash took the lead on Monday and Tuesday: although the cocks entrusted to his care on this occasion were so much superior in game to those of his adversary, he would not have won the main had not one of the Baronet's cocks broke a spur.

THE ROAD

NOBLE COACHMANSHIP.—The new road from Leeds, through Pontefract, to Barnsdale and Doncaster, under the superintendence of John L. M'Adam,[1] Esq. and which is surpassed by no public road in the kingdom, seems likely to be brought freely into use. The Royal Leeds Union Coach took this route, for the first time, on Saturday, the 23d march, and was driven into Pontefract, by Lord Pollington, amidst the joyful acclamations of an immense concourse of spectators. The six horses by which it was drawn were splendidly decorated with ribbons, preceded by a band of music, and the bells rang a merry peal.

TANDEM MATCH.—Mr. R. Houlston's match for fifty guineas, to drive a tandem fifteen miles in one hour, and to trot the first seven miles, took place April 3, over a four-mile flat on the Bromley road. The horses did the first four miles in eighteen minutes and twenty-two seconds, and the other three in fourteen minutes eight seconds, leaving

twenty-seven minutes for the eight miles' gallop. The horses did the eighth mile in three minutes ten seconds, the next four in fifteen minutes twelve seconds, and the remaining three miles in ten minutes and fifty seconds, winning the match by eighteen seconds. It was a fine performance; and the pacing of the horses at the gallop was a fine treat.—Betting was five to four on time.

TROTTING MATCHES

On Monday, the 1st of April, came on three great attempts of trotting, and on which thousands were pending. The first match was that of Mr. Willan's horse, which beat the slate-coloured American, backed to trot three miles in nine minutes for one hundred guineas. It was reported that the horse was lame, and up to the evening before the start six to four was the betting on time at the Tun Tavern, and more than two to one was bet before starting, as the horse shewed a little lame in going from Hampton to Sunbury Common, where the match took place. Mr. Dyson's man Jack rode the horse, and when at speed, the lameness was not apparent, but the horse was more than three minutes doing the first mile, and there was no increase of speed during the match. The horse broke into a gallop near the George Inn, when about one hundred yards from home, and the pressure of horsemen was so great at his heels, that his jockey turned him with difficulty, and the match was lost by forty seconds.

Captain Halford's match to trot eight miles and a half in half an hour, and to carry eleven stone, with a horse *bona fide* his property, for one hundred guineas; and a second match for a like sum, to trot a horse seventeen miles in an hour, also his property, took place the same day as the above, over a two-mile piece of ground at Merston Vale, Surrey. The eight miles and a half match was done as follows:—

	min.	sec.
First two miles	7	7
Second ditto	7	3
Third ditto	7	4
Fourth ditto	7	8
The half-mile	1	35
	29	57

A manœuvre not dreamt of was here practised. A jockey of ten stone immediately mounted the same horse, and proceeded on the second match, to the astonishment of all present. The horse had evidently been kept *in*, as the figures underneath will shew.

	min.	sec.
The mile and a half, making eight miles, including mounting time, done in	6	10
The sixth two miles	6	54
Seventh ditto	6	53
Eighth ditto	6	47
The last mile	3	29
	30	13

—The match was lost by thirteen seconds, when the Captain backed the horse to do the seventeen miles within the hour on the Thursday following, over the same ground, for 200 gs. carrying 10 st. 7 lb: and this he accomplished in 58 min. 36 sec.

Two great trotting matches for one hundred guineas a-side, made on the 12th of March, took place on Wednesday, April 3, in Chorson Park inclosures, in Essex, over a two-mile piece of ground. The first match was between Major Hawbrey's brown mare and Mr. Phillip's Arabian, ten miles, to carry 9 st each. The two miles were done by each as follows:

HAWBREY	m.	s.	PHILLIPS	m.	s.
1st two	6	40	1st two	6	41
2d	6	42	2d	6	39
3d	6	41	3d	6	37
4th	6	43	4th	7	10
5th	6	50	5th	6	41
	33	36		33	48

The match was lost by Mr. Phillips's horse breaking into a gallop. The other match, for a like sum of one hundred guineas, was made to do the same ground in less time than the winner, by Mr. Wilkinson, to ride his own horse, 11 st. He did his two miles as follows:—

	min.	sec.
First two miles	6	32
Second ditto	6	30
Third ditto	6	34
Fourth ditto	7	14
Fifth ditto	6	29

—This won the match in 33 minutes and 9 seconds, although the horse broke into a gallop in the eighth mile.

STEEPLE CHASES

Prior to Monday, April 1, it was industriously circulated, at Rochester, that Mr. Comfort's celebrated pack of fox-hounds would, at six o'clock on that morning, draw the Elms Cover in the neighborhood of Upnor, and the consequence was that a very considerable number of sportsmen, including several officers of the Coldstream Guards, met at the specified time; after waiting an hour or more, and no hounds making their appearance, it was suggested by one of the party, that it was the *first of April,* and they immediately supposed they had been hoaxed. However, not choosing to separate without some sport, a sweepstake was made by ten of the party, of five guineas each, for a steeple chase to Chalk, a distance of about six miles, as the crow flies. It was won in the most gallant style by C. W. Harvey, Esq. who rode his favourite horse *Ranter,* and did the distance in about seventeen minutes. This gentleman was offered, and refused on the field, 300 gs. for his horse. The race was admirally [sic] contested by H. Thacker, Esq. on his well-known hunter *Skim.*

A sweepstakes match of 20 guineas each, between Mr. Coxhead, Captain N. Peters, and Mr. Roebottom, took place on Friday, April 12. The start was from Frimley Furzes, near Blackwater, to Arborfield, Berks. The race for the first five miles was over heath, and the horsemen kept the steady cuts until they came to Topham Cover, when they separated, and pursued their own course through a woody country. They left the ridge of Golden Farmer Hill to the left, and were within sight of each other again on Shinfield Common, when Mr. Coxhead made all play, and reached Arborfield church-yard in one hour and three minutes, a distance of 18 miles in a straight direction. Capt. Peters

lost by six minutes, and Mr. Roebottom's horse fell, and he was thrown out altogether.

On Monday last the inhabitants of Haverfordwest were highly gratified by a novel sport in this part of the kingdom, a steeple chase of eight miles for 100 guineas. At half-past twelve o'clock, the Carmarthen road, for four miles, was thronged with horsemen, and every *prad* [horse] was in high requisition, and the Scotchwell boasted of all the belles belonging to the town and its neighbourhood. At ten minutes past one, the combatants, Mr. Morgan James, on his famous horse *Sir Peter*, by Spoliator, and Mr. W. B. Williams, on his well-known horse *Bergami*, by Vividus, mounted in high glee, both eager for the fray. *Sir Peter* took the lead for five miles, when all his gold came off his gingerbread, and he was well planted in a field near a brook, which completely floored him, and he stood contemplating its beauties, much longer than his master bargained for, who, at this critical moment, prudently gave up the chase, that *Sir Peter* should not give up the ghost. Mr. Williams, unconscious of his victory, kept sailing away with *Bergami* in grand style, and completed the distance in thirty-one minutes and a half, with perfect ease to himself and horse. On his arrival at the Scotchwell House, he was greeted by his friends, and partook of an elegant collation, consisting of all the delicacies of the season, liberally provided by the worthy host. The day proved delightful, and all parties returned highly gratified with this novel scene.—*Carmarthen Journal, April 5.*

PIGEON SHOOTING

The late defeat of the Midgham Crack Club, brought about this match, which took place on Saturday, April 6, at Farnham Heath, on the Forest. The Club, consisting of eighteen members, were challenged to produce nine to shoot against as many picked men from six counties, for a sweepstakes of 15 gs. each, at thirteen birds from the trap, at twenty-one yards. The following was the order of the sport;—

CLUB KILLED		COUNTIES KILLED	
Mr. Pearson	12	Mr. Grosvenor	13
Mr. Sadler	12	Mr. Halland	12
Capt. Smith	11	Mr. George	11
Mr. Thorn	11	Mr. Figg	11
Mr. Fielder	11	Mr. Parsons	10
Mr. Lomax	11	Mr. R. Smith	10
Mr. Simpson	10	Mr. Knight	8
Mr. Fowler	9	Mr. Rose	8
Mr. Gee	8	Mr. Martin	7
	95		90

A second match followed for 5 gs. each by the three first on each side, which was decided thus, at the same quantity of birds:—

KILLED		KILLED	
Mr. George	11	Mr. Sadler	12
Mr. Grosvenor	10	Capt. Smith	8
Mr. Halland	10	Mr. Pearson	8
	31		28

A match for 5 gs. each, between Capt. Shee, and ten from the counties of Middlesex and Berks, and J. A. Bouverie, Esq. with ten from Herts and Oxon, took place April 23, in the range near Gerrard's Cross, Bucks, at eleven birds each, twenty-one yards from the trap. There was a bye bet of 20 gs. between the two gentlemen who promoted the match. The following were the number each killed:—

Middlesex and Berks	Herts and Oxon
KILLED	KILLED
Capt. Shee 9	Mr. Bouverie 10
Mr. Norman 11	Mr. Smart 10
Mr. Gilchrist 10	Mr. Richards..........10
Mr. Webb 10	Mr. Wells 10
Mr. Smart 8	Mr. Jefferson 9
Mr. Odell 8	Mr. Bedmeade 8
Mr. Mason 8	Mr. Martin 7
Mr. Pottinger 8	Mr. Fuller 7
Mr. Kell 7	Mr. Marshall 7
Mr. Broadhurst 7	Mr. Fothergill 7
Mr. Mills 7	Mr. Hart 6
93	90

After the Captain's party had won this match, he challenged Mr. Bouverie to shoot at eleven other birds, for a dinner for the whole twenty-two. Mr. Bouverie won by killing nine birds from eleven, to the Captain's eight.

PEDESTRIANISM

BARCLAY MATCH.[2]—MR. SOMERVILLE, who had been trying the match of 1000 miles in 1000 hours, at Dance, in Oxfordshire, resigned on Saturday, April 6, after labouring at it more than five weeks. He was too lame, and too much exhausted, to proceed. It was for 200 guineas.— The Barclay match has also been attempted, at Sheffield, by WRIGHT, a pedestrian, who had on Thursday, April 18, gone 856 miles. He had then a bad cold, and his legs swelling. Notwithstanding he was so much broke down, his resolution was unshaken, and he anxiously looked forward to the Wednesday following, at twelve o'clock, to accomplish his task. We have not heard the result.

NEWCASTLE.—On Tuesday, April 15, GEORGE WILSON, who had undertaken to walk ninety miles in twenty-four successive hours, completed his task fourteen minutes within the time. He commenced on the race-ground at Newcastle-upon-Tyne, at twelve o'clock on the Monday, and though the ground was in a very bad state, owing to a fall of snow and rain, he finished, as above stated, at fourteen minutes before twelve on Tuesday. There was an immense concourse of people, amounting to no less than 14,000 or 15,000, who loudly cheered him, and raised a subscription for him. Wilson is fifty-six years of age. A worthy Baronet, seeing that the pedestrian was going to walk home, after his great exertion, hastened in his gig to the Queen's Head, in Newcastle, and sent a chaise and four, in which Wilson was conveyed to the said inn, with colours flying; and the bells greeted his achievement with several merry peals.

On Tuesday, April 9, a man of the name of PITTERS, a native of Salisbury, undertook for a trifling sum to run eighteen miles within two hours, in a circle of 110 yards, on Twyford Down, near Winchester. A large concourse of people assembled to witness the arduous undertaking, and, to the astonishment of every one, he accomplished the task with apparent ease in five minutes less than the given time: he performed ten miles within the first hour.

A pedestrian, named W. PILL, undertook to perform the task of walking forty miles in eight hours, at Brecon, on Thursday, April 4, which he easily accomplished in seven hours and forty minutes.

MARTIN, the boxer, undertook, this month, within two miles of Brighton, to run eight miles and a half within an hour, for a bet of ten guineas. He did the first two miles within fourteen minutes, and completed the distance with three minutes to spare.

MR. COURTENAY, a farmer, undertook on Tuesday, April 9, to start to Coventry, from Mile End New Town, near Bow, and return in three days. The distance is 188 miles. He started at two o'clock in the morning, passed through Dunstable, Stony Stratford, and Towcester, and accomplished seventy miles at twelve o'clock. He touched on Coventry at five o'clock on Wednesday morning, and did thirty miles on his return at two o'clock, and halted four hours, and was lame at starting again, which increased, and he reached Dunstable at three o'clock on Thursday, and rested until six. He had eight hours left to do thirty-six miles, when he resigned the task.

H. RAYNER, on Saturday, April 6, undertook, for a bet of ten guineas, to go five miles in twenty-eight minutes. He started on the Lewisham road, and performed as follows, over a mile piece of ground:—First mile in 5 minutes. 12 sec.; second, 5 min. 24 sec.; third, 5 min. 25 sec.; fourth, 5 min. 20 sec.; fifth, 5 min. 51 sec. winning the match in 48 seconds within the given time, and which is one of the greatest performances on record.

MATCH TO DOVER.—MR. WEST, the celebrated pedestrian, who is considered the best of his day at a long journey, undertood this month to go on foot from Holborn [London] to within two miles of Dover, making seventy-two miles, in thirteen hours. He did fifty-four miles in nine hours and fifty minutes, and then resigned the task, having won a bet that he did fifty miles in nine hours, which he accomplished, with eight minutes to spare.

POACHING

"Some weeks ago," says the *Bury Gazette*, "a man of the name of Crannis was convicted in the sum of 15 £. for having been found on the lands of Mr. Newton, of Elden, with three pheasants in his pockets, he being a person not qualified to kill game; and for non-payment of the penalty, was committed to the gaol here for three months; on his arrival at the prison, he was put into the receiving ward to be examined, as is the usual mode before admitted into the interior of the gaol; he was left there alone nearly half an hour; during the time, he amused himself by drawing three pheasants upon the walls with a piece of charcoal, and writing under them the following lines:

> "I am a carpenter by trade, I never was incroaching,
> I had no work, no money, which made me go a poaching,
> Three hen pheasants I had got, and homeward I was making.
> Two fellows stop'd me on the road, so poor Joe was taken;
> Then to the Justice they did bring me, with him I could not prevail,
> For my mittimus [prison warrant] he did sign, and sent me off to gaol.

The pheasants I should have caught, I have now left for store,
And this summer, if they have luck, they'll breed plenty more,
And as soon as ever the next season do come in,
If I am alive, and not confined, I shall be ready to begin,
And if that I am taken again, the money I will pay,
For I shall never stand for money, while pheasants look so gay.
            "Joseph Cannish, March, 1822."

OBITUARY

At Charleston [South Carolina], by the bite of a rattle snake, Mr. ROBERT WILSON, of Liverpool, aged about 30. He was bit the day previous, and died in great agony. He had collected a number of those reptiles to send to Europe, and being in the habit of handling them, was incautious enough to allow himself to be bit by one of them.

THE RING

April 4, PETERS, the Bath tinman, and FLOWERS, the coachman, from Dunsdan, Oxon, met to fight for 40 gs. a-side, at a place between Oakingham and Maidenhead, agreeably to the desire of the backers, Captain Hans for the coachman, and Mr. Meadows Fuller for the tinman. But the Magistracy interfering, the men met in a field across Windsor Forest, at Apsley, Surrey, ten miles distant. H. Ford seconded Flowers, and Wheeler officiated for Peters. Both men had fame for various successful combats, and the tinman was rather the favourite. The battle lasted forty-four minutes, in which ten very gay rounds were fought. In the first the claret flew from the heads of each, and the tinman was thrown, being the lightest.—The second terminated by Peters being floored by a heavy *tie-up* on the loins. Peters had the best of the next round, but in the seventh a chance hit placed Peter's head upon his right shoulder, and a pistol could not have dropped him more neatly. It won Flowers the battle, although the tinman fought the other three rounds under every disadvantage. A purse was collected for the loser.

On Monday, April 8, ISLE-OF-WIGHT HALL, of pugilistic celebrity, had a *turn-out*, at Leap, in the Isle of Wight, with SUTTON, commonly called the *Gipsy*, whom he beat in the second round, by giving him a tremendous blow behind the ear, which stunned him for several minutes.

A pitched battle took place this month, in St. George's Fields, between *two women!* The combatants had their hair cut for the occasion, and fought twenty desperate rounds.

LENNEY AND HARRY HARRIS, A NEW ONE.—The above battle took place in Ridge Meadows, three miles from Virginia Water, Friday, April 19. The stake was for 20 gs. a-side, and a purse, and Harris, who is a Wiltshire butcher, was patronized by Mr. Courtenay, to weigh 10 st 6 lb. and who had never before exhibited in a prize ring. Six rounds were fought. Lenny made the best use he could of science, but the novice, a fresh young man of 22, kept at his work manfully, and bothered good fighting, by readiness and hard hitting. In twenty-three minutes Lenney was all abroad, and hit so senseless that he was deaf to time. Both were good natural fighters, and they took punishment like *winking*.

MARTIN AND BELASCO.—The stakes of 200 gs. a-side, for the battle on the 7th of May, between Martin and Belasco, were to have been made good April 25, at the Fives' Court, 100 £ a-side having been already staked. No money was forthcoming from Belasco's backer, and the forfeit of 100 £ was demanded from the stakeholder, but refused, he having had an attachment from the Lord Mayor's Court issued against him that morning. Thus baffled, the fight is off, to the disappointment of the sporting world.

BELCHER AND SCROGGINS.—The latter having taken liberties with Belcher's *cookmaid* at the Castle, she *smacked his chops,* and then told her master. This caused an energetic row, and a turn-up between Tom and Scroggins. They fought twenty minutes, by which time Scroggins's visage was quite *transmogrified,* and he gave in.

SPORTING ANECDOTE

A well-known veteran sportsman, in the neighbourhood of Mansfield, and a constant fieldsman at Lord Middleton and Mr. Saville's Hunts, has, this season, pursued bold reynard, on the *same horse,* not less than *seventy-five times,* and, on a fair statement, went each meeting a distance of *twelve miles to cover!* This truly famous and favourite animal was not once bled, or had . . . the slightest injury or appeared the least distressed; but, on the contrary, to the very last day in the field he maintained his undaunted spirits, gloriously triumphing in the blithe echo "Hark forward, tally-ho, gone away!" This extraordinary feat stands unprecedented in the annals of sporting history.

HORSE FAIRS

A correspondent has favoured us with the following memorandums of STOURBRIDGE FAIR, Worcestershire, which took place on the 29th March:

Anderson, of Lamb's Conduit-street, purchased sixty-three horses, which it was supposed cost him upwards of 5000 £—Between 3 and 4000 horses were sold; most of them high prices; still many capital ones remained undisposed of.—The owner of one Irish horse refused 300 gs. for him: many Irish hunters sold at from 100 to 150 quineas.—Cobs were in great request, and went at high prices.—Machine horses also were in great demand.—This fair, which boasts of having perhaps as many good horses as any in England, is held on the 29th March, but the dealers attend a week previous, and all the business among the good horses is nearly done by that day in the stables of the innkeepers.—A singular custom prevails, that every person selling a horse of this description always buys a white leather head collar, a small rug, and a sircingle [girth], for the purchaser to take the horse away with.

LINCOLN HORSE FAIR, April 22, was crowded with sellers and buyers. Some fine cattle exhibited, and prices on the advance. Three horses sold for 600 guineas. Some Frenchmen made extensive purchases.

FISH

An extraordinary large jack was caught by Mr. Rhodes, of Claydon, Bucks, April 23, weighing 30 lb.

A large cod fish having been brought to Muirtown this month, the cook observed a fish-line protruding from the cod's mouth, and, on opening the fish, a large flounder, eleven and half inches long, was found entire in its stomach, with the hook and line in its mouth—this cod being taken by having swallowed the flounder on the fisher's hook and line....

Part II

The Equestrian Sports

Riding to Hounds

"Nunc agili cursu, cunctos anteire solebam."
[For it was my custom to outrun the field.]
                                            Tibullus

From the days of the young Ascanius to the present hour, riding to hounds has formed one of the chief amusements of men of all ages, and in all situations in life. . . . What figure these ancient Nimrods would have cut by the side of a good Meltonian of the present day, it is not in my power to conjecture. The best Kings and Emperors, however, encouraged all such manly exercises; and Horace wrote his *Carmen Seculare* in their praise. The pursuits of the field, in particular, being more or less attended with risk, have a tendency to increase natural courage; and by rendering men familiar with danger, make them less liable to lose their presence of mind when in it, and less anxious to get out of it. As the foil is the semblance of the naked sword, the chase is the image of war; and after all, "it is the contempt of danger which ennobles the life of a soldier."

Riding to hounds on paper, or over a bottle of wine, by a good fire side, is one thing; and riding along side them for an hour, when going their best pace, over a strongly enclosed, and deep country, is another. Than the one, nothing is more easy—gates, stiles, brooks, and fences, are all taken in stroke, and nothing is too high or too wide. Than the other, nothing is more difficult; body and mind are both at work, and every now and then the "courage must be screwed up to the sticking place." Like most other things, however, there are two ways of doing it; one in comparative safety and supreme enjoyment; the other, like Damocles at the feast, in the midst of pleasure, but in constant apprehension of destruction. All this depends on the goodness of the horse we ride, and our skill in riding him. "Hand without head," will not do, neither will head without hand. Judgment, here, must be combined with execution.

Independent of the pleasure arising from *the chase*, I have always considered a covert's side with hounds that are well attended, to be one of the most lively scenes in nature. The pride of the morning—the meeting of friends—and the anticipation of diversion, contribute to raise the spirits, and expand the soul. In my experience in life, I have found, or heard of, but few friendships formed on the associations of very early years; and for one lasting friendship, founded at a school or college, I have known a dozen proceeding from fox-hunting; and I have no hesitation in adding, that the best introduction for a young man of fortune and fashion of the present day, is to be found at Billesdon Coplow, or Oadby toll-bar.

Leicestershire is the place of all others, where riding to hounds is put to the test. The excuses of "I was the wrong side of the covert—I did not get a start—or, the hounds slipped away from me," will seldom serve here, as every man can get a fair start if he is *awake*, and every man has an opportunity of distinguishing himself. As in my future letters on this country—which I hope to resume when I have concluded those upon Warwickshire—I shall have occasion to introduce some of the distinguished characters which have been going well in this *clipping country*; I shall proceed to a detail of such observations as have presented themselves in my own experience in riding to hounds.

It is a remarkable fact, and a striking proof of the difficulty attending it, that barring Leicestershire, there are not, in other countries, more than half a score men, calling themselves sportsmen, and well mounted, who can ride to hounds;—that is to say, who can live with them for an hour, over a strong country, and at their best pace. There are, however, I will venture to assert, in each of these countries, twice that number of men whose nerve is equal to any fence that the others will ride at; yet, from certain causes, they cannot get near hounds. Now, how are we to reconcile this? Here are two men, with nerve equally good, and equally well mounted, get a fair start with hounds. One of them shall never be a field from them, and the other shall be dead beat, or, perhaps, lost, before he gets half through the run, if it is a good one. Nay, I will go one step farther;—the one man shall ride three or four stone heavier than the other! This appears paradoxical; but every day's experience proves it. Let us endeavour to account for it.

If hounds always ran straight over a country, the difficulty of riding to them would be materially lessened. A good horse, with a good hand upon him, and boldly ridden, would, nineteen times out of twenty, carry a man up to them, provided no insurmountable difficulties, such as rivers, intervened. The hand, without much assistance from the head, would then do the business; but the difficulty consists in turning to hounds, and riding *inside* and not outside of them, and thereby cutting off the angles. Whoever considers the proportion of the diameter to the circumference of a circle, will be convinced of the great advantage of riding *inside*, of hounds in their turns, and avoiding angles.... How often have I seen one set of men riding as hard as their horses could carry them, and stopping at nothing, but still losing ground, and being beaten; when at the same time, others, better judges, were going by the side of hounds, quite at their ease, and merely because they have turned *with* them, and not *after* them, by which the angles have been avoided.

There is another point in riding to hounds, not sufficiently considered. Your sporting readers will know what I mean by the difference between a quick horse, and a fast one. Very few countries require fast horses, but all require quick ones; and a quick man, upon a quick horse, would beat a slow man upon Eclipse. The speed and *stride* of Hambletonian would be useless in any country, however valuable at Newmarket; but it is a quick man upon a quick horse that, in nineteen countries out of twenty, gets best to hounds. By a quick man, I mean one who has a good eye to the direction his hounds are going in;—who turns as his hounds turn;—has a good eye to practicable places in his fences; and when he comes to them, is *decisive in his determination to go at them.* In many other things besides riding over a country, he who stops to consider is lost; but in this, decision is every thing. The "non progredi, est regredi," may be particularly applied to riding to hounds. When we stop, they are going; and catching hounds, with a holding scent, is what few men and horses are equal to. The celebrated Dick Knight's speech to Lord Spencer, when he hunted his hounds, proved he was of this opinion. He had just ridden over '*a rasper,*' which his Lord stopped to look at.—"Come along, my Lord," said Dic, "the more you look, the less you'll like it."

By a quick horse, I mean one that is quick on getting on his speed again after having been stopped at his fences; and is handy in being pulled up or turned. This is the horse that will distinguish himself in enclosed countries, where hounds seldom run, or men seldon ride, straight. It was this wonderful quickness at his fences, independent of his speed; that gave that famous horse, 'the Clipper,' such an advantage over a country when hounds ran hard. Whether the ditch was towards him, or from him, he would not suffer himself to be collected, or pulled together, therefore lost no time in his fences. He was on his speed again, as it were, before other horses had scarcely alighted on the ground. Thus taking all sorts of fences in this rapid way, without suffering himself to be collected, might do very well with Mr. Lindow on his back, but it is not every man's nerve or finger that it would suit. It enabled him, however, to go a mile and a half over a country, on the Clipper, whilst many others were going a mile.

In my experience of men riding to hounds, I have made the following remark;—that it is not because a man is a good horseman—that he puts his horse well at his fences, and is not afraid of them, that he can live with hounds. On the contrary, I have seen numbers answering this description that never could see a run, when the pace was quick. The

reason of this was—*they were not quick*. They lost time at their fences, and *they would not gallop*. I am willing to admit that the act of *extending* a horse over rough ground, and among grips—particularly, if that horse has a long stride, and does not pull together, is a greater trial to nerves, than the generality of fences, and is attended with more danger. The worst falls are those which happen in the open field, when horses are going at nearly the top of their speed; and it requires a finer finger to put a horse along, his best pace, over rough ground, than to ride him if he knows his business, over the stiffest and most difficult fences. In the one case, he sees his own danger; in the other his rider must see for him, and, by the finger, caution him against it. It is in this way alone that I can account for so many persons that I have known and met with, who, with all the necessary qualifications for riding to hounds, as far as fencing and horsemanship are concerned, yet never see a run at the best pace, because they will not gallop.

There is another description of persons who are generally defeated when *business is to be done;* and those are, your very light weights. In my experience of fox-hunting, I have observed that men above eleven stone, for the most part, beat men under eleven stone—and for this reason. The very light man says, "any thing will carry me;" and if he hears of a slight bit of blood, which no man of any size will buy, because he cannot carry weight, he goes and purchases him, calling him 'a nice little horse to carry his weight." The consequence of this is, as force must be opposed to force, this nice little horse and his rider, are knocked backwards, and thrown over by fences, which, a heavier man, on a heavier horse, would break through, if he could not clear. I am no advocate for large horses, but they must have substance and weight, or they cannot get through a strong country.

Putting fences out of the question, we may view this matter in another light. We know that weight equalizes all horses, of all ages, and all sizes. If, therefore, a man weighing only ten stone, gets horses only fit to carry ten stone, he can go no faster in a deep country than the man who weighs fifteen stone, provided he be mounted on horses equal to carry fifteen stone. This only applies to galloping; but if they come to fencing, the heavy man has it hollow. The heavy man says, "I *must* get horses to carry me." The very light man says, "those which can carry no one else will do for me," and thus he is, too often, defeated. To this must be added, in favour of the heavy man, that strength in the rider, as well as in the horse, is necessary in getting a horse across a stiff and deep country, where the fences are large and frequent.—"The gentleman rode very well," said Buckle, the jockey, of a gentleman rider, opposed to him in a race, "but he *tired before his horse;*" and this applies to the very light man over a country.

Riding to hounds, like most other things, has undergone a revolution in the march of time. Some years back, the best man was he who, after never being near the hounds for nineteen miles (supposing them to run so far), came up to them at the twentieth, and got the brush, which he carried home, in triumph, under the front of his bridle. The best man now is he who goes best through the best part of the run, even should he be "dead beat" at the last. As to riding, or asking for the brush, a man would as soon ask for the scalp of the huntsman's head, in the regular hunting countries, as for the brush of a fox. I once did see, and in one of the crack counties, a man ride over a fence into the middle of hounds as they were in the act of worrying their fox; and on the owner of them asking him why he did so, he replied that he wanted the brush. "You shall have the brush, Sir," said the master of the pack, "and let it serve you for the rest of your life. Take off that red coat when you get home, and never come a hunting again."

There are many of your readers, particularly those whose hunting has been confined to ploughed, and light-scenting countries, who can form but a faint idea of the speed of hounds in those countries which are capable of holding what is called a burning, or more properly, a lasting scent, such as will enable hounds to *run straight.* The circumstance, however, which I am about to mention, at the same time that it will shew the pace which hounds, under certain circumstances, are able to maintain, will warrant the assertions I have made as to the difficulty of seeing a run, when the pace is very quick; as also the necessity of horses being in the very best tune to attempt it....

In some countries, getting well away with hounds is difficult, and uncertain. Where coverts are large, on windy days, it is almost even betting whether a man gets a good start, or not. It is true, though singular, that in woodlands, foxes will often run the same line of country for generations in succession; but this is not to be depended upon, neither is there much reliance to be placed upon the wind. I remember telling an old and very good sportsman, one day, in Leicestershire, that the wind would, most probably, take us to his country; when he observed, that by the time I had been a fox-hunter as long as he had, I should learn to trust but little to the wind. "A fox," said he, "will make his point in spite of the wind; and it is only when he finds himself pressed, that he will cease to face it." This, I believe to be the case; but one observation I have made is,—that when a fox starts up wind, and then turns, he seldom faces it again. All they, however, who consult the wind, and ride to it, instead of to the hounds, will too often find themselves in a wrong latitude.

It is one of the drawbacks upon the pleasure of fox-hunting, that a man sometimes rides twenty miles to meet hounds, and then loses a fine run, by not getting away with them. The rose, however, is never without the thorn; and this must sometimes happen in large woodlands, which most commonly produce the best foxes. As foxes generally hang a little in large coverts, the best sportsman is often puzzled how to act. If running down wind, it is difficult for him to hear them. If he follows them up and down a deep covert ofte, his horse is half beaten before the run begins. It is necessary therefore to be wide awake upon these occasions; and I have always thought it to be the safer plan, when a man comes out determined to have a day's sport, to keep as near to hounds in covert as it is possible—even if he does take something out of his horse in doing so. By getting well away with them, he has not got to catch them, which may be still more against him, than even going two or three times up and down a deep ride in a covert. At all events, a sportsman's object is to be with hounds; and it is better to be with them on a horse half beaten, than to be riding about the country asking the old question—"Did you see the hounds?" on a fresh one....

NIMROD

On the Letters of Nimrod

Looking over the columns of the "Morning Post," a few days since, I saw a paragraph noticing the communications of our friend "NIMROD," in words to this effect, "that a sensation had been created in the sporting world by the letters of a gentleman in the *Sporting Magazine,* who appeared to have passed half his life among hounds, horses, and coachmen; and that his style was so excellent, it was a pity it had not been more worthily directed." I cannot help noticing to you my belief, that it would be well if some of the readers of the "Post" had passed their time no worse than NIMROD appears to have done. Is not that one of the best maxims ever broached—"Whatever is worth doing at all is worth doing well?" Every reflecting mind must acknowledge, that if people are to ride hunting, it is better to return to one's family safe and sound, than to be brought home senseless or mangled; we as sportsmen happen to know, that a good day's hunt is a most delightful recreation, and that such can only arise from a practical knowledge of principle in the conductors of the sport, seconded by our being well carried; and we further know that nothing is more disheartening, than deprivation of this manly gratification, by being astride an animal which we run the hazard of killing by keeping him in his place. I say that every friend to the horse, to humanity in general, is under obligation to any man who will so communicate the result of experience, as to diminish suffering arising from ignorance of a proper mode of treatment—who will shew the best plan of developing capability of performance with ease and

safety: for my own part, I have, in my humble stud, followed every advice of NIMROD. You shall hear the consequence: on the 28th of last month, I had a severe day; that is, although the country was rather deep, and the fencing frequent and strong, when I reflect, I and my horse thought nothing about it; for he came home, fed as usual, and was hunted again the fourth day as gay as possible. Since that one of the whippers-in told a friend of mine, that he knew of three dead ones. What does this go far to prove? Why that they might probably kick up their heels at exercise and yet be about as fit to go as so many dog horses. I recollect too, there were many very fine horses out, which makes the case more pitiable. NIMROD must not imagine that I thought any detail of his subject beneath his pen; the fact was, I could not have hoped he would trouble himself so far, and we are the more obliged by his doing so; one favour I particularly beg, which is, that before he concludes, he will state his mode of diet and treatment in the summer, supposing the horse to finish the season sound and up to his mark, with the run of a paddock dry of succulent food, as pointed out by him some numbers back; but I fear I am anticipating unfairly, and will conclude.

H.

Nim South's Southern Tour

The season which has just drawn to a close has been one of the most unpropitious to sportsmen in general, and to myself in particular, that I remember. As a body we were laid up in ordinary for several weeks during the very heart of it; and, individually, I was prevented making a sporting tour into the midland and northern counties, for which I was all prepared, the particulars whereof (with your permission) I intended to have inflicted upon the public through the medium of your valuable pages; therefore though I sustained a loss, the public, perhaps, *gained one.*

I was baffled in almost my first attempt to get to hounds. Being very anxious to see a friend at Brighton, and thinking to have a day with Colonel Jolliffe *en passant,* I sent a horse to Reigate on the 24th November for the following day (the fixture I think was Outwood, or some place a few miles south-west of Reigate), and rode down on the evening of the 24th myself, forwarding my hunting apparatus by coach.

The weather, which at first had the appearance of being favorable, towards night became so boisterous that I was almost blown away, horse and all, from the top of Reigate Hill. About nine o'clock, however, when I went into the stable to see my horses done up for the night, the wind had somewhat abated, and it rained a little; so giving my orders for the morning, and finding my own company getting rather dull, I shortly after retired to my bed-room, when I made the pleasing discovery that the coach had taken my things on to Brighton, leaving me with nothing but what I had ridden down in. The waiter consoled me by saying he had no doubt they would be returned by the mail; so hoping he might prove a true prophet, I crept into bed, having borrowed a white cotton nightcap, &c. of mine host of the White Hart.

Punctual to the hour the chambermaid made her appearance with hot water, but no portmanteau had arrived, neither were there any tidings of it; and after kicking about in bed in a tremendous fume for some half hour or so, I had just made up my mind to increase the weight of obligations to mine host by borrowing a pair of spurs of him also, and to hunt in my preceding day's dress (viz. trowsers), &c. sooner than not hunt at all; and just as I was going to put my resolve in execution, in walked a porter from the opposite inn (the White something else) with the identical portmanteau on his shoulder.

You may suppose with what alacrity I sprang out of bed and released the *red rag* and white cords from their confinement; but oh, how transient is human happiness! I drew up the windowblind, and found the face of the earth was obscured by snow at least a foot and a half in depth!!

This was the severest cut of all. If they had had the gumption to tell me so on awaking me, I should not have minded much whether the portmanteau made its appearance or not; but tantalizing me by bringing it, and then letting me shiver out of my snug bed to make the discovery myself, was rather a refinement of torture.

To proceed on my journey on horseback not seeming either very desirable or safe, from the balling of the snow in the horses' feet of the passers by, I got into the first coach that passed, which, after braving all dangers, landed its cargo safely in Brighton.

Though there was a pretty deep fall of snow, it did not lie long, and seemed merely a forerunner of the old-fashioned winter that succeeded. In the neighbourhood of Brighton at least it was all gone before many days had elapsed; and from the novelty of the place to me, and constant gaiety, the time slipped away imperceptibly, and the country had resumed its natural colour before I had been properly lionized over the town....

The first time I met them [the East Sussex Hounds] was at the kennel at Ringmer Green, shortly after the snow storm I mentioned. I had sent a horse on to the Black Horse Inn (or Falkiner Arms, as Mr. Kemp facetiously calls it, from the worthy Baronet of the name patronishing it on hunting days), at the entrance to Lewes from Brighton; where by the way there is an excellent breakfast set out every morning the hounds meet near Lewes, as also luncheon, the chief delicacy consisting of sausages, which, as every person alowed to be excellent, I did not take the trouble to spoil my dinner by eating.

The hour of meeting was a quarter before eleven; and having changed my horse I rode on in order to have a look at the hounds before they went into covert, in case I might not see them afterwards. On the Green, on the left hand side of the road which runs through the picturesque village of Ringmer, sat George Hennessey, formerly whipper-in to Colonel Jolliffe, afterwards to the Puckeridge, since to the Union, late a post-boy, and now huntsman to the E.S.F., with some twenty couple of hounds (ladies and gentlemen), attended by two whippers-in.

Though they had only come from the kennel (a few hundred yards), the men's boots looked as if they had performed a day's journey, at least so much of the boots as were visible for immense corduroy overalls, which hung like sacks from above the knee nearly to the ancle: in other respects they differed little from the generality of the brotherhood....

Independent of the button, I found that the Members of this Hunt might be known by their overalls and cloth caps to their boots. I never saw so many red (or *had been* red) coats with so few top boots; and some of the wearers looked more as if they were going to plough than to hunt.

I got hold of a good-natured looking man to tell me the names of some of them; and began asking who such a Gentleman was in the old hat or ragged coat; but I could not get on at all with these descriptions, there being scarcely any difference, except from bad to worse, though Lord Gage and Mr. Donovan certainly had the worst....

It was an excellent scenting day, and the pace for the first half hour was as quick as heart could wish. The fencing was very formidable and difficult for horses not accustomed to blind-ditches; and most of the field seemed to prefer the hang gates, reckoning upon their Sussex punchers either clearing or breaking them down. I thought myself singularly fortunate in getting only one tumble, by my horse preferring a flying to an on-and-off leap.

A short distance from where I fell a broad brook somewhat inter-

rupted the progress of the field, and when I came to it I found some ten or a dozen of those who *could* take it were over, while two or three who *would* take it were floundering about in it, and some twenty who *would not* take it were craning and looking at those who could and would.

Looking for a good landing place I discovered that a lady had joined the field. Her costume and appearance were not a little singular. She had on a beaver hat, a scarlet spencer or waist to her habit, with a sky blue body; and, from the state of her hair and glow of her complexion, had evidently been going "the pace that kills." She was accompanied by a sporting-looking Gentleman in scarlet, on a fine white horse, who was in a monstrous hurry to get her to ride at the brook, well knowing that the longer she looked at it the more unlikely she was to take it.

"O'd d—n it, come along," said he; "you had much better stay at home if you are afraid to ride over such a place as this," at the same time putting her horse straight to it, and riding over it himself. She followed his example—and cleared it, though I assure you it was no trifle. I was told that a cottager who resides close by makes a good thing every year by fishing Gentlemen and their horses out who get in; and he seemed to be pretty busy that day.

I need scarcely say that the lady was Mrs. Russell, of sporting celebrity; the Gentleman was Mr. Brackenbury, a very excellent rider. Mrs. R. used to be a bold rider I believe; but, like many of us, she is getting one of the "has beens," and she makes but a poor fight of it without Mr. B. I saw her out with Col. Wyndham's hounds one day, attended by a Gentleman in *trowsers,* who was more timid a great deal than she was; and instead of riding boldly at his fences, and making her follow, they kept looking at them together, he saying, "do you think we can manage this?"

I do not know how it was, but we made very little of our fox after we got over the brook; the pace, which has been killing, gradually relaxed into a cold hunting one; and though the pack persevered on their line, and worked extremely well, we ultimately lost our fox near Glynde....

Several foreigners took up their quarters at Brighton last season, French, Germans, Danes, Saxons, &c. Nearly all came for the purpose of *hunting,* though some followed their game in the drawing-room in preference to the field.

As field-sportsmen the Germans took the lead most decidedly. At the commencement of the season there were three from that country—viz. NIMROD's friend Count Hans, Count Pazwaites, and Count Patiawney; but the flower of the flock was the Saxon Baron Gablentz. Count Hans and the other two left in December with the intention of going into Leicestershire. I saw them out a few times, and they were all hard riders. Some, if not all, were mounted by Tilbury, a mode which I strongly recommended to all wandering sportsmen, for reasons which I shall take another opportunity of stating.

The Baron had his own horses, for one of which he gave 170 £., notwithstanding which he was decidedly the worst mounted of the party; but being a light weight, he generally kept in the foremost rank, unless (which he was somewhat apt to do) he took up a line for himself.

Not knowing what fear was, he neither cared what sort of a horse he got on to, nor what sort of a place he rode him at; in consequence of which, and a naturally loose military seat, he seldom went out without saluting the earth a few times; and one day he had so many falls, he said he could not count them.

I think he was the boldest rider I ever saw in my life. Of course, from the novelty both of the country and the sport, he could not be expected to do it with much judgment, and sometimes attempted impossibilities. One day he rode at the Ouse about two miles above Lewes, observing, if his horse could not jump quite over, he would get part way, and might swim the rest. As it was, he got into the middle of it, where (as he said himself) his horse and he *lived* for a quarter of an hour.

I never either saw or heard of a foreigner who entered more fully into the spirit of the English nation, or took such delight in hunting, as the Baron. Of English Gentlemen he had a very high opinion, and used to say, "By my word, an English Gentleman is the first Gentleman in the world." It was not, however, to every one who claimed it that the Baron accorded this title, having as nice a discrimination in these matters as though he had been residing in this country all his life.

Not being able to speak a word of English on his arrival (a few months previous to the time of which I am writing), it was quite astonishing with what rapidity he learned, and confidence he spoke it, generally expressing himself in more comprehensive terms than an Englishman, and his stories and descriptions used to be rich beyond measure.

Coming to covert one morning on a lame hack, some one said to him, "Why, Baron, your horse is lame."—"No, my good friend, him not lame," he said, "but he *beaucoup* fatigue *in one leg.*"

Another morning he appeared in a prodigiously smart red and gold waistcoat (fresh from Paris), in which he had been figuring at a ball the night before; and a friend observing that it was too good to hunt in, he answered—"So said my valet ven he dressed me; but I told him, by my honour, there is nothing too good for *foxing* in." . . .

. . .

Having in my last sent you an account of Mr. Craven's, or the East Sussex, fox-hounds, I now arrive at Colonel Wyndham's, or the West Sussex.

The nominal boundary between the country of these two packs is the river Adir, though they have some coverts on the Brighton side as joint property. The Colonel has the whole of the West side of the county of Sussex, and I believe a covert or two in Hampshire. They are a private pack of hounds, and no appointments are advertised, which makes it rather difficult, in Brighton at least, for a stranger to find out where they meet: and the Colonel, like most other fox-hunters, not being fond of riotous fields, leaves the Findon side of the country about the commencement of the Christmas holidays, and does not return until February, after which there is no difficulty in meeting them.

When a Gentleman keeps a pack of fox-hounds for his own amusement, and allows his friends and neighbours the privilege of hunting with them free of expense, and also does not object to seeing an occasional stranger in the field, I believe it is generally understood that those who avail themselves of his kindness are to take things as they find them, and no one is considered to be at liberty either to find fault or to advise.

Private packs of hounds, like every other species of private property, must be respected; and a man has no more right to find fault with the contents of another's kennel, than he has to censure his domestic establishment.

But still, when acting up to this principle, the gallant Colonel's hounds run no risk of wasting "their fragrance on the desert air;" for, though the use of illiberal criticism is forbidden, the just tribute of praise must not be withheld.

The badness of the weather prevented my meeting them until their return to the Brighton side of the county about the middle of February, when, accidentally hearing that they were to meet at Bramber Castle on the following day, I sent a horse on to Shoreham, and went by the turnpike, not caring to trust myself over the Downs in foggy frosty weather. . . .

The first day was on the 22d February, when we met on the Downs on the Brighton side of the Shoreham river, and, after drawing the hangers which skirt it, we proceeded to try the gorses, where we soon found; but although the place was within a mile of where we met, a main earth in a quarry or precipice which extended down the hillside to the road was open, and the consequence was that we lost our fox. After persevering on the Downs for a couple of hours, Arber at length trotted off over the Dyke Hill, to some gorses below, whence we went to Toddington Wood, and found the gallant fox which gave us the run so ably described by DASHWOOD; though I think he will agree with me that the persons who think best of a run are those who are not present at it. Not but that this day's run was a very superior one, though it was attended by many disagreeables, to say nothing of having to ride a severe chase on a horse, which, before unkennelling this fox, had been on his legs at least five hours, and for my own part I should have liked it better if they had not gone quite so fast. The sport at Applesham, on the day following but one, was the most curious I ever saw; and for men, who, as I said before, prefer "racing to hunting," it must have been delightful. . . .

Of the pleasant gentlemanlike manner in which these hounds are conducted, there cannot be a difference of opinion; and the fields with Colonel Wyndham's hounds excel those with the East Sussex hounds, as much as John Arber excels George Hennessey as a huntsman, or as much as the former pack excels the latter in point of speed: but, after all is said, I am not ashamed to confess, that I would rather meet the East Sussex hounds, with their riotous fields and all their other imperfections, than Col. Wyndham's pack, with all their high breeding and other Leicestershire qualifications; because, with the one I should be sure to see hunting, while with the other the chances are frequently very much against a stranger seeing the hounds after they once leave the covert. . . .

. . .

FAIN would I pass from the Sussex fox-hounds to those in the neighbourhood of London; but the world has long accorded precedence to the stag-hounds; and when we remember that Royalty itself is at the head of the list of owners, we cannot, perhaps, repine at the decision.

I am aware there are many men in London whose occupations are such, that, unless it were for the stag-hounds, they would never see a day's sport throughout the year. These, I think may be divided into two classes—your dandy cockney-sportsman, perhaps a fashionable tailor's son, with his neat new pink, natty leathers, and well-cleaned "pipe cases," who likes to ride through "Brentford" or Croydon, to exhibit his person to the "ladies:"—the other is your regular Mark-lane man, or, perhaps, "a black diamond merchant" from St. Mary Axe, who, nearly suffocated with bad air, and dying from indigestion, gets upon the outside of a rough-going nag, to shake his intestines about, and to have what he calls a "good gallop."

The regular stag-hunters are mostly veterans from the fox-hunting ranks, who, finding "the pace begins to kill *them*,["] discard the red coat, and adopt the "merry merry green" to follow the staghounds, and "M'Adamize" with them until death closes the scene.

In my opinion stag-hunting, as followed in England, is the tamest of all possible sports; there is neither stimulus nor science about it; and, by heavens! I would rather ride thirty miles to covert to meet fox-hounds, though the chances were five to one against a find, than be driven ten miles on the best drag that was ever built to see a stag uncarted before hounds....

Great change has taken place in the management of the different stag-hounds about London within the last few years. Those which were formerly hunted by the Berkeleys are now managed by Mr. Sullivan; and the Earl of Derby's seem to belong to a joint stock company, with Messrs. Maberly and Richard Tattersall as directors.

I was out with Mr. Sullivan's hounds on the 9th of March, when they had one of the best runs of last season. We met, or turned out, at Mr. Tattersall's farm, at Dawley Hall, about fourteen miles from Hyde Park Corner, between the Windsor and Uxbridge roads. I took a "Cockneyshire" friend[1] with me, who had lately purchased a hunter of me, but who himself had never seen a hound of any sort, and, by bumping about in the riding-school, had acquired a pretty stiff military seat, ill adapted for riding across a country. However he was a very apt pupil indeed; and before I had got him through Hammersmith I had shortened his stirrups considerably, and given him a few directions about putting his horse fairly to his leaps, and never to mind a

tumble—so long as he did not break his neck—and to stick by his horse if he wished his horse to stick by him, &c. &c. Some one had told me that Dawley Hall was only twelve miles from Hyde Park Corner, and I had not sent a horse on, but set off on my hunter, to ride quietly down with my friend, intending to do it in two hours and a half. It looks very cocktail to be seen riding through the streets of London in a scarlet coat; so I hid mine under a great coat, but found it so warm that I was obliged to cast it before I got to Holland House; and then I had to ride through Hammersmith, Turnham-green, Brentford, and Hounslow, which form almost a continued street for ten miles; in fact, one is not in the country on this side on Hounslow.

We got to Dawley Hall about half-past eleven (eleven is the nominal hour): here we found thirty or forty horsemen assembled in the court in front of the house; the hounds were in a barn behind. The deer was shortly after handed into his travelling carriage, and we all proceeded to a very large long grass field at the back of Dawley Hall, where he alighted....

After the stag had been at large a quarter of an hour or so, Mr. Sullivan and the hounds came up, attended by two whippers-in. Mr. S. is a young man rather tall then otherwise, with a nice figure, and is a light weight. He sported the black velvet cap *à la Oxendon,* with a plain scarlet frock, and a black or dark blue collar to it, and a horn (which he could not blow) slung over his shoulder. The servants were dressed in the same manner, and seemed handy fellows. The hounds are small, but a beautiful pack, with plenty of music, and can go "the pace that kills." Like all stag-hounds they were rather riotous at first; but as soon as ever they settled on the scent, they got together in good style....

After the stag cleared Staines, he took up a line of country, and persevered in it, pressing below Colnbrook. Here I threw a shoe and pulled up, twenty miles from town. I got it replaced, and set my horse's head towards the smoke of London.

Stag-hunting seems to be the popular sport in these parts. Not a wagoner did I pass on the road but inquired what sort of a chase we had had; and all the little boys kept hallooing after me, "I say, measter, vere did you take him?"

I knew they would not believe me if I said I had thrown a shoe, so I told them we had run him to Great Marlow in Bucks, some ten miles father than I had been, and they all went away quite satisfied.

Coming home from *fox*-hunting, there is nothing I like so much as to be asked by a farmer or a labourer what sport we have had. I have often been amused, watching for the next question, which is sure to follow, "did you kill him?" If I say "no, we ran him to earth in such a place," my friend is done; but tell him we killed him, and his eyes sparkle with pleasure, and nothing but an account of the run will satisfy him.

I got back to town about five o'clock, having ridden between forty and fifty miles, and stopped half an hour at Cranford Bridge to feed my horse.

The following day I thought I would go and see how my friend was after his day's hunting, and took his stable in my way to his residence to have a look at the horse he had ridden.

"Well, John, what time did your master get home last night?" said I to his groom.

"O, Sir!" said John, shaking his head, and with a face like a *travelling donkey's*, "he's not cast up yet."

"Not cast up yet, nor his horse either?" said I.

"No, Sir! neither *on* them," said John, with a sigh; "I much fear they have happened an accident."

"Good God! what have I done?" said I, as I bolted out of the mews; "I have taken an eldest son, an heir-at-law, and I do not know what else, out hunting, and broken his neck I dare say, and on a horse too that he bought of me." I do not think I ever was in such a fright in my life; and as I hurried along the street I was cursing myself for my folly, wondering what the deuce I should say to his father and mother, and his grandmother, and his uncles and aunts, and his godfathers and godmothers, and all the relations and connections of this world, and resolving never to take another cockney out hunting.

While all this was going on in my mind I arrived at the door of his brother's lodging in — Street, having in my hurry upset a blind ballad singer, and run foul of the barrow of a dog's-meat man. "Is your master at home?" said I to the servant. "No, Sir, he is gone down to Eton," said the fellow. "What has happened?" said I. "Don't know, Sir!" said the man (as I thought in a very suspicious and mysterious manner); "he went out suddenly, and merely told me that."

"Then, by G—d, it's true!" said I; "he is dead, and his brother is gone to bring up his *remainders*." And away I ran to his lodgings; and oh, what a relief it was to my mind, when, knocking at the door, his servant said his master was "up stairs."

And sure enough he was there, reading *Zimmermann on Solitude*, and eating eggs and muffins for his breakfast—the only damage he had sustained being the loss of a little leather.

It seems they had run the stag to Sunning-hill, where they took him; and my friend had accomplished the run in good style without a single fall. However he said he found his horse very lazy after it; and returning through Windsor Forest some one informed him that he had lost both his fore-shoes. So reaching the town of Windsor, he abandoned the vessel and put himself into the hold of the stage coach, and came up to town; and thinking the horse would be quite fresh the next day, his brother, from want of amusement, had gone to act the part of groom, by riding him up. However he was disappointed, for he could only get him as far as Slough, where he was a second time housed, and it was some days before he recovered from the effects of the hunt.

I am sorry to say my good resolution failed me the first time it was tried; for about a fortnight after I found my friend at my side again, going to the "Epping Hunt."!!! . . .

NIM SOUTH

Not "THIN SOUTH," as the *Age* newspaper facetiously
calls me, because I happen to be rather corpulent.

P.S. Since my Cockneyshire friend has discovered that I am a contributor to the pages of the *Sporting Magazine,* he has become very careful in his conversation, and always concludes his observations by saying, "I hope I have not said any thing sporting, have I?" In what I have written my fears lay the other way; but as I do not profess to be a stag-hunter, I hope the honest avowal of it will be sufficient apology for anything I have said unsportsmanlike.

Fox-Hunting

As I know you are always anxious to present your readers with authentic and original information of what is going on in the hunting districts, I have sent you a few remarks, founded on my own personal observation, beginning with LEICESTERSHIRE; and if acceptable, will hereafter furnish you with some particulars relating to other counties.

NIMROD

LEICESTERSHIRE

It being twenty years since I first hunted in this celebrated country, it may not be unpleasant to many of your readers to hear a little of its "history," and the different changes which have taken place in its establishments, during the period I mention.

72 Hounds in the Morning

Leicestershire may justly be denominated the Montpelier of hunting countries: in the eye of a sportsman, it is the Vale of Cashmere; and in comparison with it, all others retire "longo intervallo."

Both nature and art have contributed to render Leicestershire the country for fox-hunting. To the former, it is indebted for the depth and richness of its soil—favourable to holding a scent; and to the latter for the large size of its inclosures—for the general practicability of its fences—for the greatest portion of the land being old pasture; and for the numerous gorse coverts made for the purpose of breeding and preserving foxes.

There is another circumstance also, which gives Leicestershire a decided advantage over other countries; and that is—the few *large* coverts which the better part of it contains—thereby affording such *room* for sport, that if a fox once gets away, and is a good one, a run (barring accidents) must be the consequence. He has no where to hide his head—he must fly for his life. Woodland foxes are generally supposed to be better, and stouter, than those bred above ground; but every one who has hunted in large coverts must be aware, what an advantage both hounds and horses must have by coming away at once with a fox from a small piece of gorse, over those which may have been, perhaps, three or four times up and down a large covert, where the hounds have had to contend with strong underwood, and the horses with deep and boggy ridings, to say nothing of the certainty of gentlemen getting well away in the one case, and the chance of not getting away at all in the other.

In a quick thing with hounds, a good start is every thing; and in Leicestershire it is our own fault if we do not get it. This advantage, however, is too often abused. Mr. Meynell[2] was once heard to describe a run, and he began thus:—"The fox came out of the gorse close to my horse's heels, then came Cecil Forrester, then my hounds."

These artificial coverts being, of course, properly arranged as to distance from each other, a burst is secured. If the fox live to reach one of them, a check for a minute or two may take place; but this check may be beneficial to the sport of the day. Hounds and horses get a puff—tail hounds come up, and those who were not fortunate in getting away with the pack, secure a place. The fox, finding delays are dangerous, and that he has nothing for it but to fly, makes his point for some distant earths, the attainment of which nothing but death will prevent.

Having said this, it is not to be wondered at that, besides being encroached upon by other hounds, Leicestershire, though a small county, should contain three packs of fox-hounds, which are attended by the best and hardest riders in England; to which it may be added, without any reflection upon other establishments, that no other country could find such hounds to ride to. What benefit must they derive from such a country!

I have not yet done with the advantages of Leicestershire. To say nothing of the benefit arising from hounds being never out of the sight of the huntsman and whippers-in, unless (as it sometimes has happened) they run away from them, there is another advantage which it enjoys above all others, and that is,—when, at the end of the season, from the effect of long-continued drought, aided, perhaps, by harsh cutting winds, and hot sun, all others, where fallows are to be hunted over, are hard and dry, and incapable of holding a scent, or being ridden over with safety, either to a horse or his rider, this county is as capable of shewing a run, as at any other period of the season. As a proof of what I have said, I have only to mention a day's sport which I saw when Mr. Smith (*the Tom Smith*) had the Quorn hounds, which, I have no doubt, is fresh in the recollection of many who witnessed it, for it was a brilliant one, and such as no other country in the world could have shewn *on that day*. It was on the 17th of April; and, as Tom Wingfield (then whipper-in to Mr. S.) observed, "a kind of day more fit for growing cucumbers than for hunting," It was, however, allowed to be the second-best day's sport of the year.

The place of meeting was Slawson Town, in the Market Harborough country; but there was no fox in the gorse. In our road across the country to try another covert, one jumped out of a hedge-row, and was killed after a burst of sixteen minutes, without a check—best pace—heads up, and sterns down. We killed him near to Shacon Holt covert; and as soon as the hounds and horses had recovered their wind, we drew the Holt. Without waiting to be found, away went a gallant fox, and, putting his head nearly straight, was also killed at the end of twelve miles (point blank), in fifty-eight minutes, with only one trifling check, about eight minutes before he died.

The country he went over could only be compared to Newmarket Heath, inclosed with strong fences; but many had reason to wish that neither the fences nor the inclosures had been so large. That there was much distress among the horses, it is needless to observe, after the description I have given of the day and the pace. Mr. Smith rode the famous *Jack-a-lantern* in his usual style; but, at one time, his *light* was out. He stopped: but whilst Mr. Smith waited for Tom Wingfield, whom he saw coming up, with the view of a change for the better, the good old horse recovered his wind, and came up to us at the check. Seeing Mr. Lindo on "The Clipper" (more of them in a future Number) encouraging the hounds to a scent at a gateway, he was beginning to

rate us, saying that the hounds had been pressed upon, and that we only wanted a puff for our horses. At this moment the chase was renewed, and Lindo, turning round, aptly remarked that "*he* had had *his* puff, or he would not have been there." The fox lived about eight minutes longer; and Mr. Smith, observing two couples of his young hounds leading, *appeared transported with delight.* He never turned his horse's head ten yards to the right or to the left for an open gate, or for a gap, but rode by the side of his pack, cheering them to their fox (which he knew must die), in a manner and at a pace that I shall never forget: neither shall I ever forget the fever we were in, from the exertion of such a run on so warm a day. I could hear the pulsation of my temples as plain as I could that of my horse's heart.

The fences in the Market Harborough country are the strongest in Leicestershire. The richness of the soil throws the quick [living hedge] to a great size; and to guard against the bullocks in the summer season, very few weak places are to be found. If a horse be not a superior fencer, and good at timber, he has no business there. The inclosures also are large, which is very trying to horses. An anecdote on this subject is related of Mr. Smith. He observed to a friend of his, that "he never saw him out in the Harborough country." His friend replied that "he did not like it, the fences were so large." "Oh," said Mr. Smith, "There is no place you cannot get over, with a fall." Perhaps, however, he thought rather more of a fall than Mr. Smith did.

Apologising for this digression, I return to my subject. The first year I was in Leicestershire, was the last of Mr. Meynell's, and the first of Lord Sefton's hunting the Quorn country. In mentioning the name of Mr. Meynell, I feel a degree of respect due to it, which all sportsmen must acknowledge and appreciate. So long as fox-hounds and fox-hunters are to be found in England it will never be forgotten; neither is there a kennel which is not, at this moment, indebted to him for some of its best blood. As, however, I may have occasion to mention the name of this justly celebrated sportsman again, I shall only add that, as a master of a pack of fox-hounds, Mr. Meynell never has been excelled. Independent of his knowledge of every thing relating to hounds and to hunting, his conduct in the field was such as should be handed down as an example worthy the imitation of every master of fox-hounds. From his rank in life, and from the sphere in which he moved—to say that he was well bred and polite to his equals, and to his friends, is saying nothing; but towards every man who hunted with his hounds, he conducted himself with that general urbanity and condescension, which *alone* secure to a person in his situation the esteem of the country, and with it, the foxes. In his time, a man's life was not more secure from violence and murder, than was that of a fox.

To every man who is a fox-hunter, it is well known how much it is requisite for a master of hounds to stand well with the yeomen and farmers of his country. They have much in their power, and to them Mr. Meynell was uniformely civil, and even polite. He has been seen more than once to pull out his watch at the place of meeting, and to observe, that the time of throwing off was expired; but, he would say, "I see Jack. . . .'s horse here, and he is not come. It is Leicester fair this morning—he is a good fellow, and we will give him a quarter of an hour." I need not add that he alluded to a sporting grazier, who he knew, was obliged to attend the fair; but as at those fairs the cattle market is early in the morning, a farmer can do his business there, and attend hounds afterwards. Ye masters of fox-hounds, bear this in mind! This is the way to preserve a country!!

The last time I saw Mr. Meynell in the field was, I believe, nearly the last time of his being with hounds: it was after Lord Sefton had taken to them. We met at Thrussulton Wolds, a seat of Lord Ferrers's, and found directly in the plantations close to the house. We went well away with our fox for about two miles, and thought we were in for a run; but he was met and attacked by a shepherd's dog, which grappled with him: he disengaged himself and went on; but in a few fields more we found him drowned in a canal which he attempted to cross; so that, no doubt, the cur dog had injured him. I observed Mr. Meynell very forward in this short, but sharp burst—frequently cheering as he went. As we were drawing for a second fox, I witnessed a remarkable instance of the quickness of his ear—more remarkable at his period of life, when that wonderful organ is seldom so correct. The hounds were in a small covert, about one hundred yards from the place where he stood, which commanded a view of it. Lord Shefton went with the hounds, and stood close to the gorse. A hound spoke, but he spoke cautiously. There was no cheer to him, so he was suspected;—but "one *word*" (as we say) from a hound in a Leicestershire covert, sets every man on the alert for a start. It is like the sound of a bugle to prepare for the charge; and, on some nerves, has much the same effect. However, in this case, the alarm was false; there was no fox; and Lord Sefton rode up to Mr. Meynell and asked him what hound spoke in the covert. "I think it was Concord," said Mr. Meynell. "It was *not* Concord," said Lord Sefton—"he was at my horse's heels." "It was either Concord, or Caroline" (brother and sister, and their first year), replied Mr. Meynell. In five minutes the point was decided. Raven, the huntsman, came by us with the hounds. Lord Sefton asked him the question. "Concord, my Lord," was his reply.

Mr. Meynell's eye to a hound was not less quick than was his ear. It has been asserted that on seeing a pack of strange hounds drawn to feed, he could call almost all of them afterwards by their names.

To return, however, to my original subject. Leicestershire never witnessed more splendour than during the period of Lord Sefton's hunting it. The price of horses (and he set the example) was never higher than in his time, and, I conceive, will never be so high again. From five to eight hundred guineas was a common price for a hunter that could go forty minutes, best pace,—and even more was asked and given. Mr. Lorraine Smith had a magnificent horse, called Hyacinth, got by Hollyhock. He asked a thousand for him, and I believe Lord Sefton offered nearly all the money. He had, afterwards, the misfortune to break a blood-vessel under Mr. Smith, and died in the field. His Lordship, of course, for his great weight, was obliged to get the best of horses, and price was only a secondary consideration:—the first was, to procure the horse that could carry him; and such animals as his Plato, Rowland, and Gooseberry, were at any time difficult to find. He had always three out each day for his own riding. Young Raven (son to the huntsman) rode one of them, and the other was ridden by a groom, both good horsemen, and riding in his Lordship's stirrup-lengths. One of them was always close to him, so that the moment he perceived symptoms of distress, he jumped upon the second horse. The third was kept at a proper distance, going easily to himself, till an opportunity presented itself of getting up to his Lordship, in case he also should be wanting. Lord Sefton had one of the best grooms that England could produce. His name was Potter. His horses were always *high in flesh, but strong in work,* which is the perfection (if not the *sine qua non*) of condition for horses that carry high weights. *Good* flesh is strength. His Lordship had a quick eye to hounds, and his nerves were very good, though he avoided timber if possible. Considering his weight, however, he went brilliantly over a country.

With all these advantages, it is generally believed that he found himself unable to get horses that could carry him up to his hounds when they went their best pace, and for that reason he gave them up, and took to the road; where his merits are too well known to require any observations from me, he being allowed to be one of the steadiest and most masterly coachmen in England.

When Lord Sefton retired from the sporting world, it lost one of its brightest stars. The splendour of his establishment gave to spectators more the idea of an imperial hunting party in a foreign country, than that of an English pack of fox-hounds. It brought to our recollection Dido's hunting party to the godlike Æneas. If the covert was accessible to a carriage, he always appeared in his barouche and four, accompanied by several others; and ladies were often of the party, though they never quitted the carriages. His hounds were perfect, and well might they be so. The celebrated John Raven hunted one pack; and the no less celebrated Stephen Goodall (afterwards many years huntsman to Sir Thomas Mostyn), hunted the other, both pupils of Mr. Meynell's.

Mr. Beckford observes, that were he obliged to have either a good huntsman and a bad whipper-in, or a bad huntsman and a good whipper-in, he should decidedly prefer the latter. Of what importance then must he have considered a good whipper-in; and what advantages must Lord Sefton's hounds have possessed in having two such whippers-in as Joe Harrison and Tom Wingfield, besides other assistance; for a feeder was always out well mounted, as also Young Raven, on one of Lord Sefton's spare horses, both ready to act when wanting.

The command which these hounds were in, could only be compared to that of a regiment on parade. A whip was scarcely ever used; and as far as a "yo-go-it" could be heard, nothing more was wanting to bring them back. A horn also was scarcely ever heard to sound. I was particularly struck with the latter circumstance, having never heard it for six days in succession; and it was only had recourse to on the seventh, in consequence of Stephen Goodall, whose voice was never strong, giving a blow for a hound, called "Cruiser," who was missing in a fog. This, in some degree, is connected with the nature of the country, for we all know that in woodlands a horn is as necessary as a hound.

Exclusive of the old Melton Club (at this time very well attended),

Lord Foley, Sir Henry Peyton, and Sir Stephen Glynn, had a house between them at Quorn. They all rode well to hounds; and I believe it was then that Sir Henry took a leap, which was recorded in the *Sporting Magazine*. Lord Foley has now retired from the field. Sir Stephen Glynn is, unfortunately, no more; but Sir Henry Peyton goes as well as ever he did with Sir Thomas Mostyn's and the Duke of Grafton's hounds, residing at Tusmore Park, in Oxfordshire, where on the road, as well as in the field, he is, and I hope will long continue, a leading character.

OXFORDSHIRE—SIR THOMAS MOSTYN'S COUNTRY

That part of Oxfordshire hunted by Sir Thomas Mostyn,[3] is known by the name of the Bicester country. On the western side of it the land is light, resembling the hill part of the county; but on the Buckinghamshire side, there is a fine grazing district, with good sized fields, a deep soil, and strong fences—not much unlike the better part of Northamptonshire, and good enough for any hounds....

In addition to this country, Sir Thomas has a kennel at Chipping Warden, in Northamptonshire, on the road from Banbury to Daventry, six miles from the former, and ten from the latter place, from whence he hunts part of that country running up to the Pychley and the Warwickshire countries. This part of Northamptonshire is uncommonly fine to ride over for those who are not afraid of large fences, but *the draw* is apt to be uncertain. A blank day has never been an unusual thing here—a circumstance which I never could account for, from the real fox-hunting spirit that pervades the farmers who inhabit it. It is no uncommon thing to see a hundred of them out in a day; all anxious for sport; many of them riding good horses, and selling them for large prices; and their farms being for the most part grass, no damage can be done to them.

Sir Thomas Mostyn, though a young man, is an old master of fox-hounds, having kept them entirely at his own expence, nearly twenty-five years. It is twenty-two years next August since he took possession of the Bicester country: and previous to that period, he hunted part of Gloucestershire, and part of Oxfordshire, having a kennel at Stow-on-the-Wold, in the former county. Few men are better qualified to be at the head of a pack of fox-hounds than Sir Thomas. A single man, possessed of a fine fortune, and at ease in his circumstances, the expence is not an object to him; and his conduct in the field is particularly gentlemanlike—added to which, no man, did his health permit him to enjoy it, is more fond of the sport. His attention to his kennel is great; and in the field he is a pattern to all masters of fox-

80 Hounds in the Morning

hounds. It is much to be lamented that severe fits of the gout prevent his deriving that pleasure from his hounds to which he is entitled; as there are many days in the season on which he cannot go out at all, and on others he is obliged to return home without following them far. This circumstance, however, has not abated his zeal to shew sport to others, though he may not have it in is power to partake of it himself....

Sir Thomas Mostyn's hounds have had the advantage of three celebrated huntsmen, Shaw, Stephen Goodall, and Tom Wingfield, who is now with them. These men are all so well known in the sporting world, that nothing I can say, can add to or diminish their fame....

When, however, I say that in Stephen Goodall's time Sir Thomas Mostyn's hounds were the speediest in England, I do not say they were the best; but my assertion of their being the speediest, is founded on the best grounds—on comparison with others. Every hound, and every horse, goes fast by a bush or a thistle; but it is by comparison alone that their speed beyond others is ascertained. At the period I allude to, I was in the habit of seeing two, and sometimes three other packs in the same week, and it certainly appeared to me, that so long as a good scent held, and all was right, the speed of these hounds was tremendous, and their fox, if killed at all, was killed in a brilliant and decisive burst. But, on the other hand, if things went wrong—if, at the end of ten or fifteen minutes, a flock of sheep, a dry road, a short turn, or any of those ill-natured, but sometimes convenient, accidents occurred—they wanted a little of that *condescending stoop*, if I may be allowed the expression, which they have now got in their kennel. Their pace in those days was such, that not a word could be heard from them; and the man who could not follow them by his eye, had little to depend upon from his ear.

Not professing to be a judge of hounds, I only speak of Sir Thomas Mostyn's at this period, as any other casual observer would do; and the first thing that struck a stranger to them was, that they appeared too much like one family, or, in more technical language, bred too much in-and-in. There was a particular character and style belonging to them, unlike most other hounds. They were firm and compact, shewed a great deal of high breeding, and would not tire; but they were not hounds for a bad-scenting day, or a short-running fox.

Sir Thomas's hounds, as I before observed, are very well attended; and there are several very hard riders amongst the number. The fields in the Bicester country are not large, generally consisting of from sixty to seventy horsemen; and, with the exception of, now and then, an Oxford man, rather too much in a hurry to get on, they go very pleasantly together over a country. There is no jealousy amongst them;

neither is there any of that riding over men and horses, as well as hedges and ditches, which is now become so prevalent in Leicestershire, and which is a great bar to the pleasures of the sport. Having witnessed the sad accident Mr. Osbaldeston met with in that country last season, and having been ridden over three times myself, I may be allowed to say a word or two, as I can speak *feelingly*, on the subject.

There is no horse, however perfect he may be, but may make a mistake at a fence, however small, even when *fresh*, and the *puff* is in him; but when he gets weak at the end of a run, he is of course more liable to it. A fall, then, may always be calculated upon; and allowance should be made for it by the one who comes next to the fence, supposing he is obliged to go over the same place, which is often unavoidable. He should never ride at it till he sees the horse that goes before him *well on his legs*, in the next field. I say, "well on his legs," because, having cleared the fence is no insurance against a fall, when a horse is weak, as, should the ground be deep, he may not be able to support himself on landing. In Leicestershire, they charge the fences like a flock of sheep through a gateway, and if you fall, you are certain to be ridden over. I remember, a few seasons back, in that country, as I was in the act of landing over a downhill fence, with a horse so beaten that he was never worth a shilling afterwards, I looked up and saw a hard-riding man in the air above me. I called out to him, "Pray, don't come so near!" His answer was, "I beg your pardon, but my horse has carried me so well!" Thus, then, was I to be jumped upon, because his horse was fresher and better than mine.

Sir Thomas Mostyn may justly be said to have as good a pack of fox-hounds at this time as ever went into a field; and any true lover of the sport would ride fifty miles of a morning to see Tom Wingfield hunt them. Who Tom Wingfield is most of your readers are aware; but as the history of every man who is great in his way, has more or less of interest attached to it, it may be no harm to inform those who do not already know it, that his education has been complete for the situation he fills, having whipped-in to the late Mr. Meynell, Lords Sefton and Foley, as also to Mr. T. A. Smith, all in the Quorndon country. Considering that he was not educated in woodlands, it is wonderful as well as delightful to see him (as I have seen him) stick to his fox for two hours in those "little spinies," as he calls them—the great Clayton Woods—and kill him without leaving him for a moment.

In the open country Tom is preeminent. A beautiful and determined horseman, he is never out of sight of his hounds, and he can see more with that one eye of his, than many would if they had three. When his hounds are at check he invariably stands still, as coolly as though he were looking at a prospect, and never intrudes his opinion till they appear to ask for it. This is the way to give confidence to hounds, and nine times out of ten, as Tom knows, the instinct of the hound may be backed against the judgment of the man.

Wingfield is a man of few words, but what he says is to the purpose, and he can be a bit of a wag. A friend of mine was riding over Leicestershire with him when he lived with Mr. Smith, and coming to "a rasper," [an irritating person] which a third person, who was of the party, did not fancy, Tom turned around and observed, "I think, Sir, that gentleman has no business *in our shire*." Tom is, however, an excellent huntsman and a careful servant, and it is to be hoped that his master and himself will long continue to enjoy the benefits which they derive from each other....

NIMROD

Sporting Trifles

The Hertfordshire hunt had what they call a most gallant day last week: having run a burst of more than an hour, they crossed upon a fresh fox at Branfield, and clattered him two hours and a half more, when he was run to *earth* near *Baldock*. The two chaces, which admitted of no interruption from hard running were full forty miles in extent! Out of a field of fourscore, only *nine* were in at the earth, at the head of whom was Lady Salisbury.[4] After giving honest Daniel, the old huntsman, the go by, she pressed Mr. Hale *neck* and *neck*;—soon blowed the Whipper-in, and contrived indeed through the whole chace to be always nearest the *brush!* ...

The Prince of Wales[5] has lately met with an unexpected interruption to his field sports in Hampshire. Having hunted a part of the country, hitherto reserved for the County Subscription pack, a remonstrance has been sent to his Royal Highness, and he has been formally warned to refrain from many of the best covers in the country, not excepting some in the neighbourhood of his newly-purchased seat of the Grange.

His Majesty's Stag-Hounds

On taking up the COUNTY CHRONICLE of the 12th inst. I saw an account of a run with his Majesty's hounds, when the deer was turned out at Salt-hill; and crossing the country by Farnhamchurch—over Stoke common, &c. &c. he was taken *near* to the Earl of Essex's park, at Cashiobury, in Hertforshire—adding, that this is the course which this deer always takes.

Many years ago, with the late King's hounds, I witnessed a beautiful run over this identical country; but which, for the lapse of time, would not be worth mentioning now, were it not for two or three circumstances attending it, which may amuse your readers, some of whom, no doubt, recollect it.

I was asked by a friend of mine, residing near Maidenhead, to come and spend a fortnight with him, and to bring a couple of horses with me, as I should see some excellent sport with his Majesty's stag-hounds. Having just quitted Leicestershire, and having never seen stag-hunting, I confess I held it cheap. I had heard of something like a calf being turned out of a tilted cart, which could be seen for two miles a-head,—that the hounds were stopped, when the master of them, or any of his particular friends, was thrown out, and that a whipper-in, or some such person, took care never to lose sight of the animal to be pursued. The first two days that I went out with his Majesty's hounds, certainly did not remove my prejudices against stag-hunting; for, having no scent, we made a sorry business of it. In spite of a very sharp fellow, one of the yeoman prickers [riders], whose name was George Gosden, riding after the deer, and "slotting" [tracking] him as it is called, in (to me) a wonderful manner, we could have no music from the hounds, nor could they get away from under the horse's feet. Notwithstanding this, it was a pleasing sight to see the good old King [George III], then far advanced in years, looking so happy and cheerful in the midst of his subjects, in his snug bob-wig, and stout buck-skin breeches, conversing with those around him, with the affability of a private gentleman. The third day, however, in some degree, altered my opinion of stag-hunting, for a finer run was never seen; the deer having turned out at Salt-hill, and taken in Cashiobury Park, a distance of upwards of twenty miles, as the crow would fly! The scent was so good, it was with difficulty the hounds could be stopped, which they were twice for his Majesty to come up; but after that it appeared useless to attempt it, and supposing that the King, from the pace they went, *had declined,* the Duke of Cambridge said, "let them go;" the result of which

was, that with not more than three or four trifling checks, he was taken as before mentioned. There was a large field of horsemen, many of whom stuck close to the pack, though the fences were in some parts stiff and in all parts frequent. The Duke of Cambridge, I remember, rode remarkably well, taking his fences without hesitation, and turning, judiciously, with his hounds. When we arrived at the Park, there was much distress among the nags, but their work was then done. It was beautiful, however, to see our deer hunted through two different herds, with which he mixed, without once changing from the scent, and when, finding it was in vain to elude his pursuers, he took soil in a large piece of water in the park, where he was secured. This hunting him around the Park, and getting him out of the water, having occupied a considerable time; to our no small surprise, we saw the King coming cantering along, between the Earl of Sandwich and General Gwynne, who had conducted him to the end of the chase. He had no sooner entered the Park, than a tall, handsome black servant of the Earl of Essex's rode up to him, uncovered, and informed him that his Lord was unable, by indisposition, to attend him in person, but that refreshment would be ready for him by the time he arrived at the house. His Majesty and his suite availed themselves of the Earl's hospitality; and on my road home, I was passed by one hack-chaise and four, in which were the King and his son, and by another, in which were General Gwynne and the Earl of Sandwich, then Master of the Horse, all of whom appeared much pleased with the sport of the day.

On the second day of my being with these hounds, the horse I rode attracted the notice of the Royal party, as likely to carry one of the Princesses, being equal to a good deal of weight, and very temperate, and well on his haunches, in his canter. Mr. Gosden was dispatched to sound me as to whether he were for sale; when, thinking to stop any further questions, as I did not intend to part with him, I said his price was 300 guineas, and that he was fourteen years old. An offer, however, was made me the next day, of 150 guineas, and the horse to be returned to me, or turned out for life, when he had done his work. I concluded the business by informing the General, to whom I had the honour of being known, that I believed he must live and die with me; and I shot him seven years afterwards. . . .

NIMROD

Lord Derby's Stag-Hounds

On Tuesday, the second of April, LORD DERBY's stag-hounds met at Wickham Cross for the last time this season; and, as usual, the field was numerous, but the morning was cold, and apparently unfavourable for sport. At eleven o'clock, his Lordship arrived, accompanied by Lords Grosvenor, Belgrave, Stanley, Wilton, and Palmerston, as also Prince Esterhazy. A beautiful deer, called *Alexander,* was then uncarted for the day's sport: and after short law being given him, the hounds were laid on, but the scent being light, they went at a moderate pace towards Barrows; then turned for Goodham Lodge, through the covers at Crown Ash Hill, where the scent improved; then turned to the right for Chelsam Common to Tatsfield Church, when he crossed the vale for Westerham Charts, to Four Elms, then to Penshurst, crossed the Medway to Cheddingstone, leaving Tonbridge to the left, through the lawns on the right of Tonbridge Wells, across the common for Summer Hill, when the hounds ran into him, after a chase of three hours and forty minutes. A finer run was never seen—the hounds having crossed over eleven parishes, and must, on a moderate computation, have run fifty miles. Many horses were, of course, beaten a long way. Several were led from the field, and bled immediately. Five died before Wednesday night; and Mr. Claggist's famous horse, "Sir John," died on the following Saturday.—Thus ended a season, through which these hounds can boast of having had a succession of runs, seldom equalled, but never surpassed by any hounds in England.

They left the *Oaks* on Monday, the 15th, for Knowsley Park, to recruit for another season; when we shall anxiously look for their return to this country. They have been particularly fortunate with their deer, two only having been killed during the present season.

CERVUS

A Brief Review of the Racing Season of 1828

Want of leisure has prevented my having the pleasure of addressing you for some months past; but I now resume my pen for that purpose. It is my intention at present to review the proceedings of the past racing season, and therefore proceed to headquarters at once.

The Craven Stakes at Newmarket, which used formerly to be considered as an index to the betting book for the young ones, and mustered a strong field, and generally included some of the flyers, has, the last two or three years, sadly "fallen from its high estate," having given place to the Abingdon Mile *Handicap*. Lamplighter, in the Craven, fully maintained his last year's ground, by beating some high-sounding names; but the Handicap contained, amidst all the quantity, but a very moderate lot indeed. The three-year-olds came out worse, probably, than had been seen for years—the Riddlesworth having been carried off by a very middling nag indeed, though of a good family; being nothing less than own brother to Emilius—"akin, but oh! how different."

The First Spring Meeting has by far the most interest of the three, as the One and Two Thousand Guineas' Stakes are usually the criteria for the betting on the Derby and Oaks. Lord Grosvenor's Navarino, in Dilly's hands, had been exalted to the top of the tree, through some *private* performance (said to have been with Mameluke), which, that the public might *benefit* by it, had been kindly suffered to transpire: but, like most of the *private* flyers, when he comes to run in *public* for the "two thousand," he proves any thing but one; and, though backed nearly against the field, he was nowhere; and Cadland (the only South-country *race-horse* of his year) won easily. Among the mares, as it turned out, the race for "the thousand" afforded no judgment for the Oaks—for, though won cleverly by Zoé, who was able to scratch over that flat mile, yet her subsequent illness never gave her another chance and I doubt, after all, if Lord Lowther has much to regret in getting rid of his mare at so small a sum in the preceding autumn, as, I should think, she has been any thing but a cheap one to the party. As to Trampoline, she cut out one of the greatest jades living in her first race....

At Chester, this year, Sir Thomas Stanley's usual good fortune deserted him, and passed over to Mr. Houldsworth. Indeed, through the whole year, I am happy to see that this latter gentleman has recov-

ered something like his former position on the Turf—having been very successful at Newmarket, as well as nearer home. As another proof of what rest and coming fresh to the post does, here is Mr. Clifton again, with a second Brutandorf, carrying off both the Cups, and with a very indifferent nag too—Fylde, by Antonio:—and who, having performed so much at once in the Spring, has done nothing since. On the whole, Chester this year quite maintained its station as one of the first of provincials; and, to those who are content with plenty of sport, without requiring the excitement of heavy betting, (though there is no lack of that, at least to the extent sufficient to give an interest in the races,) Chester undoubtedly affords the best week's sport in the kingdom.

At York, the Spring Meeting was flat, though the appearance of Velocipede and Bessy Bedlam had been looked to with some anxiety—people wishing to ascertain if their public forms were as good as last year: but the respective fields they contended with were so very moderate, that they were booked as certainties. It was in this Meeting, however, that Laurel (who, it will be remembered, ran third for the Leger last year, though having been amiss all the season) shewed his superior powers, by beating Matilda and Mulatto, and is sufficient proof that the Leger would have been his, had he been up to the mark. His running since his quite confirmed him the best of his year.

At Epsom all the other stakes sink into insignificance compared with the attraction of the Derby and Oaks; and, though there is now no lack of general sport, yet the two great stakes are all absorbing. The Colonel, from his two-year-old performances, and the running of Velocipede, inducing the supposition that all the South country horses were bad; Cadland (though he had appeared in such high form as a winner, had subsequently not defeated anything worth naming) crept to the top of the list, and was decidedly the first favorite, though it was known he had been short of work. Chifney's party, a short time previous to the day, strongly fancied their horse (Zinganee), which they bought of Lord Exeter; but he was unluckily attacked with that bane to young horses (the distemper) almost immediately after his arrival at Epsom, and came to the post looking most wretchedly; though, with the help of a good heart and the inimitable hand of *the* Sam, he ran a much better horse than even the party themselves expected. After the dead heat, which by the bye forms an epoch in the annals of the Derby, I certainly fancied the Jock as much as the horse; for the Newmarket people are so used to ride single-handed races that they are down to every advantage and shift to be taken. The Derby has not been so near taking a walk into the "North countrie" for a long time. The blood of Cadland is another instance of what that which is good will do, without the need of being *fashionable:* his sire, Andrew, having had very few thorough-bred mares, and was, during the short time he covered, far from having been in any note. He unfortunately died some time last year. Andrew himself was not any thing remarkable as a runner. He was purchased by Mr. Bouverie at three years old from Mr. Andrew—hence his name; but his blood was as good as could be wished both for speed and stoutness—being by Orville out of Morel (own Sister to Truffle), by Sorcerer; and his dam also being a Sorcerer mare (Sorcery), would appear to favour the breeding-in system. The Sorcerer stock, in the first generation, have always been rather soft and washy; but by being crossed with the old *stout* blood, as in this instance with the good old Beningbrough, are sure to throw runners.

The Oaks' fillies were certainly a very moderate lot. Zoé's materials would not do for the Oaks length here; added to which she was very far from up to the mark on the day, and was one of the weakest goers to get up these hills I ever saw, as Ascot also afterwards proved. Lord G. Cavendish's Andrew filly, from some *private* trial as usual, was also a great favorite, from what reason the parties themselves in course only could tell: for anything more unlike a winner of the Oaks I never saw, being a little short scratching goer; and it must have been some very recent "spin" that induced them to fancy her at all; for it was but a very short time previously that Lord George sold the dam of her for a mere

The Equestrian Sports 91

song to go to Germany. The result proved (as it usually does), that, in nine cases out of ten, their private measurements are nothing but mistakes. Out of it all, however, the race turned up a trump for the Duke of Grafton; for his Grace's stable at the beginning of the season looked very unlike its usual form. Turquoise had, in that jumble of a race with Trampoline and Flush in the spring, been beaten, though it was afterwards decided to be no race at all; but she had then been amiss: yet the Duke's own people, like the rest, did not think much of her, or she would not in course have run for the selling plate (though unclaimed). There is no doubt she is a good honest creature, and can get a distance, but wants a turn of speed in a short race.

The munificent patronage of our Gracious King [George IV] has this year extended most nobly to the Racing World; and Ascot has, in course, been greatly benefited by it: indeed, the presence of Royalty and all the fashion and beauty of the Metropolis, combined with the local advantages of the course, which forms as delightful a parade as Kensington Gardens, give a zest to the sport, and render it beyond comparison the pleasantest course in the kingdom. His Majesty's stud appeared here in full force, though, I regret to say, not a winner among them. I had made up my mind to say a little on the management of the King's stud; but I will not *now*, though I may shortly, on another occasion, review the whole that has been done. The performance of Bobadilla (certainly a great one for a three-year-old) for the Cup, occasioned her to change masters at a very handsome premium, and placed her in the foremost rank of her year.

The second meeting at Ascot, which emanated from the desire of His Majesty to be gratified with the sports, was a very fair one, considering the short notice and the consequent disability of the principal horses to be there—being obliged to leave after the first meeting to perform prior engagements. For future years we have a good prospect—several Produce Stakes, &c. having been made. . . .

At Doncaster, the Leger, which had promised to be a very sporting one, turned out no race at all, having never been won with more ease. Velocipede was no doubt *the* horse of the party; but Nature will not be denied: and his legs, which had always been tottering refused the work necessary for such a race. But what is to be said with regard to the tales that are told of poor Bessy Bedlam! who, according to the phrase in use, was "made safe" for the purposes most beneficial to the scoundrels concerned in such a nefarious transaction, worthy only of a second Dawson. If the late exhibition do not go very far towards the extinction of the unlimited betting which has been of late carried on, I shall much mistake; and if it *should* narrow the circle, and reduce it once more within a reasonable compass, there will be at least some good arise out of the villany, and the evil will have wrought its own cure. That Bessy Bedlam, *unpoisoned, or otherwise "made safe,"* would have won the Leger, I am not prepared to assert; but certain it is, she, on the following Friday, ran her race in less time than the Leger was run for. As, however, she and The Colonel come together in the spring, the question will be decided.—Altogether, the Leger, as far as betting was concerned, was a very harmless one; and, but for the evil reports with which it was tainted, would no doubt have gone off with equal *eclat* to any of its predecessors. The Cup, always a crack race, shewed up Laurel in his brightest colours, and quite confirmed him the best of his year. . . .

On the whole, the racing season of 1828 has been a very fair one—the provincial meetings (which, after all, it would not be difficult to prove are the test of good sport) having been better attended than for many years. Though it is generally acknowledged, that betting has "fallen into the sear, the yellow leaf;" from which some people augur a falling off in the supporters of the turf; yet, it is from that *very cause* my hopes are raised: for, with the downfal of gambling, (from which only has emanated that blot which alone disfigures the annals of this year's sport,) legitimate and honorable racing, and upholders of this most national sport, will assuredly rise.

THE YOUNG FORESTER

Eclipse

This paragon of running horses, as in his actions, so in his fame, stands proudly aloof from almost the possibility of competition. Nature, we fear, her favourite labour completed, threw away the precious mould in which she had formed Eclipse. Flying Childers, indeed, stands before him in chronology, but must submit to follow him in posthumous reputation, and that on the ground of actual performance. Eclipse excelled all other racers, previous, or contemporary, in a union of the three great essentials of speed, stoutness, or lastingness, and ability to carry weight. The name bestowed upon him, appears to have been, by a fortunate conjunction of his stars, equally indicative of the date of his birth, and prophetic of the superiority which he was fated to possess over all his kind. He never in his life, felt whip or spur, or even the controul of the bit; and although no jockey could hold him against his will, neither of the two, who only had the honour of riding him, ever experienced the least difficulty in pulling him up at an ending post. Nor was there any difficulty in training him, at least after he had raced, although the most resolute and headstrong of horses. He was a strong, but thick-winded horse, and in his sweats, the blowing of his bellows was audible at a considerable distance.

Eclipse, as is well known, and as has often been stated before in the Magazine, was foaled in 1764, during the great eclipse. He was bred by Duke William,[6] the hero of Culloden, and in his pedigree has always passed as a son of Marsk; but, as was first published in the Philosophical and Practical Treatise on Horses, from the report of O'Kelly's old groom, the mare was covered by both Shakespeare and Marsk. She, Spilletta, the dam of Eclipse, was got by Old Regulus, out of Mother Western. Eclipse was a chesnut horse, just of the colour of Shakespeare's stock, with white legs behind and a blaze in his face; and, as far as recollection may be correct, about, but not above fifteen hands three inches in height, with the appearance of being able to carry eighteen stone. No horse shewed a greater difference in form, between himself in his flesh, and in his racing condition. It is not known that any portrait was ever taken of him in his flesh, and information on that head is desirable. From what cause is not certainly known, he did not appear in public until five years old, when he won the Maiden Plate at Epsom, May 3, 1769; and was taken out of training, at Newmarket, in the October Meeting, 1770, after beating Sir Charles Bunbury's Corsican, B.C.: 70 to 1 on Eclipse; and the next day, walking over the Round Course for the King's Plate. From 1771 to 1788 he covered at Clay-hill,

Epsom, when he was removed to Cannons, Middlesex, in a four-wheeled machine purposely built for him, drawn by two horses, his old groom being an inside passenger. They both had their appropriate refreshment on the road, the horse also partaking of the cakes with which the groom indulged himself. Eclipse died at Cannons in the next year, Feb. 28th, at the age of twenty-five years, the property of Colonel O'Kelly, who honoured his funeral with cakes and ale, after the example of Lord Godolphin with his Arabian. Like his sire Marsk, Eclipse's memory was honoured with an epitaph.

Eclipse had three proprietors, the Duke of Cumberland, who bred him, Mr. Wildman the sheep salesman, who brought him a yearling at the Duke's sale for about seventy or eighty guineas, and Dennis O'Kelly. In 1769, O'Kelly purchased the half of Eclipse for 650 guineas: and afterwards the other half for 1100 guineas—a bargain so cheap as to surprise every sporting man who heard of it, and no one more than O'Kelly himself. His gains by this horse were probably nearer to 30 than 20,000 £. Eclipse covered at first at 50 gs. afterwards at 20, and lastly at 30. In 23 years, 344 sons and daughters of Eclipse won 158,047 £. 12 s. exclusive of the winnings of a great number of his get, which have never been brought to account. The general character of his stock was speed and size. Perhaps he got a few decidedly stout horses, one among which was England's Whizgig.

Guy Stakes at Warwick

If there is one thing more absolutely requisite than another in a letter which is intended for the public eye, it is accuracy; or, to speak more plainly, Truth—a qualification that your Correspondent THE YOUNG FORESTER has in your Magazine of this month (February) unhappily overlooked.

In page 247 he says, "The Stake at Warwick has been awarded to the owner of Cetus, who was second, in consequence of the present owner of Birmingham having refused to pay some paltry 25 £. forfeit for a Stake at Winchester, where the horse was engaged in the name of the person whom Mr. Beardsworth bought him of."—This is notoriously untrue; and, by the manner in which the writer speaks of the transaction altogether, it is to be feared it is wilfully so.

The next paragraph I apprehend too is incorrect; but which I will not speak so positively about, because I know but little of racing, and therefore am unwilling to compete with so precocious a youth as this appears to be.

He says, "It has long been one of the best acknowledged rules of racing, that no horse is entitled *to be a winner* until all the arrears due for such animal shall have been paid up."—Is he sure of that?—Where is the rule to be found? Has he not made a mistake? and instead of the words "to be a winner," should he not have said "to start?"—This talented gentleman may not see the difference.—Great wits, they say, have short memories—perhaps they are short-sighted too!—In my humble judgment, there is a great deal of difference.—By making use of the word "start," you afford the owner an opportunity of paying the Stake in arrears *if applied for,* instead of letting the *onus* hang over his head till he has defeated his antagonists.

And now I would ask, did Sir Mark Wood "most honorably" make any application to the Stewards or Clerk of the Course before Birmingham started at Warwick for the paltry 25 £ forfeit at Winchester? THE YOUNG FORESTER answers this question partly, asserting, "he apprised both trainer and master, previously to the race, of the objection he had to make." Now if he had done so, I should say they (that is, the trainer and master) were not the proper persons to apprise. The Stewards (or at all events the Clerk of the Course) were the proper persons; but, unfortunately for THE YOUNG FORESTER's veracity, here is another untruth: Sir Mark Wood did *not* "most honorably" apprise Mr. Beardsworth (the owner), previously to the race, of the objection he had to make.

"Save me from my friends," he says, "has been the cry through many ages:" but, instead of Mr. Beardsworth echoing it, I guess the Jockey Club and Sir Mark Wood are more likely to apply it to this doughty genius, and conjure him, if he is determined to attempt to take their part, that he will assert only that which is true.—I am, Sir, your humble servant.

J. MYTTON[7]

Part III
A Miscellany of Sports

Pedestrianism

With a Sketch of the Life of
MR. FORSTER POWELL[1]

This being an exercise which with others of an athletic stamp, has lately risen into much notice, it is our intention to collect an account of every extraordinary performance of this kind, whether ancient or modern. Our resources, and the diligence we have made use of in obtaining many rare instances that are scarcely known, (through a lapse of time, or the obscurity or locality of their first relators) with others which have occurred within the circle of our own memory and observation will, we presume, supply our curious readers with a gratification never before exhibited. But with respect to the importance of pedestrianism, and its comparative merit with other means of swiftness, it must be granted, that that of horses, and the present goodness of the roads, are not any real depreciation of swiftness in man, and, consequently, should not render this quality less estimable with us than it has been with our ancestors, many of whom kept their running footmen for extraordinary messages. And further, numerous instances indubitably prove that it is still highly possible for men to perform very long journies much sooner on foot than when mounted or assisted by the fleetest horses that can be found. . . .

Amongst the moderns, the following instances are remarkable:

In the beginning of the present century, there was one Levi Whitehead, of Bramham, in Yorkshire, who was noted for his swiftness in running, having won the buck's-head for several years at Castle Howard, given by the grandfather of the present Earl of Carlisle. He also won the five Queen Anne's guineas given by William Aisleby, Esq. of Studley, near Rippon [Ripon] beating the then famous Indian and nine others, selected to start against him. In his 22d year he ran four miles over Bramham Moor, in nineteen minutes; and which is still more remarkable, in his ninety-fifth and ninety-sixth years, he frequently walked from Bramham to Tadcaster, (full four miles), in an hour. He died in the hundredth year of his age, on the 14th of March, 1787.

About the year 1740, Thomas Calile, a lamplighter, was known as a very swift runner; he beat all his competitors with ease, and once ran in the Artillery-ground [London] twenty-one miles in two hours.

From 1760, for ten or twelve years, John Smith, commonly called the shepherd's boy, a little man, was noted as a fleet runner; he beat most who opposed him; won several silver cups at the Artillery-ground, and likewise one hundred guineas, by running fifteen miles in an hour and twenty-eight minutes, on Moulsey Hurst.

On February 1, 1759, George Guest, of Birmingham, who had laid a considerable wager that he walked a thousand miles in twenty-eight days, finished his journey with great ease. It seemed as if he had lain by for bets, for in the last two days he had one hundred and six miles to walk, but walked them with so much ease to himself that, to shew his agility, he walked the last six miles within an hour, though he had full six hours to do it in.

In July 1765, a young woman went from Blencogo in Scotland, to within two miles of Newcastle in one day, which is about seventy-two miles.

Robert Batley, of Hutford in Norfolk, was famous in his youth for extraordinary speed in running, and was well known when an old man, among the gentlemen at Newmarket, as a great walker, having frequently gone from Thetford to London in one day (eighty-one miles), and back again the next. He died in the 66th year of his age, in October, 1785.

Reed of Hampshire, is a noted pedestrian. He, in 1774 ran ten miles within an hour at the Artillery-ground; walked one hundred miles in one day at Gosport; in 1787 and in 1791 walked fifty miles in little more than nine hours on the sands at Weymouth.

Colin Macleod, a Scotchman, (who is now in the 104th year of his age), in the autumn of 1790, walked from Inverness to London and back again; and afterwards to the metropolis again; and on the eighth of October following, for a considerable wager, he set out from the obelisk at Hyde-park-corner to the five-mile-stone on the Turnham-green-road, and back again in two hours and twenty-three minutes, which was seven minutes less than the time allowed him.

Last, not least, is Mr. Foster Powell. This extraordinary man was born in the year 1736, at Horsforth, near Leeds, in Yorkshire, and being bred to the law, was clerk to an attorney in New-inn, London. While in that employ he had occasion to go to York with some leases, to which place he went and returned on foot in little more than six days. He afterwards performed several expeditions with great swiftness, particularly from London to Maidenhead-bridge, and back (twenty-seven miles) in seven hours.

In 1773 he made a deposit of twenty pounds for a wager of one hundred guineas, the conditions of which was, that he should begin, some Monday in November, a journey to York on foot and back again in six days....

What rendered this exploit more extraordinary was, that he set out in a very indifferent state of health, being compelled from a pain in his side, to wear a strengthening plaister all the way; his appetite, moreover was very indifferent, for his most frequent beverage was either water or small beer; and the refreshment he most admired was tea, and toast and butter....

In September 1787, he offered a wager of twenty-five guineas that he walked from the Falstaff-inn, at Canterbury, to London-bridge and back again, which is one hundred and twelve miles, in twenty-four hours, which being accepted, he set out on the twenty-seventh of that month, at four o'clock in the afternoon; reached London-bridge at half past two the next morning; and was again at Canterbury at ten minutes before four in the afternoon....

In 1790 he took a bett of twenty guineas to thirteen that he would walk to York and return in five days and eighteen hours. He set off on Sunday the twenty-second of August, at twelve at night, and reached Stamford on Monday night; arrived at Doncaster on Tuesday night; returned from York as far as Ferrybridge, on Wednesday; on Thursday he slept at Grantham; on Friday on this side Biggleswade, and arrived at St. Paul's-cathedral on Saturday, at ten minutes past four, which was one hour and fifty minutes less than the time allowed him.

He was so little fatigued with this journey, that he offered to walk one hundred miles the next day, if any person would make it worth his trouble, by a considerable wager....

This extraordinary man, who is now in the fifty-seventh year of his age, has lately offered to walk six miles in one hour; to run a mile in five minutes and a half; and to go five hundred miles in seven days!—He requires a bett of one hundred guineas to fifty, on the last undertaking, and twenty pounds upon either of the others. After which he intends to decline all performances of the sort for wagers.

Mr. Powell is about five feet eight inches high; his body is rather slight made, but his legs and thighs are stout, and well calculated for performances of this kind.

102 Hounds in the Morning

Pedestrianism

On Monday, Oct. 14, at Sheffield, the pedestrian, Townsend, performed another surprising task, by gathering with his mouth one hundred stones placed at the distance of one [hundred?] yard, and walking four miles backward, and running eight, making in the whole eighteen miles, which he performed in three hours and fifty-six minutes, being four minutes under the time specified. He gathered the one hundred stones in forty-seven minutes, equal to a distance of nearly six miles.[2]

Skipper, the pedestrian, finished his arduous undertaking at Newmarket on the Wednesday at four o'clock, p.m. in high style, having walked 1000 miles in 1000 successive half hours.[3] He appeared in good health at the close. He had no backers.

Captain Fairburn, on the 14th instant, undertook to walk, fair toe and heel, 18 miles in three hours and a quarter, for 200 £. The ground selected was Epping Forest, and he won in three hours nine minutes and ten seconds.

Mr. Abernethy, the Scots pedestrian, this month performed a match to go from London to Nottingham and back, making a circuitous route of 260 miles, in four successive days. He started on the 16th.

Match to Maidenhead and back to Kensington.—Mr. Barnard West, the pedestrian, started at twelve o'clock on Monday, Sept. 30, to go from Kensington to Maidenhead Bridge and back, forty-eight miles, in seven hours, for a stake of 200 guineas. Betting was six and seven to four on time. The pedestrian, on his return, halted at Brentford, having the last five miles to do in forty minutes. He won the match with great difficulty, having only three minutes to spare.

A great pedestrian feat was performed this month by Mr. James Tinney, at Oundle. He engaged to walk 96 miles in 24 successive hours, and performed the task one minute within the time, in gallant style, without apparent distress, coming in to the winning point at the rate of six miles an hour. He walked on the Peterborough road, a mile out and in—twelve or fourteen miles of the journey was on pavement as bad as any in the kingdom.

A match, which equals any pedestrian feat on record, took place on Wednesday, Oct. 2, in Cranbourn Grove, Windsor Forest. Bumstead, a gentleman's groom, was matched by his master, for one hundred guineas, to run ten miles in fifty-six minutes. The pedestrian is twenty years of age. The five miles were done in twenty-seven minutes and twenty-five seconds, without visible fatigue, but in the ninth mile there seemed something amiss, and betting was 2 to 1 on time. It was a momentary loss of wind, which the pedestrian recovered, and won in 55 min. 51 sec. He is a Yorkshire man.

Friday, October 18, a match, which excited very great interest at the Club-houses, and upon which there was heavy betting, was decided on the Kilburn-road. Captain Smith, well known in the sporting world as a good pedestrian, undertook to run five miles in thirty minutes, for a stake of 50£ pay or play, and time for the favourite at odds. He started at eight o'clock from Maida-hill, a mile in and out, and finally performed the match, not even having a second to spare.

The Game at Golf

In the *Annals of Sporting,* No. 28, there is an attempt at the description of the Scottish game of Golf, by Mr. C. Curlewis, which does not convey a proper idea of the game, either in the manner of playing it, or the instruments used. The proper spelling is *golf,* although pronounced *gouf* in the North. The club, the figure of which is as follows, is from three to four feet in length, according to the height and length of arm of the player:—

At No. 1 it is covered round with list [strips of cloth], as far down from the top as is necessary for the two hands, when striking. The upper part above No. 2 is generally of some very pliant tough wood, as hickory, and is joined slantingly to the head by strong glue, and strengthened by well-resined cord. The head, from the joining at No. 2, is of hard wood, such as beech, and tapered off according to the grain of the wood, so as not to be liable to split when striking the ball. A want of due attention to this will render the head liable to split and fly off at the first hard stroke. The face of the club is secured by a piece of hard bone, let in at the bottom at No. 3, extending as far as the lines, about three quarters of an inch broad, and half an inch thick. No. 4 shews the reverse of the club head, which slopes off from the flat front, and shews a half oval reverse. The opening left in the figure (5) is filled with about six ounces of lead, to give additional weight to the head.

The ball which is played with is made of leather stuffed with feathers; the sewing is turned inwards, leaving a small opening for inserting the feathers, which is then closed with about two stitches. The ball is then boiled, which contracts it so that it is reduced to the size of an egg, but nearly round. It is afterwards painted several coats of white paint, and, when dry, is fit for use.

The game is played by two or more, an equal number on each side; but only two balls are used, one of each party striking in turn: but if the last striker does not drive his ball so far on as that of his opponent, one of his party must then strike *one*, or perhaps *two* more, and the game is thus marked by calling out *one, two,* or *three more,* as the case may be. If more than two are playing, the same person does not strike twice in succession: a miss is counted one. The party who puts the ball into the hole at the fewest strokes wins the game.

The grounds for this amusement vary in different parts of Scotland. Some are nearly square; in which case there is a hole at each corner; and, if irregular, there is one at each angle: so that the party go quite round to the spot whence they started. Generally there is a quarter of a mile between each hole. Besides the club described, there are occasionally two others carried by an attendant for each party. These are called *putters*—one being a short stiff and heavy one of the same form, but larger in the head, for making a steady and direct stroke when near the hole: the other is of iron, for making a hit out of a rut, or on a hard road, where the first club would be in danger of breaking. When a ball falls into a hole or rut, from which it is impossible to *strike* it out, the party is allowed to take it out with his hand, and throw it up in a line with the spot, which is accounted as *one,* and he then strikes from where it chances to rest.

This game can be played on sands at any season when the weather is favourable; but, when the grass is long, the balls are impeded, and not easily found again when struck to any distance. A good player will strike his ball over the tallest tree; but if there be an opening sufficient to allow it to go through clear of branches below, he will send the ball farther, by striking it so as it may not rise higher than thirty feet. The holes made in the sand or turf are generally about seven to eight inches in diameter.

This is a very healthful but not laborious amusement, as some time is allowed for conversation between each stroke, which, if they are good players, impels the ball several hundred yards [!?], and several minutes elapse ere the party come up to where the balls have rested. When more than one party appear on the ground, the first that starts is allowed to go on two strokes ahead before the other party strikes off. This prevents confusion.

The chief places where this game is played are—at Edinburgh, on a fine green to the South of the city, called the Links; on the Sands at Leith; on the Sands at St. Andrew's, in Fifeshire; and the Green, near Glasgow; and on the two Greens, called Inches, north and south of the city of Perth. At other places the game is also played, but these are the chief.

It sometimes happens that one of a *morning* party indulges rather a little too long in the arms of the sleepy deity, or sleeping partner, so that one is wanting to make up the party—in which case, if a respectable person in appearance should chance to be looking on, he is invited to take a turn with them, if he can handle the club. This gave rise to a rather ludicrous circumstance some years ago at one of the above-mentioned places, where a party of three had waited for some time for the appearance of their drowsy acquaintance.

They perceived a respectable looking person approach them in his morning walk, whom they politely asked if he had ever amused himself at the game of *golf*. He replied it was some time since he had played, but, as he perceived they wanted one, he consented to make one of the party, until the other gentleman should make his appearance. A round or two gave them an opportunity of conversation, in which he bore an aggreeable part, and so far gained upon the good opinion of his new companions, that they, and in particular the Chief Magistrate, who was one of the party, felt much gratified by his company. At last the drowsy gentleman made his appearance, and on coming up to the party, found the worthy Provost and the stranger in friendly converse; on which he exclaimed, with some surprise, "Why, Provost, d'ye ken wha ye are playin' wi?"—"To be sure, a' but this gentleman, who seems to be an excellent player, an' pleasant company:"—and so he was, although reduced to accept of a degrading yet *necessary* office, for the support of himself and family.—"Why, Sir, I thought you wou'd hae kent your ain *hangman*, that is, the town hangman." This *surprising* notification aroused the sensitive feeling of the worthy Chief, who advanced to the *finisher* of the law, and, striking him, demanded how he dared to intrude himself into the company of gentlemen? To this the unfortunate wight mildly replied, that "a man's *profession* does not so often disgrace him as he may disgrace his profession," and immediately made his bow and walked away. This reply disarmed the choler of the Provost, who afterwards shewed some kindness to the unfortunate agent of the public.

D. A.

THE GAME AT GOLF

With reference to the observations on the ancient game of Golf in your Number for August last, under the initials D. A. I beg to correct one or two inaccuracies as detailed in that communication.

The *club* to begin with, is properly enough described; but in place of two or three, there are at least eight or nine, carried by the attendant or caddy, of different shapes, as well of wood as of iron, to strike the ball in whatever situation it may chance to be found by the player, who, according to the rules of *some* societies, is never allowed to touch his ball till holed.

The ball is, as stated, stuffed with feathers; but the leather of which it is made is boiled *before* the feathers are stuffed into it, and *not afterwards,* in order that it may be softened to receive the thread with which it is fastened.

The game is correctly described; and in addition to the places mentioned, where, principally, this game is played, I may state that every Saturday in the season it is practised at Blackheath [near London] where there is a Golf Club of very old standing; and at Manchester there is one lately established.

I may just farther mention, that instead of the game being played on the *Sands* of Leith, St. Andrews, &c., it is on the *Links* at these places—certainly not far from the Sands.

By inserting this, any of your curious readers may have an opportunity of seeing the game played in the vicinity of London.

An Admirer of the Game

Skating

On Tuesday, January 14, a grand skating match took place, on Portyfoot river, near Carter's Bridge, Chatteris, Isle of Ely, for a prize of 10 sovereigns. It is customary for eight persons only to enter; but on this occasion sixteen were allowed to start: the half of a measured mile, twice round, for a heat. The spectators were 10 and 12 deep on each bank of the river, and there could not have been less than 7000 or 8000 persons present. The racing continued, without intermission, from one till past four o'clock, and the Chatteris band played favourite airs. One race, of two measured miles, was done in five minutes two seconds.[4] Young, of Northdelph, was the final victor.

The amateurs of this healthful exercise had another treat on the Maze Lake, Herts, on Saturday, January 18. The first match was for a sweepstakes silver bowl, value 25 sovereigns, between the following gentlemen:—Messrs. Harewood, Blenkinsop, Hayward, Rogers, and Smithson. The match took place round a half-mile circle, and the distance to be completed was five miles. The skaters went off in fine style on the outside of the half-mile boundaries, affixed by weights. The first half mile was done by Mr. Rogers in two minutes and a second. He was passed in the second mile by Messrs. Blenkinson and Smithson. Mr. Hayward fell at the commencement of the third mile, and gave in; and

Mr. Rogers was beat soon after. Mr. Harewood, who had evidently reserved his powers, shot a-head at the end of the fourth mile, and the race was between him and Mr. Blenkinsop. It was a fine struggle in the last mile, and was won by Mr. Blenkinsop, in 19 minutes and 37 seconds. The ice was not so good as on the preceeding Saturday, when some matches took place, the snow having adhered to it in parts.

Another match of a mile took place between Captain Smith and Mr. Jenkins, for a rump and dozen for the skaters. It was a good race, and was won by Mr. Smith in three minutes and two seconds.

A subscription purse of ten guineas was skated for this month, near Crowland, and the diversion attracted a large company. As the sum was to be a free prize to the winner, sixteen men entered for it, and drew to run as in coursing matches, two and two, so that 15 two-mile heats took place. Mr. James Eager, of Thorney Fen, was the winner, beating the noted skater, Charles Staples, who had challenged to run any man in England for 100 guineas. Mr. Samuel Eager, the father of the successful competitor in this race, has three sons, and he offers to match them against any three brothers in England, to skate two miles each, for fifty pounds.

At the starting for the last heat for the 10-guinea purse, 50 £. to 10 £. was offered to be betted on Staples against Eager, but the race was won by the latter in good and easy style.—*Stafford Chron.*

An extraordinary skating match lately took place on Aqualate Meer, in the county of Stafford, the beautiful sheet of water belonging to Sir J. F. Boughey, Bart. in presence of most of the beauty and fashion in the neighbourhood. The match was undertaken for a considerable sum, by a gentleman of the cloth, to skate thirty miles in three hours, which was accomplished with ease. At starting the bets were 5 to 1 against him; but all the knowing ones were sadly taken in.

Fish and Fishing

... All nature, indeed, is a scene of wonder, and the study of it is one of the most pleasing amusements that can engage the mind of man; and as it appears beyond all doubt that this lower world was intended for our use and amusement, he pays a bad compliment to the Maker of it, who

goes blundering through it, without stopping to inquire into the wonderful works it contains. Nature is liberal to those who cultivate her; and by no one are her inmost recesses more minutely explored, than by the scientific fisherman, who may be said to penetrate into her very womb.

However simple the amusement of fly-fishing may appear, by its general use, yet a fishing-rod in the hand of an expert fisherman is as complete a triumph of art over nature, as any that I am acquainted with. That half a dozen sportsmen, each, to a certain degree, a proficient in the art, should go to the same river, on the same day, and at the same hour, and that five out of the six should not kill more than thirty brace of fish between them, and the sixth should kill more than that number with his own rod (which I once saw happen), proves fly-fishing to be an art of no easy acquirement.

It is not necessary for a fisherman to be an entomologist; and, if equal to it, it would far exceed the limits of these letters, were I to enter fully into the history of the different sorts of flies we meet with on the banks of brooks and rivers, which appear to belong to them as part of the food of the fish which they contain: but I will take upon myself to assert, that in no part of natural history are the works of the Creator more wonderfully displayed, than in the tribes of those ephemeral beings which, animated by the generative warmth of the sun, are seen sporting in the air, quite unconscious of the short time they have to live....

However well the imitation of flies is effected, yet it is by the use of the natural fly that the best and largest fish are killed. This method of fishing, however, is held comparatively cheap by the scientific fisherman, and consists of bobbing, or dapping, as it is called, with a line, not quite so long as the rod, and is thus divested of the graceful motion of throwing the fly, and considered more for the pot than for sport. This is also a cruel method of fishing, as the goodness of the fly is appreciated by the length of time it will remain "*in exercise;*" or, in other words, in the agonies of death, all which is called "playing on the hook." Hunting and shooting have been termed sanguinary amusements; but I think when we come to read the humane Charles Cotton's account of some of his practice in this apostolical recreation, as he was pleased to style fishing, we shall be almost induced to observe, that, in this one instance, it is a refinement on cruelty. When * speaking of the green drake fly, he says, "Having gathered a great store of them, we put them into a long draw-box, with holes in the corner to give them air, where

*See Isaac Walton.[5]

they wll continue fresh and vigorous a night or more. We then take them out thence by the wings, and bait them thus on the hook:—We take one (for we commonly fish with two of them at a time), and, putting the point of the hook into the thickest part of his body, just under one of his wings, run it directly through, and out at the other side, leaving him spitted across upon the hook; and then, taking the other, put him on after the same manner, but with his head the contrary way—in which posture they will live on the hook, and play with their wings, for a quarter of an hour, or more."

It has been remarked that there is an analogy between fish and the female sex in their pastimes and appetites, each being said to be fond of variety, and attracted by shewy and gaudy objects. When speaking of fly-making, the poet Gay[6] observes—

> To frame the little animal, provide
> All the gay hues that wait on female pride;
> Silks of all colours must their aid impart,
> And every fur promotes the fisher's art.

The success of all field sports depends upon the weather, but fishing is, above all others, subject to its dominion; and the greatest trial of skill in the fly-fisher is to suit his fly to the day, or even to the hour, the difficulty of which is attributable to the existing state of the atmosphere. To obviate this, may not be in the power of a whole book of ready-made flies, for which reason a fisherman who knows his business should never be without the materials to make a fly upon the spot, in imitation of the one he sees on the water. . . .

NIMROD

Billiards – The Dutch Baron

The gentlemen of the green cloth have been put out of *queue*, by a hero of a *hazard table* imported from the Continent, within a few weeks, by one of the squad, who, while he pretended to be playing the *losing game*, is shrewdly suspected of going snacks in all that rolls into the *pocket*.

The Dutch Baron was introduced to the billiard-table at Bath, a few weeks ago by his friend, who *happened* to have known him at Hamburgh. He played in a crowd of billiard amateurs and professors, many of whom are rich, and lost about one hundred and fifty guineas with the utmost *sang froid.*—Upon his retiring, his *friend* told the company he was a fine pigeon, a Dutch Baron, who had emigrated from Holland with immense property, and who would as readily lose ten thousand pounds as ten guineas. Some asked, "Is it the *Gala Hope?*" "No, (replied others) he is in hands that will not let him slip a-while."—"Is it the Princess Amelia's house Hope?" asked another.—"Who is he?"—"Who is He?" was eagerly enquired—"A Dutch Baron, as rich as a Jew," was answered in a whisper.

No Batavian ever laid out a hundred and fifty guineas so well as this Dutch Baron. The whole corps of *riflemen* flocked round him, like a swarm of fish at a piece of bread. But little P. well known at Bath, who thought he knew best how to make his market, like a *man of business,* applied to the Barons' *friend* to have the first plucking.—The friend, as *a great favour,* engaged to use his influence; little P. was at the billiard-table the first man in the morning, that he might secure the play in his own hands; the Baron came—to it they went: Little P. kept back his play; the Dutch Baron played but poorly—fair strokes he often missed; but whenever he was at an important point, he won, as if by accident.— On they went—Hambletonian and Diamond. Little P. was afraid of frightening the Baron, by disclosing the extent of his play; the Baron played so as to persuade every one he knew little of the game. The contest was, who should play worst at indifferent periods, and who, without seeming to play well, should play best at important points. The Baron won on all great occasions, till little P. had lost about 1000 £. But the Baron managed so well, that no one thought he could play at all; and although little P. was *sickened,* yet the bait of 150 guineas found plenty of customers. Some of them the greatest adepts in the kingdom gave the Baron at starting three points in the game; but the Baron's *accidental* good play was so superior, whenever a great stake was down, he at last gave three points to those who had given him three, and still he beat them—by *accident.*—And before the billiard knowing ones at

Bath would stop, the Baron had won nearly ten thousand pounds, with which he made a bow, and came to London.

And here he is!—He has been at the billiard tables about St. James's Street. But this *Dutch Nobleman's* fame travelled almost as fast as himself, and he is *found out!*—Not however till he had sweated some of the most knowing gentlemen of the queue.

He conceals his play so well, that no one can yet form an idea of its extent. To the best billiard players he gives points, and always wins on important occasions. He seems to be a very conjuror, commanding the balls to roll as he pleases; and there is nothing to be named that it is not supposed he can accomplish.

But the most entertaining part of his story, is the stile of reprobation in which the *professors* of the queue, speak of his concealment of his play. They execrate him as guilty of nothing short of cheating; they, whose daily practice it is to conceal their play, and angle on the gudgeons with whom they engage—*they* bitterly revile the Dutch Baron for retorting their own artifice, and entrapping them in their own way.

And who is the Dutch Baron?—asks every one who hears of his achievements.—In Hamburgh, he was the marker at a billiard table!

[Pierce Egan?[7]]

Pistol and Rifle Shooting

Having observed, in No. 5 of *The Naval and Military Magazine,* some remarks by Colonel Maceroni on pistol and rifle shooting, and having been present several times when my friend Colonel M. has been practising, I think it may, perhaps, be interesting to some of your readers—amateurs of this description of shooting—to be informed what may be done by an expert marksman provided with good weapons.

I therefore send you the copy of a memorandum which I made at the time, and which you can, if you think proper, insert in your next Number. T. W.

MEMORANDUM OF SHOOTING, JUNE 25, 1825

Pistols—Scratch rifled, percussion, calibre 32, by Forsyth.
Rifle—Percussion, calibre 15, by Forsyth.

Dined on the banks of the River. After dinner Colonel M. was requested to practise.

First. Fired at three half-crowns in cleft sticks, four feet high, at fifteen paces—pistol pointed to right toe; count four to raise and fire—missed first shot, but cut the stick in two, all but touching, under the coin: second and third shots hit plump.

Second. Fired at a wooden chair, upright—desired to hit the edge of the seat; count six, aim from toe, at fifty-two paces—hit edge of seat, and knocked out a large splinter: chair in my possession.

Thirdly. Fired three rounds at fifty-two paces, at three half-bricks—count four, pistol pointed to toe—hit two plump, and grazed the third.

Fourthly. Fired five rounds from same spot, at five different willow trees, of about five inches diameter, all at different distances, from seventeen to fifty-six paces—count four, aim from toe—hit all five trees at from two to five feet from the ground.

Fifthly. Fired at a dock leaf by the side of the river, distance one hundred and seven paces, five shots—aim at discretion; dock leaf seven inches long, stem out of water, four inches broad in the middle—two right through.

Sixthly. Returning home in the punt, fired at a white owl flying slowly across us, at about fifty yards—put the ball clean through him under the wing. It being nearly dark, and the owl falling in long grass, did not find him till next morning: had him stuffed.

June 22.—Going up the River in the punt, Colonel M. shot two water rats on the bank, through the body—distance about twenty paces.

After dinner Mr. F.'s groom asked leave to hold up in his hand a flat tile for the Colonel to shoot at, at twenty paces—fired at fifteen paces, and hit it about the centre. The man did not flinch, but remained with his arm extended, and a fragment of the tile in his hand.

Rifle.—At two hundred *measured* yards, put six balls in succession against a blackened board placed against a white wall: the board six feet high and thirteen inches broad—three shots from off the hat, lying; three standing, without a rest.

Blackened a three-feet square on the old summer-house—measured three hundred and fifteen yards. M. fired eighteen rounds; put fifteen shots in the square, mostly near the centre; three shots a little below, but in good direction. Four out of these eighteen shots struck the ground within five or seven yards of the wall; but from the smoothness of the turf did not diverge laterally. Colonel M. prefers shooting rather too low than too high; as, he says, if the ground be pretty level you are sure to have the advantage of the recochet. Shot kneeling; rested the rifle against a tree.

Washed the rifle; measured out the utmost extent of our ground, four hundred and forty-two yards; augmented the charge; filled the trap with very small shot. From an undulation of the ground could not see the black square, except standing. No tree handy for rest; fired standing, without rest, five rounds—four in the square. One shot only six inches above the center point; another between seven and eight inches below it, nearly touching the perpendicular middle line. A strong breeze up: left off.

In the evening, fired with pistols at a cast iron plate in the garden, at twenty-five paces; plate fifteen inches by twenty-two, blackened; two chalk lines down the middle, four inches apart; a one-inch square in the centre. Colonel M. pointing his pistol to his foot, raised and fired by command—count three—fixed twelve shots *all* within the four-inch space; four shots touched the centre square inch.

As it was getting dark, and we were returning to the house, Colonel Maceroni fired at a pole of two inches diameter. I could hardly see it at all. In order to get the top of the pole between him and the light, he sat on the ground, slowly raised his pistol, and put the ball through it, at about four feet six inches from the ground.

All this I consider most excellent shooting, not to be equalled even by the first shots of the Tyrol, whose rifles could not do execution at one half the distances mentioned above.

The great rifle matches in Germany are never at more than from one hundred to two hundred yards.

Archery

The second meeting of the Herefordshire Bowmen took place last month at Oakley Park, near Ludlow, the seat of the Hon. Robert Clive, M.P. The company was numerous, and the shooting was at a target sixty-one yards distant. The skill displayed, particularly by the ladies, was excellent, and excited the surprise of all who witnessed it, considering the distance. On the conclusion of the "pastime," the company sat down to dinner, where mirth and wit enlivened the board. A ball concluded the festivities of the day.

A grand field day of the Tottenham archers took place on the 22d August at the Society's Archery-ground, in Tottenham, on which occasion a splendid silver medal, manufactured by Messrs. Hamlet, bearing the arms of the Society richly chased on the face, and a suitable inscription on the reverse, was shot for by the members, and after a close and well-contested struggle, was won by Mr. J. Fourdrinier, of Tottenham, by a majority of a single arrow only. The ground was most numerously attended by all the beauty and fashion of the village and its vicinity. After the termination of the shooting, the whole party adjourned to the house of one of the mem[b]ers, adjoining the ground, where an elegant entertainment was prepared for their reception: music and dancing then occupied the remainder of the evening.

At Firle-place, Sussex, on the 21st of August, the good taste of Lord and Lady Gage was made manifest by a grand display of archery there, to which most of the neighbouring gentry were invited. Soon after three o'clock, a sumptuous dinner was served up to the company (composed of nearly one hundred ladies and gentlemen) in the great hall of the mansion; after which, at about five o'clock, the archery commenced, and was pursued with great spirit and pleasantry until its close, when it appeared that the arrow entitled to the prize had been discharged from the bow of Miss Campion, of Danny, at the distance of sixty yards from the target. The amusements of the day were followed by a ball and supper.

Royal Kentish Bowmen

On Saturday, July 31, the above Society met at their elegant Lodge, on Dartford Heath, to shoot at a target, placed at the distance of an hundred yards, for an elegant inlaid Indian bow, quiver, and twelve arrows, valued at fifty guineas. The shooting commenced at two o'clock; much skill was displayed by all who entered the lists. Several of the first bowmen in England were present. The prize was won by Mr. John Mattock, who pierced the bull's eye. A gentleman of the name of Wright gave the prize. The shooting lasted two hours. At five o'clock, the company, consisting all of gentlemen, sat down to an excellent dinner: Lord Eardley was in the chair. The dinner consisted of turtle, venison, &c. When the cloth was removed, *Non nobis Domine*, was sung in very fine style, by Messrs. Nield, Vincent, Leete, and Master Smith. The first toast drank was, "The Royal Kentish Bowmen, and success to the meeting." "The King" was next given, "The Prince and Princess of Wales," &c.—Captain Sutton, of the Navy, sang "Here's a health to all good lasses."—Captain Sowden was proposed as a Member, by Mr. Maddocks, and seconded by Mr. Charles Calvert. He was then ballotted for; and, it appearing there was no black ball, he was elected.

About nine o'clock, a party of distinguished fashionables arrived, among whom were Lady Say and Sele, Lady Melbourne, Mr. Mitford, Mrs. Culling Smith, Mr. and Mrs. Smith, General Pattison, Mr. Latham, Mr. and Miss Maddocks, &c.

The ball commenced, at half past nine o'clock, with *Mrs. Gardner a troop*. The company danced in two sets, of thirty couple each. The supper took place at one o'clock, of which about two hundred persons partook. It was one of the most elegant entertainments ever seen. The desert consisted of the finest fruits the season has produced, such as pines, peaches, nectarines, &c.; the whole was a present from Lord Eardley.

Catches and glees were sung, after supper, in a very fine style, by the professional gentlemen from London, particularly "When Winds breathe soft," a favourite glee of Webbe: it was given in a beautiful manner; the treble by Master Smith, and the bass by Mr. J. Maddocks. It was four o'clock before the company separated, the greater part of whom resided in the vicinity of the lodge.

The tickets to the ball and supper, were one guinea each.

A Town Besieged in Time of Peace: Kingston Taken by Storm

We were greatly surprised in proceeding through a part of Surrey on Tuesday last, on arriving at the town of Kingston, to observe that the whole place—whether inn, public-house, shop, factory, public-building, or private dwelling—was closely shut up, and to all appearance bore the semblance of a Sabbath-day, or some General Fast. Curiosity led us to inquire into the cause; and the answer that we obtained induced us to remain and witness the result of so strange an event. Most of our readers—whether juvenile or adult—are no doubt well aware of a certain fable, and as far as recollection carries us without reference, we believe the following is the substance:—

"A town once in danger of being besieged, a consultation was held with the inhabitants, in order to ascertain which was the most secure and safest way to fortify and strengthen it. A mason said there was nothing like stone: a carpenter said, stone might do very well, but in his opinion, good strong oak was much better: a currier said, gentlemen, you may do as you please, but there is nothing like leather."

This fable goes in illustration of the various modes adopted by the different occupiers to guard against a common assailant about to be put into motion. In most popular commotions we have observed the lower parts of premises closely fastened up; but in the present instance even the windows of the first and second stories were all barricadoed, and to an extent that we were at first at a loss to define the reason. A variety of opinions were manifested on the nature of the materials used to guard against the intended offender, as interest or convenient motives directed: some houses displayed the handicraft work of the carpenter, some of the hurdle-maker, some of the currier, some of the carpet vender, and others of the sail-cloth manufacturer; in short all vulnerable parts, such as windows, fan-lights, lamps, and the like, were promptly converted into a shape of resistance—but to guard against what? A Shrapnell-shell?—No!—A Congreve-rocket?—No!—A cannon-shot?—No!—A *foot-ball?*—*Yes!*

It was nearly ten o'clock when we first entered the town: all was then in active preparation, and by eleven the entire number of edifices were declared in a state of siege. Ancient usage has handed down many curious customs and amusements, and among others this is one; and it is the more especially so from the circumstance of bringing into requisition nearly the whole population of an Assize town—whether high or low, gentle or simple, female or child—such being the attraction of annual custom. Curiosity likewise led us to examine the formidable ball that had given rise to so much trouble and expense to guard against. It consisted of a large bullock's-bladder well filled with air, and secured in a stout leathern case, made perfectly round, and in size and appearance not unlike a 68 lb. cannon shot. We understood that many persons of a particular and fastidious class had been making exertions with the law authorities to put down this day's amusement of the people (*annoyance*, so termed by them), but without effect; and this circumstance seemed rather to have increased the anxiety of many to go on with the sport, without the least shade of diminution of the intention of its original propagator.

The moment for starting the ball being announced by the tolling of the town bell, which struck off exactly at eleven o'clock, Rumbold, an old sporting hand, made his appearance with the dreadful machine secreted in a basket; and the task devolved upon Mr. Redford, of the Castle Hotel, to give the starting kick, which he executed in a lofty and effective manner. By this time an immense concourse of persons, of all denominations, had assembled in the grand market street, the roadway being filled by the *canaille,* and the foot-paths by shopkeepers and other respectable persons. To describe the immense noise and cheering that followed the first mounting of the ball would beggar description; but it strongly reminded us of the following lines of Casca in the tragedy of *Julius Caesar:*—

—"The rabblement hooted,
And clapp'd their chapp'd hands, and
threw up their sweaty night-caps,
And utter'd such a deal of stinking breath,

that, for mine own part,
I durst not laugh, for fear of opening my
lips and receiving the bad air."

A simultaneous motion and rush followed the falling of the ball to its centre of gravity, every one being anxious for the second and ultimate kicks or buffets: and the scene that presented itself by the alteration of the apparel of many who had fallen to the ground, and in consequence got well bedaubed with mud, was truly ludicrous.

The competitors at the ball were divided into two classes—namely, the inhabitants at Thames-street-end of the Castle, and those of the Town's-end: and it appeared that the utmost energy and exertions were resorted to by the partisans of one and the other districts, in order to drive the ball home to its wonted destination. No obstacle appeared to daunt the anxiety of either side. To surmount the roofs of houses, scale the walls, and to plunge into the creek or river, were comparatively trifles; for wherever the object of attraction happened to be cast or buffeted to, whether in or out of doors, there were persons at hand ready to dash after it, regardless of any ceremony. Had a mad-bull been let loose it could not have afforded (as far as we could judge) greater satisfaction to the Kingston people than this leathern ball. The day happened to be congenial to the amusement, owing to the partial showers of rain that had fallen; and by the time the hour of victory approached (five o'clock), the appearance of almost every person was altered, either by being mud-splattered, apparel all disordered, or otherwise being soundly ducked in the creek, or river Thames—very frequent instances of the latter occurring, notwithstanding the coldness and inclemency of the weather; and it will be a matter of surprise to us should many escape their death by their temerity.

The folks of Thames-street-end, on time being called, and after six hours hard contention, were declared the victors and lawful possessors of the ball, amidst a general shout from their numerous partisans; and we are happy to add, that at the conclusion of the scramble no accident of any consequence happened to mar the proceedings of the day, excepting a few bloody noses and bruised shins.

Mr. Moor, of the Griffin Inn, Kingston, at whose house we took up our quarters, provided an excellent anniversary dinner for the gentry on the occasion, consisting of the very best fish, flesh, fowl, and game, as well as wine of the first quality; and we regret to state that the number of the company was not so bountiful as anticipated, arising, as we understood, from the divisibility of visitors with mine host of the Castle.

Mr. Kempster, the respectable distiller, was in the chair, assisted by Dr. Harding, as deputy.

The toasts and sentiments were of a loyal and sporting kind; and the evening passed off exceedingly pleasant, and quite in accordance with the day's diversion.

From what we could learn of the innkeepers of Kingston, we wish that party spirit and envy were entirely annihilated, as it would tend most materially to promote their interest, and of all other parties, whether in that or any other line of business.

The Laws of Cricket
As revised by the
CRICKET CLUB *at* ST. MARY-LE-BONE

The Ball: Must weigh not less than five ounces and a half, nor more than five ounces and three quarters [still the weight]. It cannot be changed during the game, but with the consent of both parties.

The Bat: Must not exceed four inches and one quarter in the widest part [still the maximum].

The Stumps: Must be twenty-two inches out of the ground, the bail six inches in length.[8]

The Bowling Crease: Must be in a line with the stumps, three feet in length, with a return crease.

The Popping Crease:[9] Must be three feet ten inches from the wicket, and parallel to it.

The Wickets: Must be opposite to each other, at the distance of twenty-two yards [still the distance].

The Party Which Goes from Home: Shall have the choice of the innings, and the pitching of the wickets; which shall be pitched within thirty yards of a center fixed by the adversaries.

When the parties meet at a third place, the bowlers shall toss up for the pitching of the first wicket, and the choice of going in.

It shall not be lawful for either party during a match, without the consent of the other, to alter the ground, by rolling, watering, covering, mowing, or beating: this rule is not meant to prevent a striker from beating the ground with his bat near where he stands during the innings, or to prevent the bowler from filling up holes, watering his ground, or using saw-dust, &c., when the ground is wet.

The Bowler: Shall deliver the ball with one foot behind the bowling-crease, and within the return-crease, and shall bowl four balls before he changes wickets, which he shall do but once in the same innings.

He may order the striker, at his wicket, to stand on which side of it he pleases.

The Striker Is Out: If the bail is bowled off, or the stump bowled out of the ground.

Or if the ball, from a stroke over or under his bat, or upon his hands, (but not wrists) is held before it touches the ground, although it be hugged to the body of the catcher.

Or if in striking, or at any other time while the ball is in play, both his feet are over the popping-crease, and his wicket is put down, except his bat is grounded within it.

Or if in striking at the ball he hits down his wicket.

Or if under pretence of running a notch,[10] or otherwise, either of the strikers prevent a ball from being caught, the striker of the ball is out.

Or if the ball is struck up, and he wilfully strikes it again.

Or if in running a notch the wicket is struck down by a throw, or with the ball in hand, before his foot, hand, or bat, is grounded over the popping-crease. But if the bail is off, the stump must be struck out of the ground.

Or if the striker touches or takes up the ball while in play, unless at the request of the opposite party.

Or if the striker puts his leg before the wicket with a design to stop the ball, and actually prevents the ball from hitting the wicket by it.[11]

If the players have crossed each other, he that runs for the wicket which is put down, is out; if they are not crossed, he that has left the wicket which is put down is out.

Whan a ball is caught no notch to be reckoned.

When a striker is run out, the notch they were running for is not to be reckoned.

When the ball has been in the bowler's wicket-keeper's hands it is considered as no longer in play, and the strikers need not keep within their ground till the umpire has called *play;* but if the player goes out of his ground with an intent to run before the ball is delivered, the bowler may put him out.

If the ball is struck up, the striker may guard his wicket either with his bat or his body.

In single wicket-matches, if the striker moves out of his ground to strike at the ball, he shall be allowed no notch for such stroke.

The Wicket-Keeper: Shall stand at a reasonable distance behind the wicket, and shall not move till the ball is out of the bowler's hand, and shall not, by any noise, incommode the striker; and if his hands, knees, feet, or head, be over or before the wicket, though the ball hit it, it shall not be out.

The Umpires: Are the sole judges of fair and unfair play, and all disputes shall be determined by them; each at his own wicket. But in case of a catch which the umpire at the wicket cannot see sufficiently to decide upon, he may apply to the other umpire, whose opinion is conclusive.

They shall allow two minutes for each man to come in, and fifteen minutes between each innings; when the umpire shall call *play,* the party refusing to play shall lose the match.

When a striker is hurt, they are to permit another to come in; and the person hurt shall have his hands in any part of that innings.

They are not to order a player out, unless appealed to by the adversaries.

But if the bowler's foot is not behind the bowling-crease, and within the return-crease, when he delivers the ball, they must, unasked, call *no ball*

If the striker runs a short notch, the umpire must call *no notch.*

Bets: If the notches of one player are laid against another, the bets depend on the first innings, unless otherwise specified.

If the bets are made upon both innings, and one party beats the other in one innings, the notches in the first innings shall determine the bet.

But if the other party goes in a second time, then the bet must be determined by the number on the score.

Amazonian Cricket Match

This extraordinary performance, between the Hampshire and Surrey heroines, commenced on Wednesday, the 2d instant, in a field belonging to Mr. Strong, at the back of Newington-green, near Ball's Pond, Middlesex. The wickets were pitched [stuck in the ground] at eleven o'clock. It was made by two Noblemen, for five hundred guineas. This grand match was to have taken place at Clapham a few weeks back, but, owing to some unforeseen misunderstanding, it was put off till the time mentioned. The ground, which is spacious, was enlivened with marquees and booths, well supplied with gin, beer, and gingerbread. The performers in this contest were of all ages and sizes, from fourteen to sixty: the young had shawls, and the old, long cloaks. The Hampshire were distinguished by the colour of *true blue*, which was pinned in their bonnets in the shape of the Prince's plume. The Surrey was equally as smart; their colours were *blue*, surmounted with *orange*. Those Amazonians' names were as follows—they consisted of eleven on each side:—

The Surrey side consisted of—Ann Baker (sixty years of age, the best runner and bowler on that side), Ann Taylor, Maria Barfatt, Hannah Higgs, Elizabeth Gale, Hannah Collas, Hannah Bartlett, Maria Cooke, Charlotte Cooke, Elizabeth Stock, and Mary Fry.

The Hampshire side consisted of—Sarah Luff, Charlotte Pulain, Hannah Parker, Elizabeth Smith, Martha Smith, Mary Woodson, Nancy Porter, Ann Poulters, Mary Novell, Mary Hislock, and Mary Jougan.

Very excellent play took place on Wednesday; one of the Hampshire lasses made forty-one innings [turns to bat] before she was thrown out; at the conclusion of the day's sport the Hampshire lasses were eighty-one a-head—the unfavourableness of the weather prevented any more sport that day, though the ground was filled with spectators. On the following day the Surrey lasses kept the field with great success, and on Monday, the 7th, being the last day to decide the contest, an unusual assemblage of vehicles of all descriptions surrounded the ground by eleven o'clock; tandems, dogcarts, hackney-coaches, &c., formed a complete ring; several handsome females, dressed in azure blue mantles, graced those vehicles. The Earl of Barrymore, in a single horse-chaise, was amongst the spectators. His little friend, who goes by the name of *Tiger*, was on his poney. At three o'clock, the match was won by the Hampshire lasses, who not being willing to leave the field at so early an hour, and having only won by two innings, they

128 Hounds in the Morning

played a single game, in which they were also successful. Afterwards they marched in triumph to the Angel, at Islington, and took some refreshment.—After their departure, the remainder of the spectators were entertained with a foot race: it was between a Hampshire barber, residing in the neighbourhood of Chick-lane, and a Surrey man. The ground was measured (one hundred yards); as much ceremony was practised as is customary at a race-course; a gentleman on a grey poney, and another on a chesnut mare, cleared the ground. At five o'clock the two champions appeared in full array, the Hampshire barber being no *sans culotte,* but in buff; his antagonist, the Surrey man, had a white handkerchief round his head. He was allowed five yards in advance, but he was distanced by twenty-five yards. This concluded the sports of the day.

[Pierce Egan?[12]]

On Throwing the Cricket Ball

The event of the bet of one hundred guineas, between Lord Kennedy and Captain Barclay, whereby the latter was to produce a man before Christmas Day, to throw a cricket ball one hundred yards (who failed in the performance), has by no means surprised me. It has recalled a few circumstances of a similar nature to my recollection; and the following observations, if you think proper to give place to them in the *Sport. Magazine,* are much at your service.[13]

I beg to premise that I am an ardent admirer of the game of cricket, though my affinity to "three score years," has compelled me to become merely a spectator, and this, when the game is well played, is a rich treat to me.

I think when a ball is well hit away, and pursued by a good fieldsman, and thrown back to the wicket from a long distance with precision, to be one of the finest features of the game, and never fails to command the approbation of the surrounding multitude. I have, Mr. Editor, seen many matches of throwing the ball, and have been intimately acquainted with many good throwers, and I think I can account for the failure of this fine *athletic young man* produced by the Captain, in not covering the one hundred yards. I have no doubt that he was recommended to Captain B. as having done much more, and that his performing it was a certainty. The Captain should have chosen a cricketing month, when the blood is in free circulation, the limbs and muscles flexible (for there is a sleight in throwing, which strength alone cannot accomplish), instead of December's frost, the very idea of which is almost enough to repel a cricket ball.

I remember Mark Cobden's winning a match of the late Earl of Winchelsea, in Goodwood Park, by pitching the ball one hundred and nineteen yards. The same Nobleman matched a man against Mr. Wm. Lillyhett, of Havant, to throw on Broadhalfpenny Cricket Ground, in Hants, for twenty pounds. Mr. L. the first throw made one hundred and twenty-three yards, and won. I saw him soon afterwards very easily beat in Kingslay Bottom by Mr. Wm. Bailey (since deceased.) I saw Mr. Hackman, of this city, beat Mr. E. Cosens on Hunston Common, pitching fairly one hundred and eighteen yards. I know at present of some "long arms," as they are termed, who think little of one hundred yards. My reason for stating the above matches is, that neither of the men (and I have conversed with them all) would attempt *one hundred yards* in winter, though competent to a much greater distance in summer.

I am a total stranger to the man produced by Captain B. yet so confident am I of his ability (judging from what he has done) that I have bet my neighbour, should the match be attempted again in *season*, a dozen of wine, that he exceeds one hundred and eight yards, once in three throws.—I remain, Sir, yours, &c.

CH. CHESTER

P.S. Mr. W. Bailey, and Brown (the bowler), of Emsworth, before he hurt his arm, were the best throwers I ever met with. They were each of them equal to one hundred and thirty yards; the latter has exceeded it: they would both chuse a ball up to its weight of five ounces and three quarters.

. . .

A match was made some time ago, for 100 guineas a-side, between Lord Kennedy and Captain Barclay, which was agreed upon to be decided before Christmas Day; the latter gentleman undertaking to find a man who should throw a cricket ball the distance of 100 yards forwards; and in order that no advantage might be derived from the wind, he should throw the ball back again the same distance. Hyde Park was the place fixed upon, and on Tuesday morning, Dec. 24, the Noble Lord and his sporting adversary met, when the latter produced a fine athletic country man, to all appearance, who attempted the undertaking, with the disadvantage of an unfavourable morning, and failed in it, not getting beyond 98 yards in his best throw; consequently the Captain lost his money.

Cricket

The fine summer we have experienced has not been lost to the amateurs of cricket. Never was this manly sport pursued with more ardour than during the present season; but as it is impossible for us to find room for a detail of the numerous matches which have taken place, we select the following as the most interesting one that has lately come before us.—The account is extracted from the *Norwich Mercury*.

An extraordinary match at cricket, which from the circumstance of the best players of three counties having to contend in it, had excited intense interest, began on Monday, August 7. The match was played between the best men of Leicester and Sheffield, called the Union, and those old and experienced players, the Nottingham Club—in a ground made by subscription, for the express purpose of cricketing, cut from the side of an immense hill, and surrounded by a high stone wall.

The game might be regarded in some degree as a trial of superiority between the old and steady style of playing, and the new and dashing method adopted by the young players of the present day. Both sides were composed of picked men. On the Union side were Shelton, Barber, Davis, Marsden, Gambles, Owston, Woolhouse, Dearman, Rollins, and Squires.—On the Nottingham, Smith, Warsop, C. Jervis, Kettleband, Dennis, Clarke, G. Jervis, Barker, Goodhall, Bramley, and Thorpe. The Union won the call, and put the Nottingham in about one o'clock.

Barker and C. Jervis, of this side, now commenced the game. The utmost attention prevailed. The general feeling amongst the amateurs at this moment was certainly in favour of Nottingham. The players, however, had not continued for one hour (during which the unprecedented number of eight overs[14] had been bowled by Rollins and Marsden, with the loss of only six runs) before the best judges most confidently expressed their opinion of the safety of the Union. The manner in which the field acted together, and the power and general precision of Marsden's bowling, were universally admired. As a slow bowler, Rollins gained much credit; and his peculiar style of giving the ball, contrasted with the tremendous delivery which his colleague had adopted, appeared literally to confound some of the old Nottingham players. The experienced Dennis blocked two of Marsden's balls, got a run from a third, but the fourth he appeared to have no sight of, and was bowled out. This likewise happened to Clarke: he stood but two overs of Marsden's balls, and then with the most delightful unconsciousness, suffered a ball to pass under his bat and take the middle stump. In three hours nine wickets were down, and the score was seventy. The two last men, Bramley and Thorpe, played for an hour very carefully, and made the score up to 101. In remarking upon the merits of the veteran Nottingham players as batsmen, we cannot help confidently expressing our opinion, that they have depended on that old steady line of striking, which when opposed to the bowling and fielding displayed by the yound players of Sheffield and Leicester, can *never* make a great game.

After a short pause, Union commenced the innings. Shelton and Barber went in; the field was arranged; and perfect silence was observed by the multitude as Clarke delivered the first ball. It might have been perceived by the least curious spectator, that the friends of the Union feared every thing from the bowling of Clarke; and this apprehension of danger increased, when on the next over, Clarke proved that he still retained his speed and exactness. To sink the confidence of the Union still lower, Shelton, a good batter of the Leicester party, touched one of Clarke's twisted balls, and was caught out without a notch by Dennis the wicket keeper. Davis, an accomplished general player and known good batter, took his place; and appearing to take either Clarke's balls or those of his colleague with the utmost ease and confidence, the hopes of the Union were quickly restored. As he was getting into good play, the time fixed for striking the wicket arrived, and the ground was reluctantly abandoned.

The second day's play commenced about half-past eleven, when Davis, who was left in with Barber at the termination of the first day's innings, continued in excellent play and with good judgment; and

Barber risked nothing for a run. They fell, however, after getting 38 notches, under the bowling of Barker, and were succeeded by Vincent and Marsden. When the latter walked up to his post, a buzz of expectation arose from the spectators, and he opened his play with the confident expectations of some, but with the hopes of all. He commenced striking in the grandest manner at the very first ball, and in fifteen minutes, the Nottingham bowlers seeing their balls, however varied, struck to all parts of the field, apparently at the will of the batsman, took counsel on the ground, and put G. Jervis in the place of Clarke. From this time Marsden began a course of batting, of which the oldest annals of cricketing afford scarcely any parallel. The highest state of physical strength, the most perfect confidence, and the greatest practical talent, combined to produce such an exhibition of fine play, that the oldest records of double wicket afford but one example of any thing superior. At a quarter past three o'clock the Nottingham first innings was cleared off, with the loss of four wickets only. Gamble, a very safe batter, and capable of doing great execution, was now in with Marsden, but he appeared for some time to attempt nothing but the running Marsden's notches, which, with scarcely any exception, followed each ball in regular succession. The Nottingham field could not conceal their astonishment, and the admiration of the spectators was unbounded. Soon after three o'clock the play was abandoned for refreshment. At the return to the field, Gamble (Marsden's fellow-batter) began to take his share of the game. From this time (about four o'clock) the two players struck at nearly every ball; and in the short space of two hours actually ran 119 notches between them. Out of these the greater number arose from *three* strokes. The Nottingham balls became weak from absolute hopelessness, and it was evident that, if Marsden could maintain his grand style of batting, bowling him out was the very last thing to be expected. Among some of the very extraordinary balls that rebounded from Marsden's bat, one may be remarked which may convey to the amateur some idea of his great powers. At the near wicket to the tents, he struck at a well-pitched ball, which rose somewhat high, clearly out of the ground. It was driven over the highest part of the stone wall, on the right of the entrance to the green, at the height of forty-five feet from the ground, and alighted at the distance of *one hundred and thirty yards* from the place where it was struck.

Third day.—The news of Marsden's success, and the desire to witness what may almost be termed his second innings, caused the ground to present a busy appearance at an earlier hour than usual. At eleven o'clock the players resumed their stations. Those who had been disposed to attribute the extraordinary score which Marsden had made the previous evening to good fortune, must have admitted, after witnessing his inimitable manner of meeting the first balls this morning, that his success was the honest result of his talents: his terrific bat produced seven notches from the first over. It would be needless to follow Marsden for the following three hours and a half, during which he maintained his post. The office of wicket-keeper behind his play was absolutely useless; and with a very few exceptions the balls were driven forward, or struck over the heads of the fielders, into the crowd. The vexation of the Nottingham men displayed itself in various amusing ways; and as the impossibility of bowling him out became more apparent, they undoubtedly relaxed their exertions. It was ludicrous to see the fielders shifting themselves from one extremity of the ground to the other, with the invariable ill fortune of leaving some passage uncovered, which Marsden's fine eye never failed to discover. Barker, the Nottingham bowler, at one time so far lost his temper as to give a full pitch at the face of the player instead of his wicket. Marsden regarded the ball with a look and a manner which seemed to say, "What will come next," and struck it down with sufficient power as to cause it to enter the tents. The admiration of the spectators was now loudly expressed, but the next shift of the losing players caused still further amusement. Dennis having with much care and some solemnity arranged the field, ventured to try a few balls against the invincible wicket. After Barker's strong bowling, Marsden appeared to receive the change with much satisfaction, and, striking each of the four balls of the over, made 10 runs. Dennis now gave the ball to Clarke, admidst the laughter of the crowd, and retired to the end of the field, in the hope of catching one of the long balls. Marsden had now scored 227, and had been in play a little more than eight hours in two days. The fatal ball which was to close Marsden's glorious career was now given by Barker. Marsden struck as usual, but the ball for once went lightly off the bat, and was caught by the bowler at mid wicket. He retired from his post with the applause of the spectators. The innings was over at three o'clock, yielding the unprecedented score of 380.

The Nottingham second innings soon after commenced, but we can go no further into detail—it must suffice to say, that the Union was declared to be victorious in one innings—Nottingham two innings 176—Union one innings 380.—Nearly thirty thousand persons, it is calculated, visited the ground during the three days.

Part IV

The Bloody Sports

Billy, the Rat-Killer

Thursday night, Oct. 24, at a quarter before eight o'clock, the lovers of rat-killing enjoyed a feast of delight in a prodigious *rat*icide at the Cockpit, Westminster. The place was crowded. The famous dog *Billy*, of rat-killing notoriety, 26 lbs. weight, was wagered, for twenty sovereigns, to kill one hundred rats in twelve minutes. The rats were turned out loose at once in a 12-feet square, and the floor whitened, so that the rats might be visible to all. The set-to began, and *Billy* exerted himself to the utmost. At four minutes and three quarters, as the hero's head was covered with gore, he was removed from the pit, and his chaps being washed, he lapped some water to cool his throat. Again he entered the arena, and in vain did the unfortunate victims labour to obtain security by climbing against the sides of the pit, or by crouching beneath the hero. By twos and threes they were caught, and soon their mangled corses proved the valour of the victor. Some of the flying enemy, more valiant than the rest, endeavoured by seizing this *Quinlius Flestrum* of heroic dogs by the ears, to procure a respite, or to sell their life as dearly as possible; but his grand paw soon swept off the buzzers, and consigned them to their fate. At seven minutes and a quarter, or according to another watch, for there were two umpires and two watches, at seven minutes and seventeen seconds, the victor relinquished the glorious pursuit, for all his foes lay slaughtered on the ensanguined plain. *Billy* was then caressed and fondled by many; the dog is estimated by amateurs as a most dexterous animal; he is, unfortunately, what the French *Monsieurs* call *borgne*, that is, blind of an eye.—This precious organ was lost to him some time since by the intrepidity of an inimical rat, which as he had not seized it in a proper place, turned round on its murderer, and reprived him by one bite of the privilege of seeing with two eyes in future.

. . .

The dog BILLY, of rat-killing notoriety, on the evening of the 13th instant, again exhibited his surprising dexterity; he was wagered to kill one hundred rats within twelve minutes; but six minutes and twenty-five seconds only elapsed, when every rat lay stretched on the gory plain, without the least symptom of life appearing.[1] Billy was decorated with a silver collar, and a number of ribband bows, and was led off amidst the applauses of the persons assembled.

Bull-Baiting at Bristol

"About the lordly bull they crowd"
                                    Pullein

Some of the fifty thousand readers of the *Sport. Mag.* have doubtless cantered over the bright green sward of peerless Durdham Downs. . . . It is the finest spot in the universe for a bull-bait.

The bull was led into the ring and tied to the plug a few minutes after our arrival, at this choice and delicious little vale; he walked coolly round the circle, at the full length of his rope, for some time, and then contracting his revolutions by degrees, at length took up his station in the center of the ring, ever and anon lashing his finely rounded sides with his tail, and testily stamping with his fore-foot, as if impatient for the commencement of the fray. A fine two-year-old dog was the first that was turned in upon him. He rushed up to the bull's head like lightning, and made a desperate snatch at his leather; but the bull, who had placed his curled head close to the turf, and almost between his fore-legs, by a slight, but most effectual jerk, loosened the hold the moment it was effected, and whirled the dog to a very considerable height. He fell, however, within a yard of the bull's heels, and immediately crept, unperceived, beneath his belly, through his fore-legs, and nabbed him by the down-dropping nether lip. The bull had been looking about to see where his assailant fell, and was somewhat startled at feeling the dog's teeth rioting in his beef so soon again, in a quarter too from whence he least expected him. But in the twinkling of an eye the dog was hurled out of the circle by a desperate uptossing of the bull's head. The noble fellow, however, contrived to elude the many snatches made at him by the spectators, and crawled up towards the death-striking horns again. The bull met him half way, and placing his head askance gored him very severely in the shoulder, and would certainly have sacrificed this fine fellow to his rage had he not been instantly relieved, and the bull's attention forcibly diverted to another quarter.* The play now went on in gallant style; the old bull's head appeared scarcely to move while he sent between two and three dozen dogs successively in the air, to the infinite alarm of their owners, who often essayed to catch them in their arms as they "toppled down head-

---

*This brave young dog was castrated. Some say the operation deprives the animal of pluck; we have seen several instances to the contrary, but nevertheless we must say that we altogether disapprove of the practice. "Fie on't."

long" to the earth. Some of the noble-hearted animals, after receiving repeated gores and infuriate tosses, still tottered up to their punisher, and fell under his feet, where they were almost trampled to death, still, however, endeavouring to clutch their terrible opponent by the jowl.

There were as usual a few of the "Jack Rugby," or "follow-my-heel" breed, whose currish propensities were punished with such tremendous and crushing doublers-up, as invariably sent them away hopping on one, two, or three legs (as the case happened), yelping most prodigiously, and turning deaf ears to all the fierce interrogatories and terrific vituperation of their disconsolate and enraged proprietors. The uproar was immense—the gossip of the dogs; the low tones of the bull, growling "curses not loud but deep;" the continual and many-voiced chatter of the ring-clearers as they took away the punished dogs, kept back the heavy-pressing crowd from the reach of the bull's rope; and persuading the many intruding tykes to retire from the circle by dint of most vigorous application to their gridiron ribs, with huge, long, never-to-be-forgotten ashplants, produced such a "concatenation" of noises, as can only be conceived by those who have witnessed some such sport as a prime first-rate bull-bait. "In gude sooth it was a ryghte merrie pastyme."

In the course of the play we observed preparations making at our dexter side for turning in a fine brindled bitch, with teeth like a wolf's, and an under-jaw projecting far beyond her jet-black quivering nostrils. We think she was just about the prettiest thing in the bull way we had hitherto seen. Indeed we have never since met with above a couple who could match with her in externals. She had been most outrageous since the first dog was uncollared, and there seemed such manifest probability of pinning about her, that we unconsciously said, "that we would individually bet five to seven, that she fixed the roarer."—No sooner had the words slipped over our lips than a droll-looking old fellow, who was sitting on the ground in our front, cocked up his puckered untonsored iron-grey visage, and stretching out a bony, withered paw, clutched the tip of one of our doe-skin muffles, and with a satisfied smile, indicative of his self-sufficiency and consciousness of winning, hastily ejaculated "done." This was a closer. We could not retreat if we would. But the chances seemed all in our favour. The bitch was a beauty. There was such palpable breed about her head, and capability of clutching in her under jaw, that the least hint would have induced us to double the bet. Preliminaries being settled, according to the established etiquette of the bullring—the fees of entry being paid, and every incumbrance stripped off, the brave-looking bitch went in most gaily and gallantly, and immediately began to—nibble the bull's horns. We were of course bit, and somewhat chagrined. The old blade skrewed up his mug into a most excruciating smile of triumph, and fixing his squinting corkscrew glances upon our right pocket, put forth his palm for the indispensable. The bitch was terribly gored, and would not face the old bull's prickers again.

 He had now been a considerable time at play, and almost every dog on the sod had tried his teeth upon him without any ultimate effect. His tough muzzle was very much lacerated, and the blood trickled down his cheeks in several distinct streams from sundry deep bites which he had received about the eye. There was a cessation of hostilities for above four minutes. The owners of the untried dogs seemed half afraid to let them loose. Those who had been pierced were under the hands of their friends and admirers, having their gore staunched and their wounds sewed up. At last a crippled white bitch, at the command of an old butcher, by whose side she had hitherto been standing, (calmly watching the flight of the numerous dogs in the air, and the clever and effective motions of the old bull), slowly hobbled into the ring; she was covered with scars, blind in an eye, and altogether deprived of the use of one of her hind legs. Unlike many good dogs we had before seen, she did not run directly up to the bull's front, but sneaked cautiously round him, with her remaining eye vigilantly bent upon his every motion, and apparently watching for an opportunity to bolt in for a grab. This was rather *unbulldoglike* behaviour, we must say; but when we consider the infirmity of the old bitch, and the little chance of success she would have in running in like a strong, fleet, and unmaimed dog, it may in some measure be excused. 'Tis very certain that she had pinned this same formidable bull above a dozen times, and we were informed (by a person to whose assertion we are inclined to give the most implicit credence) that she and the bull had slept many a night together in the same stall. In the stable they were as amicable as doves, but on the turf it was very different. The bull's fiery and bloodshot eye was fixed upon her the moment she made her appearance. He seemed to be perfectly aware of her tremendous qualifications, and steadily kept his front towards her, turning as she turned; and disregarding all other objects, kept his keen optics fixed on her alone. Another dog unexpectedly burst into the ring while the two quadrupeds were thus steadily eyeing each other, but the bull sent him curvetting and gamboling over the heads of the spectators, without deigning (or perhaps daring) to honour him with a momentary glance. It was some time before an opportunity occurred for the bitch to get in. At length she suddenly darted forwards with a velocity of which we had deemed her incapable, and at one bound reached the bull's nose. On this occasion, however, she was unsuccessful. Her sturdy old friend tossed her off several times; but her disasters only tended to prove her invincible courage. She repeatedly went into the old bull; and at one time contrived to evade his horns so cleverly, and grappled with him so stoutly, that she would, in our opinion, eventually have pinned him, had he not trod her off by main force, and running clean over her maimed body, left her to be picked up by her fond old master.

After another irregular and very short contest, with a few fresh dogs, the particulars of which we do not remember, the bull had a very protracted breathing-time, and he was just about to be led off the ground unpinned, when a lanky, wire-haired, dingy-red coloured dog was brought to the extremity of the circle. His head was more like a lurcher's than a bull-dog's, and his tail short, thick, and rather rough and brushy. A loud laugh arose from all sides of the ring, as soon as he was introduced: a thousand fingers were pointed in derision at the dog and his master; and the old fellow with the gimblet eye once more turned up his head, and in a most unsupportable tone of voice tauntingly said, "he supposed we would even put our money upon this cur too." The circumstances of our former defeat were still fresh in our memory. We had not an atom of faith in the long spiry snipe-nosed dog—there were no symptoms of pugnacity about him; but the old joker's look and tone were a great deal too much for our philosophy. Win or lose, we were determined to bet with him; and bet we did, to the same amount and at the same odds as before, and (we still chuckle with glee to think of it) we actually won! The ugly lurcher-looking beast went resolutely up to his beef, and, without encountering a single repulse, effected a fine full-mouthed hold on the bull's snout! It was altogether miraculous and unaccountable. The enraged bull tried all his old arts to disengage himself from the dog's gripe: he tossed him furiously upwards against his keen horns, beat him from side to side tremendously on the ground, trampled on him, gallopped round the ring, lay down, rose up again in an instant, bellowed with vexation, pain, and fury, renewed the dreadful beating, trampling, and tossing; but it was all to no purpose—the ugly mongrel-looking dog stuck to him with a most inconceivable and matchless pertinacity; and at length the old bull reluctantly gave in, and suffered himself to be quietly led round the ring by his brave but plain-looking conqueror. So much for externals!

C.

P.S. Jack Cabbage (who, we were told, would most certainly buff with a friend) did not exhibit; but we had the usual quota of bouts at fisty cuffs.² They manage these matters famously in the West. They don't jaw and palaver like the cockneys. "A word and a blow" is their motto: "if thee't fight I, I'll fight thee;" and a monosyllabic response in the affirmative has been the sole prelude to many a sturdy fray among the stout Bristolians. Our best wishes to them all.

Vindication of Cocking

I am a sportsman of the old school, and have always considered cockfighting as one of those rural sports which our ancestors have handed down to us, and which we are legitimately entitled to enjoy, provided we have a taste that way. The display of the courage of the noble, the gallant cock, must surely tend to keep alive the ancient John Bull spirit, which I lament to see is sinking fast into dandyism and insignificance.

A cry has been raised against our ancient sports—the Methodists call out "Shame," the ignorant have taken the alarm, and a late Act of

The Bloody Sports

Parliament has been passed to restrain the lower classes of society from the enjoyment of their rightful diversions. Now, let us consider hare-hunting, fox-hunting, shooting, fishing, or indeed any other rural sport, in comparison with cock-fighting. Poor puss, the most timid animal in the creation, is started from her form, before fifty or sixty dogs, each five times as large as herself, and a numerous field of horsemen and footmen, with whoop and halloo, and the open-mouthed pack close at her heels. Away she starts, driven by fear, and trusting only to her speed for her safety: but her speed avails her but little; she soon gets tired with fright and terror, and her enemies, slow but sure, follow, and overcome her, as it were, by inches—

> Ah, there she lies! how close! she pants, she doubts
> If now she lives. She trembles as she sits
> With horror seized.

But concealment is vain, the quick-scented hound discovers poor puss's retreat, and behold! she is up again, and making another effort to escape from death—but in vain—she is taken, and torn in pieces. Now, here is a death of the most innocent and timid animal, by cruel means. It is true that the sagacity which the hare discovers to elude her pursuers may be a matter of considerable curiosity, or the species may increase too much if they are not destroyed; but then there are more easy modes of killing them. Now, let us look at cock-fighting. The spirited, the courageous cock, acknowledges no superior, or no competitor with himself for the favours of his female companions: if two cocks are left in the same place, battle ensues as a matter of course, and the death of one or both of them is the sure result; but in a state of nature, instead of terminating the battle in a few minutes, it is the work perhaps of hours; now, if they are furnished with weapons,[3] and put into good condition, it seldom happens that a battle lasts five minutes. The valour of the animal, so animating to the blood of an Englishman, is tried to the utmost, and his natural propensities gratified. He is equally matched, and falls a victim to the superiority of his adversary. I ought to write in stronger terms of comparison against shooting (where the poor half-killed bird struggles off to some hiding place to die a lingering death); and against fishing, (the tortures of which I need not describe); but surely enough is already written to remove false impressions from the minds of any candid reader. The ways of nature herself are cruel, from the spring of the tiger or the fascination of the serpent, to the wily acts of the spider. A truce, then, to such hypocrisy as would restrain, (by legislative enactments) the foot from being lifted up, lest, in setting it down again, it might wound or kill the harmless insect; and let us give our sympathies and our humanities where they can be substantially beneficial.—I am, Sir, yours, &c.

AN AMATEUR OF THE COCKPIT

Fight between Crib and Molineux

Tuesday, December 18, 1810. Notwithstanding the numerous pugilistic contests which have occurred during the last twenty years, I may say with more propriety from the time of Big Ben and Johnson[4] to the present (the most of which I have attended), I do not remember so great an interest having been excited amongst the amateurs of boxing, as appears to have been occasioned by the contest that took place between Molineux, the black, (a new candidate for pugilistic fame) and Tom Crib,[5] of fighting celebrity, at Copthall Common, in the vicinity of East Grinstead [Sussex], distant from London about thirty miles.— Whether this arose from the *nature* of the combatants, from the immense sums pending on the issue of the battle, or from the anticipation of an arduous struggle for victory, I cannot say, but that every spectator was feelingly alive to the conflict, was fully evident. It may be here observed, that the *sable-coloured heroes of the fist,* who hitherto have entered the list as prize fighters, have never been distinguished by their successes in the various rencontres they have from time to time been engaged in; and this has been accounted for by supposing that the African race were not endowed with such muscular powers as John Bull. In Molineux, however, this general defect was amply supplied. He is a man of robust stature, weighing 14 st. 8 lb. and therefore deemed competent in point of strength to face any man in the united kingdom. From the specimen he gave of his powers and bottom [courageous stamina] in the combat with Tom Blake, some time ago, he was deemed the best match for Crib of the present day (it having been understood that Jack Gulley[6] had declined all contests as a prize fighter). It was accordingly agreed they should fight for 200 guineas a side.

From what I have heard and witnessed, each man felt confident of victory, and so expressed himself to his respective friends: hence may be accounted for the many thousand pounds betted on the occasion. But, Sir, what alarmed the *natives* most was, the consideration that an *African* or a *tawney Moor,* was looking forward to the championship of England, and had even threatened to decorate his sooty brow with the hard-earned laurels of Crib, who, for the "honour of Old England," swore not to resign either the one or the other but with his life.

With opponents so determined, it was not to be wondered at if the conflict proved a most desperate one; how far that was the case, will be best seen by the sequel.

A more unfavourable day for the sport could not have been selected, as it rained in torrents the whole of the day; and notwithstanding the great distance from town at which the battle took place, the spectators were numerous; and those who were not provided with covered carriages were literally drenched. The last three miles of the road were almost knee deep with clay; so that it can excite no surprise to learn that many horses were knocked up, and the riders, as well as a number of pedestrians, never reached the scene of action. At twelve o'clock Mr. Jackson,[7] who did, and does on all occasions of the kind, officiate as Master of the Ceremonies, had the outer circle formed of the various vehicles, which had served to transport from the metropolis, several thousand of amateurs, who had arrived on the ground in spite of difficulties and bad weather.

The ring in the centre of the large one was strongly constructed of stakes and ropes; and, according to the terms of the fight, measured twenty-four feet every way. The spot for the *Campus Martius* was situated nearly at the foot of a hill, which protected the combatants from the chilling wind and rain from the eastward. On the summit stood a *windmill,* and several others within sight, in different directions. This spot was selected, perhaps, in preference to any other, as most emblematical of the *Quixotic expedition,* or more likely to signify that *milling* [boxing] was the order of the day. At this juncture, however, we were all anxiety for the present, and doubtful for the future. Every heart palpitated with hopes and fears for their respective champions. Even Bill Gibbons, and some other *fancy lads* of the *Westminster school,* it is said, let fall tears in the contemplation of the carnage and bloodshed about to take place. I myself, Sir, saw the *big drops* roll down the *weather-beaten cheeks* of many of them, which I *unwittingly* took for heavy drops of rain. But now the champions appear, "arm'd cap-a-pee, and eager for the fray:" no more *snivelling;* every spectator felt himself an hero, and the lads of the *fancy* seemed by their countenances to say, "What a glorious thing's a battle!"

Molineux, the Moor, not the *Moor of Venice,* but one equally brave and unfortunate, was the first to enter the ring; he made a graceful *congee* to the amateurs (a-la-Bitton), hurled up his cap in defiance of his adversary, then retired to strip for the battle.—Crib followed so bright an example, except the gracefulness of the bow, and in that Molineux had the *art* on his side.

Gulley, the second of Crib, and Richman [Richmond], that of Molineux, entered the ring with their champions.

The awful moment is arrived for setting to, and the heroes throw off their *upper benjamins* [overcoats] as the signal. They shake hands, retire two steps, put themselves in attitude, then eye each other with the most penetrating looks, at the same time each attentive to his guard.

A solemn pause for the moment ensued, and then commenced the

First round.—Molineux commenced hostilities, by placing a right hand blow on the left side of Crib's body; but which was attended with trivial effect. The native champion smartly returned the hit, with a right and left at the head, and one *for luck* in the body; the Black then closed, and was thrown by his adversary.[8] Thus terminated the first round without bloodshed or injury.

Second round.—The combatants set to very sharp, and seemed to verify the opinion gone abroad, that they were both fully determined on a manly stand-up fight, to the exclusion altogether of sparring or shifting. A furious rally took place; several hard blows were exchanged on both sides.—Crib's did the most execution; his blows having been directed straight forward, whilst those of Molineux were hand over head, given with miraculous power and resolution, but without judgment, insomuch that Crib was enabled to parry them or spoil their effect, by planting the first hit. Crib, on the whole, had the advantage of this round, although he exhibited the first blood.

Third round.—Molineux, not the least dismayed at the *taste* he had had, faced his antagonist courageously this round, who met him with corresponding resolution, and coming in contact with the Black's head, at arm's length with his left hand, made him by the blow measure his full length on the ground; the lusty Moor was on his legs in a second, and it was "*Mungo* [Negro] *here, Mungo there,* and *Mungo every where,*" who anxiously looked round for his *customer,* whom he was prevented from meeting until the

Fourth round; in which, after an ineffectual attempt to rally down Crib, the Black received a knockdown blow.

Fifth round, consisted of straight forward fighting: they both rallied in good style; Molineux persevering in the system of boring down his opponent by main strength, whilst Crib evinced a determination to prevent him by repeated blows on the head, which failed to have that effect. This, no doubt, proved to the amateurs that a man so persevering in his manner as the Moor, so regardless of blows, and so strong withal, could not fail to prove not only an *ugly,* but a *troublesome customer* in the end, to Crib, or any other *gentleman* of the *profession.* Towards the finish of this round the Black closed, when it was discerned that he was the strongest man, and was as expert in the *art of fibbing* [hitting with short, sharp, rapid blows] as Dutch Sam, who was the first that rendered that practice cognizable as a part of the science. The Black by this new manoeuvre obtained the best of this round.

Sixth round was begun by a furious onset, but Crib being over anxious to *compliment* the Black for a hit he had received, fell, partly from a slip and a blow.

Seventh round.—Crib had his revenge this round; the Black rushed on his adversary, according to custom, when he caught a violent blow on the forehead, by which he picked up a handsome *rainbow.* His countenance, however, was not the more *clouded* on the occasion, and he was the first to come to his time [to the next round].

Eighth round.—If it were not invidious to single out any particular round, I would say, that this was the best-contested round in the battle; the combatants were still in possession of their full vigour, and had been taught discrimination; they had discovered, also, the weak and strong parts in each other. Crib had found out that, if the resolute Moor got him into so reduced a state as to make his *sledge hammer* blows *tell,* that he should not like his head to be the *anvil,* and from the determined conduct of his tawney antagonist, things were fast ap-

proximating that way.—It was here, that it would seem then, the grand push was to be made, in order to give a decided turn to the battle. Crib brought into the struggle his courage, strength, and science, which were not more than sufficient to cope with the persevering and invulnerable Moor. The rally was desperate; success was alternately on the one side and the other; the Black at length fell; but the extraordinary efforts of Crib rendered him more feeble at the end of the round than his adversary.

Ninth round—Was gallantly contested, but Crib was compelled to make play, by the Black following him up, and giving him no quarter; neither would he take any, for his head was always at the service of his adversary. He never shrunk from a blow, and his great anxiety was always to return it. Crib evinced weakness, and fell from a hit. The *knowing ones* exchanged looks with each other round the ring, as much as to say, "things look a little queer, master."

Tenth round.—By this time the *conceit* was pretty well taken out of both the heroes, and it was not to be wondered at, considering how hard they had fought, and how severely they had been punished. The head of Molineux was prodigiously swollen; and if the Moor had been an artist he could not have laid on the black and red with a more regular hand on Crib's face, although Crib might think it might have been done with a more *delicate touch.* In this. as well as the seven successive rounds, Molineux appeared much the strongest man; he went into Crib, *pell mell,* without standing for repairs, and rallied him at every part of the ring; and when he got him against the ropes, he either threw him, or encircled his neck with his left arm while he *fibbed* him with his right hand. If this could not be called murder, it was something like manslaughter; for Crib seemed all the same as in a blacksmith's vice. It was here where there was shewn a little national prejudice against the Black; but being of a passive nature, he could derive no injury from it; and, to speak impartially, and for the honour of pugilism, the strictest fair play was shewn to both parties throughout.

At the termination of the seventeenth round, Crib was so completely exhausted, as to be termed *dead beat;* but it must not be forgotten, that in reducing Crib to this state, Molineux himself was in a tottering condition, but appeared more animated, more gay, and was the first to appear to his time.

From the seventeenth to the twentieth rounds, Crib appearing to be convinced that he had *overshot* his mark in supposing that he could beat Molineux *off hand,* as he had endeavoured to do, had therefore recourse to his favourite mode of retreating or fighting shy, without which, it appears to me, he must have been compelled to have given in the battle. The Black, naturally presuming this was Crib's forlorn hope, followed him up, and never quitted him until the

Twenty-third round—When seeing a falling off in the Black, and feeling himself somewhat recovered, he made play and knocked his man down for the first time for several rounds.

From the twenty-fourth to the twenty-eighth round, bets were considerably reduced; they had been about 4 to 1 on the Black, and now the bets were even.

Twenty-ninth round—was ominous to the Black; he made an effort to get Crib against the ropes, but without effect; neither could he throw him as he had done; after a short rally, he was knocked down by Crib, who seemed more alive and full of confidence than he had been for many rounds before.

Thirtieth round.—Crib had now certainly the lead, and finding his antagonist could not keep his legs well, stuck to him until he invariably rallied him down.

Thirty-first round—after a short rally, was finished by the Black throwing Crib, but he fell over him in the struggle, by which means he pitched upon his head; and I have heard it from a friend of his, that the hurt he received on this occasion affected him with a giddiness that he could not stand, and induced him to communicate to his second (Richman), that he could no longer continue the contest. Richman, however, finding that Crib was also so much exhausted that he could scarcely support himself, encouraged Molineux to try a round or two more; he did so, and on the termination of the 33d round he fell by an effort to keep his legs; which being termed by Crib's party *falling without a blow,* the victory was claimed in favour of Crib, which would have originated a dispute, had not Molineux again repeated, "I can fight no more."

Crib, no doubt, was delighted at the declaration, but did not treat the spectators with a *somerset,* according to custom. No, indeed, all the strength he had left, was insufficient to support him off the ground without assistance.

Thus terminated a battle which has not been excelled, in point of *hitting* and *execution,* for many years; and while the courage and resolution of the lusty Moor have been extolled to the utmost, the merits of Crib, as a bruiser, will not fail to be duly appreciated by the victory he has gained over so invulnerable an opponent. In this last contest, the struggle I conceive to have been between science and strength. The advantage that Crib had, by his excelling in the former, the Black had by superiority in the latter. With respect to coolness and bottom, it is but justice to place them on a par.—Before I saw the Black set to in this last rencontre, I thought him too irritable and hot, but I am now convinced that his impetuosity is only a part of that principle upon which he fights, and which, no doubt, would have proved successful against most men. To be a finished boxer, a man must be possessed of a large proportion of natural muscular powers, besides other acquirements, the chief of which is, to learn to hit straight, and with a jerk from the shoulder, without which, as Liston[9] would say, "It is all my eye and Betty Martin." The Black is only deficient in this accomplishment. His style of fighting comes nearest to that of Bully Hooper, of Russian memory, who dealt largely in the *black art.*

"On the whole I never witnessed superior manhood to that which Molineux displayed at Copthall Common; and I understand, that so far from being satisfied with the *taste* he had on Tuesday last, that he means to avail himself of the earliest opportunity of inviting his victorious opponent to a *belly-full;* and then, if his efforts prove unsuccessful, he will for ever resign the *profession,* and say with Shakespeare's hero of old, "Othello's occupation's gone." The battle lasted 55 minutes.

"An Amateur"

This letter [above] is given in the precise language of the writer; but we conceive the term *Moor,* or *Tawney Moor,* applies to the *Moors* on the Coast of Barbary, &c. and as formerly possessing a part of Spain, from which they were afterwards driven,—and not to the Negroes from the coast of Guinea, called Blackamoors.—Molineux is supposed to be of this latter race. If he has any thing of the White in him he is called a man of colour, and if either father or mother were White, then a Mulatto,— not a Tawney Moor.

A Fresh Challenge

"To *Mr. Thomas Crib*
"St. Martin's-street, Leicester square
Dec. 21, 1810
"Sir—My friends think, that had the weather on last Tuesday, the day upon which I contended with you, not been so unfavourable, I should

have won the battle; I therefore challenge you to a second meeting, at any time within two months, for such sum as those gentlemen who place confidence in me may be pleased to arrange.

"As it is possible this letter may meet the public eye, I cannot omit the opportunity of expressing a confident hope, that the circumstance of my being of a different colour to that of a people amongst whom I have sought protection, will not in any way operate to my prejudice.—I am Sir, your most obedient humble servant,
"Witness J. Scholefield" "T. MOLINEUX"

Crib has accepted the challenge. They are to fight again on the 21st of May,[10] for 250 guineas a side, and a subscription purse of 100 guineas for the winner.—Fifty guineas of the stake are the actual property of Molineux.

The [Second] Battle between Crib, Champion of England, and Molineux, the Baltimore Man of Colour

The battle took place, as we announced it would, on Saturday last [September 28, 1811]; and the spot chosen for the scene of action was near where we intimated, being Crown-Point, a short distance from Thistleton-Gap, and about twelve miles from Stamford, a place of doubtful county-ship, being situated at the conflux of three counties, Lincoln, Rutland, and Leicester. This circumstance, no doubt, occasioned its selection, with a view to avoiding the authority of any interfering magistrate. Here, in a large stubble-field, a stage was erected, twenty-five feet square, for the combatants, which was again surrounded by a rope ring to keep off the crowd. Round this, at a very early hour, the whole country began to pour from all directions.— From the barouche to the donkey, every mode of human conveyance was in use, and thousands who were not so fortunate as to possess any one of these, trusted to their own legs, and walked ten, fifteen, and some twenty miles, to witness a display of strength and courage, peculiar to our country, and apparently congenial to its spirit. As the Oak, at Greetham, which was the head-quarters of Molineux, lay in the road from Stamford, most of the company from that quarter, called on the sable hero as they passed; he seemed alert and confident. Before twelve o'clock, the appearance of the field, where the stage was erected, was of the most unusual and interesting description; several rows of people, on foot, surrounded the large rope ring, behind which were innumerable horsemen, mingled with every species of carriage, from the chariot to the dust-cart. The backs, boxes, wheels, and roofs of these, actually swarmed with spectators, and few of the horsemen were contented to *sit* on their saddles, most of them *stood*, Circus-fashion, a proceeding, in this instance, attended with but little danger, for the living mass was so closely wedged, that when once fixed, there was no moving. The display of *flash-men* [showy boxing fans] from the Peer on the coach-box, to the more gentlemanly-looking pick-pocket, was very complete: all the fighting men and fighting amateurs were down:—*flash*, in short, was the order of the day—to have appeared in a white neckcloth would have been an impeachment on a man's taste, and to have talked of any thing but *hammering* [boxing], a lamentable proof of his ignorance.

A little before twelve, the seconds and bottle-holders made their appearance on the stage; and their arrival encreased the anxiety of the immense crowd present relative to the approaching fight. Gully and Joe Ward attended to assist Crib; Richman the Black, and Bill Gibbons, to assist Molineux.[11] They stripped and put on jackets in preparation for their principals.—About twelve Molineux appeared within the ropes, but his antagonist Crib was the first to spring on the stage, which he did with great gaiety, and made his obeisances to the spectators. The air rang with shouts of applause. Molineux followed, and actively jumped over the railing; he also made his bow, and was greeted with cheering; if not quite so general as the last, yet sufficient to shew that he had many friends, for love or *money*, among those present. Crib was well dressed, in a brown great coat, and boots—and his appearance altogether was very respectable. He seemed to stand about six feet high[12]—looked smiling and confident—and appeared in high condition. Molineux wore a blue coat and nankeen trowsers: he is not so tall a man as his opponent—but is of Ajax make—broad and brawny—capacious of chest—and with arms formed for *hammering*. He eyed Crib with a vengeful sulky look, and seemed bent on doing desperate things.

The preparations for the fight now commenced in the most solemn manner; and it is impossible to express the breathless anxiety of the multitude at this moment. The determined port of the heroes, their evident strength, and the notorious animosity of the Moor, all prognosticated a *terrible mill.* The latter kept walking on the stage while the seconds were arranging the clothes, &c. in a hasty disturbed manner, indicative of violent anger. At length the combatants began to strip—and every hear beat high with expectation. When in fighting trim, both looked remarkably well—the Black is handsome for a man of colour—and Crib is well and stoutly made. He had evidently the advantage in length of arm over his challenger.

The battle, although short, was most desperate. Four more such rounds as the first five, would have given Crib his *belly full;* but his excellent training and determined courage enabled him to recover himself, while the Black, who was by no means in such high condition, and was moreover thrown off his guard by passion, rapidly lost his wind, and exposed himself to his adversary's murderous hitting. The beating which he received on the throat occasioned him to bleed internally, and it was very plain, at times, that he was almost suffocated by the blood rising.—The blow on the side, which he received when falling, descended like a stroke from a hammer: it was heard distinctly at the extremity of the crowd, and its deadly effects were very visible during the next round. It must, however, be allowed that the Black fought well. Crib himself, we understand, says, that he hits with a strength which no other man possesses; and the face of the champion bears ample testimony to the truth of his assertion. He was very much disfigured.—Molineux sparred neatly early in the fight, but he lost his science after he had been a good deal punished. We must, however, confess it struck us that the Black *shyed* his adversary: he seemed from the very first to be afraid of him,—and with the inclination to rush in and sacrifice him to his rage, to couple a dread of the consequences. During the last rounds he fought like a frantic fellow, and fell like a log: his seconds had to lift him up as they would a lump of lead, and lead him to his man as they would a child. After the 11th round he could not again by any means he brought up,—and Crib was proclaimed victor by shouts which rent the skies.—The Black, after the fight, lay extended on the stage in a most piteous manner,—as if dead. The surgeon he brought with him from London bled him, and after some time had elapsed he was enabled to crawl to his chaise, supported by two friends, with his body bent like an S.[13]—The victor, when his conquest was announced, sprung up from the stage, and cut several capers, to shew that he was yet in a condition to take and give more *hammering.*

No one can say, that in this battle Molineux had not fair play shewn him:—we would, however suggest that the cries of exultation, which proceeded from the champion's numerous friends, when the advantage seemed on his side, must have had the effect of *cowing* the Baltimore man:—we think, in decency and generosity, they ought to have been omitted.—Molineux, it is said, had provoked a good deal of feeling against him by savage denunciations of vengeance, and vapouring professions of what he would do to Crib. These are certainly sufficiently disgusting and repugnant to the spirit of Englishmen: but it ought not to have been forgotten that Molineux is a stranger—that he gave a proof of his courage by offering a general challenge—and that he came to the fight unsupported by friends of note, while the champion had all the *flash-men* in his train. It is said this latter circumstance preyed much on the mind of the Black, and occasioned him to, what is technically termed, *funck* [flinch].

On Sunday, Crib passed through Stamford, and on Monday he arrived in London in a barouche and four horses, decorated with blue ribbonds, with a gentleman amateur and Joe Ward, one of his seconds; and his reception on the road was as great as a gallant officer could have received, bearing a narrative of any glorious exploit against a foreign enemy. Not the Admiralty, but Great St. Andrew's-street, Seven Dials,[14] was impassable from the crowd assembled, and the interior of the champion's house was not sufficient to give audience to patrician congratulating amateurs; but the hall of the house is a *coal shed*,[15] and they were received in turn without respect to superior rank. Crib has suffered most about the eyes, which, however, have been well managed, but are vey black, and he has not recieved a solitary body hit. He has cut his hand severely by striking, but he is altogether well. The champion called on Molineux, at theRoyal Oak, Greetham. He has suffered most on the left side of his body, which is hideously swollen, and the right side of his head from the neck upwards: his jaw is fractured in two places, and he cannot speak intelligibly. Considerable dissention prevailed amongst persons who had previously been considered good men, and who had declared off their bets. The matter is thus—a certain number of persons had taken odds at about *two to one*, and when the odds became higher, and they found they had been badly to market, they declared themselves *off*, a thing unknown in sporting, after they had been *on*. Amongst the principal of these are some *qui tam* gentry, a *bumb trap*, a *swell*, and a *prig*, who have been followed by others of a better consideration, and the *rumpus* has put the honest better flash to his customers at least.

The champion was evidently much indebted to Captain Barclay's peculiar system of training.[16] With this gentleman he spent the three months immediately previous to the fight; and under his superintendance went through a discipline, and observed a regimen, of the strictest description. They say the champion got terribly tired of these restraints, but his scientific patron, who is supposed to understand training better than any other man in existence, kept him tightly to it. By the means pursued, Crib's body was brought into so high a state of order, that nothing gross or puffy was left about him. He was throughout firm, light, and pure; strong in wind, and hard in flesh. One of the advantages of training is, that in consequence of it the flesh does not so easily inflame or turn black through blows. A man in ill-condition would be blinded by the hits which a trained man will receive without shewing any marks. It is to the great superiority of the Captain's plan that they attribute his successful performance of the famous Barclay match, of a thousand miles in a thousand hours, which many have since tried and failed in, and which it is supposed will long remain unrivalled in athletic exertion.

It is generally understood that Molineux was by no means so strict in his training as he ought to have been. He, in company with Tom Belcher, Richman, &c. took a tour of the country, during the time that the champion was with Captain Barclay,—and exhibited sparring in the different towns. This was a mode of life by no means calculated to produce any desirable effect on the Black, but that of raising him some money. It is also reported that he lived much too freely; and indulged in certain liberties, from which he ought strictly to have abstained. On the day of the fight, he bolted a boiled fowl, an apple pie, and a tankard of beer, for breakfast; viands by no means the most proper for the occasion. His more cautious antagonist restricted himself to two slightly boiled eggs.

After Crib and Molineux had retired, a subscription was entered into to form a purse for a second fight. Twenty pounds were collected, of which seventeen were to be the meed of the victor, and three the consolation of the vanquished. *George Crib* [younger brother of Tom], a ten-stone man, and *Edward Maltby,* a countryman, about the same weight, entered the list; and an excessively smart and well-contested battle took place, of about half an hour's duration, in which thirteen rounds were fought. Young Crib was obliged to own the superior prowess of the countryman; he was beaten sadly, while his antagonist scarcely sported a mark. Both sparred well, and fought determinedly. The countryman comes from Bromley Hall, in Nottinghamshire; and it is said walked forty miles the day before. He says he has three brothers, each of whom would beat him with one hand—if so, he must come of a good fighting family.

Thus terminated the athletic exercises of this interesting day—exercises certainly attended with danger and pain to those engaged in them—but what active sport is not? Boxing is a manly and a national exercise; and we hope to see its spirit ever kept up in the country as a preventative of something much worse. The neighbouring towns have been all in a bustle; and the innkeepers have reaped a plentiful harvest. We hear of no accident having occurred. The interest excited in that part of the country was certainly without precedent; and we believe much money was lost and won. It is supposed that at least 10,000 spectators were present at the fight.

Molineux has since received a collection, made by Mr. Jackson of 49 £. 16 s. He attributes losing the battle to falling off in wind in the fifth round, and describes Crib as having done him but little injury until this failure in wind; but this is erroneous, although in the heat of action he might not have felt the effects, as Crib always was *in* and fighting with him. It has been said he was neglected by his backers; the fact is, he was backed by subscriptions from several, who undertook only to advance their subscriptions, and consequently had pledged themselves to no responsibility about training. The worst part of the Black's training was the Northern *tour,* which, although it filled his pockets (but he arrived in London pennyless), it subjected him to indiscretions not suitable to a man who was about to fight for 600 £. besides being knocked about with the gloves by any one who chose to set to with him.

A bet of rather a singular kind was made between two gentlemen of Portsmouth, depending upon the battle between Crib and Molineux. The winner (who betted upon Crib) *gets a complete suit of clothes,* including every article that can be understood as coming within the meaning of the bet; with the useful appendages of walking-stick and gloves, and a *guinea in his pocket.* The bet has been paid.

A baker in the Borough staked the whole of his personal property, together with the lease of his house (amounting to 1700 £.) on the issue of the above battle.—Crib was his favourite.

It is said that Capt. Barclay won 10,000 £. on the battle between Crib and Molineux.

Sparring

Molineux had a benefit at the Fives Court,[17] on Thursday, the 19th instant, and from the assemblage present, it was evident that he was not entirely deserted, as the Court was completely filled at an early hour, and the performances were superior to any thing before exhibited in the Court on any similar occasion; although the sets-to were but few, yet the amateurs had a treat in specimens of *real milling*. The first set-to was betwixt Molineux and Power,[18] which displayed the science in its full extent, and was managed with courage on both sides, not unlike fighting for a stake. Power, by quickness, had an advantage in the set-to, yet dexterous flush hits were placed by both. The next set to was a novel one, betwixt Molineux and an athletic Nottinghamshire man, who has a fancy for boxing, but who in this case gave very unfavourable specimens of *wapping* talent. Molineux rallied him with quickness, and had the match his own way. The next match was betwixt the champion Crib, who gave his services in support of his vanquished adversary, by setting to with him, and it was altogether a bloodless imitation of the combat at Thissleton Gap. Molineux sparred in the same manner as he fought, and Crib received him the same as on that occasion, keeping a decided superiority with the right hand.

Pugilism – between Owen and Mendoza

for fifty guineas a-side, on Tuesday, July 4, 1820

Banstead Downs, fourteen miles and a half from London, was the spot selected to decide this *rivalry of fame*—this *point of honour*—this *darling of reputation* so allied to the hearts of all brave men!

The contest, it seems, originated in what is termed "an old grudge;" being of three years standing; and so jealous were these heroes of their "tow'ring fame," that Mendoza and Owen[19] have offered to fight each other for a glass of *max* [neat spirit], merely to ascertain which deserved the appellation of being the "best man!" so far was any thing like mercenary ideas out of the question. But this was considered derogatory to their characters—both of the combatants having fought for large stakes—and more especially as Mendoza was now viewed in the light of being the "Father of the present Ring;" and Tom Owen fast approaching to that important *milling* station. However it went on so *lingeringly*, and has also been so often *chaunted* without any specific time being appointed, that it was in general looked upon by the sporting world altogether as a *hoax;* and in fact, the Pugilistic Society[20] had nothing at all to do with the match in question.

Mendoza was decidedly the favourite. Fourteen years and upwards had passed away since the *Star of the East* [Mendoza was a Jew] had appeared in the prize ring with Harry Lee (March 19, 1806), and more than thirty-three fleeting summers (April 17, 1787) had occurred since Mendoza first distinguished himself as a boxer, with [Samuel] Martin, the Bath butcher. On January 9, 1788, Mendoza was defeated after a most gallant fight, at Odiham, by Humphries;[21] but on May 6, 1789, Mendoza, in turn, gained a victory over his opponent, at Stilton. The third decisive fight between Mendoza and Humphries took place on Sept. 9, 1790, at Doncaster, when conquest again crowned his exertions. Our limits will not permit us to follow Mendoza throughout his successful career. Suffice it to state, that Bill Ward was twice defeated by him, at Smitham Bottom, on May 14, 1792; also on Bexley Common, November 12, 1794. In this year Mendoza forfeited a deposit of 20 £ out of a match of 50 guineas to Hooper. At Hornchurch, April 15, 1795, Mendoza was compelled to resign his laurels to Mr. Jackson, in ten minutes and a half.—After this circumstance, it might be said that Dan left the ring, coming again forward, as above stated, to settle a quarrel with Harry Lee.—At one period of Mendoza's life, a finer subject for an anatomical lecture, it was supposed, did not exist in England; and, although a short man, he weighed 12 st. 5 lb.

Owen derived considerable notoriety in the pugilistic world from his conquest over Hooper, the tinman, (at that time viewed as the dread and terror of the ring), at Harrow, on November 14, 1796. It was a hard fight of fifty rounds, and continued upwards of an hour. The guard of Owen was so straight, and so prodigiously strong, that Hooper, with all his talents, could not beat it down, and was scarcely able to put in a hit. Hooper was terribly *punished:* but Owen put on his clothes with the utmost indifference, and walked out of the ring. Owen also fought with *Jack Bartholomew*, on Sunbury Common, on August 22, 1797. This was acknowledged to be one of the hardest battles ever contested for thirty minutes. Owen lost it, but in a subsequent *turn-up*, it seems, Tom regained his laurels.

To the *majority* of the present *ring-goers,* it was mere *hearsay* evidence respecting the fighting qualities of the above boxers; but the once great fame of Mendoza, although 55 years of age, rendered him the favourite at 6 and 5 to 4. Owen was known to be a good man, but it was thought he had not *science* enough to oppose the *accomplished Israelite.* The east end of the town was completely drained; and the name of Mendoza likewise attracted a number of young *swells* from the west, who had not seen either of the above *ould ones* fight. A great number of the *oldest* amateurs in the *Fancy* were likewise induced to be present; and it is rather singular to state, that the same Baronet, who was Mendoza's umpire at Odiham, acted in that capacity upon this occasion. Owen is 51 years old. Owen, attended by Crib and Josh. Hudson, threw up his hat first; and Mendoza, followed by [Jack] Randall and Harry Lee, repeated the token of defiance.[22]—Mendoza was loudly cheered, and backed 5 to 4. The latter very politely bowed to all parts of the ring.

Mendoza's colours were a blue silk bird's eye, and tied over Owen's, which were yellow.

ROUNDS

1. Mendoza, on throwing off his clothes, exhibited a very fine manly bust; his eyes sparkled with confidence, and there was altogether an appearance about him that seldom characterizes an individual of fifty-five. Owen, on the contrary, looked thin; and the *tout ensemble* was rather meagre than otherwise. On setting-to, both of these *ould ones* were extremely cautious, and a minute elapsed before a hit was made. Owen at length let fly, but without any effect. Some exchanges then took place, when they closed at the ropes, and after an attempt to *fib* on the part of Mendoza, which was frustrated by Owen, a struggle for the throw took place; but in going down Dan was the undermost. Two to 1 on the Jew.

2. Mendoza ran in with great alacrity, and made a sort of *pushing* forwards, and got Owen to the ropes, when the latter went down, and his neck got *scored* from them. Great applause for Mendoza.

3. The Jew behaved extremely handsome, and shewed some good fighting; but Owen planted a tremendous hit on Mendoza's left cheek, just under the left eye, whence the *claret* flowed copiously, and Mendoza went down—yet he jumped up gaily.

4. Owen now gave the amateurs some fine traits of pugilism. Mendoza again was *nobbed* [struck in the head], and the *claret* was profusely running down his cheek. In going down Owen was undermost.

5. Mendoza now *shewed* he was completely *gone by* as to any

superiority in fighting, and Tom Owen displayed talents that astonished the ring. Mendoza received a dreadful fall.

6. Owen, in retreating from his antagonist, ran against the stakes, but the latter again planted a heavy *facer*. In struggling, both went down.

7. Here Tom Owen was the hero of the tale. He *nobbed* Mendoza, and got away with all the dexterity of a youth; it was now only Mendoza by name, his excellence as a fighter had evaporated, and his hits were generally short. Owen, in a close at the ropes, exhibited the advantages of *his stop;* he held Mendoza as firm as if he had been *screwed* up in a vice, and pummelled him at the back of the neck so dreadfully severe, that Dan at length fell down exhausted.—"Bravo" from the Christians, and the Jews were rather *funking*.

8. Mendoza came to the scratch[23] bleeding, and almost in a state of stupor, from the severity of the last round. Owen planted so tremendous a hit on Dan's face, that he went back from the force of it, and slipped down, as if on a slide, at the corner of the ring. The Jews were still backing Mendoza with confidence.

9. Long sparring, and Owen convinced the spectators that he was a perfect master of the art. He hit Mendoza in the front of the eye, jabbed him also in the face, and at the end of the ropes Owen held Mendoza by the arm, and punished him till he went down.—2 to 1 on Owen.

10. The appearance of Mendoza's face was much changed, and his left eye was encircled in *claret*. Owen got away from his antagonist in fine style. In fact, Owen was everything, and he quite satisfied the amateurs of the present period, that in his day he must have been a boxer of first-rate qualities. Mendoza was *punished* all over the ring, when Owen threw his opponent, and fell heavily upon him.[24]—Any odds.

11. Owen was determined not to give a *chance* away; and he also appeared determined not to have any more belly punches, the one he got was rather a dozer. Tom got away, and put in some sharp *facers*. He likewise gathered himself well up to hit. A short, but sharp rally occurred, when Owen fell down; and Mendoza likewise at about two yards' distance, came heavily down upon his face on the turf. "It's all your own, Tom!"

12th, and last. Mendoza was quite abroad and hit short, and at the ropes he was again held by Owen and *fibbed* down. The Jews now sung out in grief, "Its all *shiser ma trice;*" and Mendoza said he would not fight any more, as he could not win it. He was terribly *punished,* and defeated in fourteen minutes and twenty-seven seconds and a quarter; while, on the contrary, Owen had not a scratch upon his face. The latter was

carried out of the ring by Crib and Hudson, amidst the cheers of the spectators, and Owen said he was not above eleven stone.

Mendoza, while being dressed, seemed sensibly affected at his defeat. He had not the least idea of losing the battle.

Mr. Jackson collected 20 £ on the ground for him, when he was put into a coach. Owen soon returned to the ring, decorated in all the paraphernalia attendant upon conquest.

REMARKS.—Owen exhibited all the fine points of fighting, and he now *practically* illustrated all those theoretical lessons which he had previously laid down for the guide of his pupils. As a *getter-away*, few young men could have excelled him. Tom planted his hits, which were heavy, with great dexterity; and also *throwed* his opponent in a masterly style. He is a hard hitter; and a very difficult man to be got at. It is twenty-three years since he fought with Bartholomew; and we have been assured that nothing else but "this quarrel could have induced him to exhibit in the ring." He has, however, closed his fighting career, by displaying a superior knowledge of the art of self-defence quite unexpected; and he also won the battle in a style that astonished every one present. Mendoza, in appearance, is quite an altered man, as a pugilist; he could scarcely make a decisive hit—and his once fine *science* was looked for in vain....

Wrestling

The Okehampton Grand Match commenced on the 16th of August. The light weights shewed excellent play, and a youngster, called Isaac Yeo, gave promise of much future usefulness in the ring. The Thursday morning brought a shoal of players from North and West Devon, and both spectators and actors in the scene were in the highest spirits. The admirably-fenced ring was completely crowded; and among the wrestlers it was who should play first. The double play brought with it some of the crackest turns ever witnessed; the men, all fresh from their native hills, displayed a strength and vigour almost super-human; as they were stripped they seemed very Atlases, and their Herculean forms were gazed on, even by those accustomed to look on Moor-men [men of the Devon moors], with astonishment. Strangers to Devon almost fancied them to belong to another race of beings from themselves, and the witnessing their play will long be spoken of by many a passing traveller, whose good fortune it was to be at Okehampton on that day. Woollaway, who was considered much improved, had the first prize of eight sovereigns, John Drascombe the second of four sovereigns, and Jury the third of two sovereigns; besides which, several pounds were divided amongst the deserving; and every player expressed himself perfectly satisfied with his reward, and the kindness shewn him during his stay.

The Honiton Match commenced at the Baker's Inn, on Thursday, August 17; and, as was anticipated, presented a fine shew of players, doing due honour to the districts from which they came, and affording proof that East Devon is equally favorable for breeding wrestlers with any other part of the county. The men entered into the business with an earnestness that evinced a determination to preserve the honour of the county unsullied. It was with no small satisfaction the friends of the manly exercise recognised among the players the Uffculm youth, the stripling who acquired such credit at Broadclist; and though the little knight fell before the stronger arm of Vincent, he will always be deemed a credit to any ring. At half-past four on Friday afternoon, the play commenced for the second day's prize, and continued for several hours with unabated ardour: but it growing late, it was determined by consent to divide the prize of eight sovereigns amongst the most deserving players.

Shooting Parties

His Grace the Duke of Wellington, at Strathfield-say, Hants; Earl Verulam, at Gorhambury, Herts; Lord Granville, at Wherstead, Suffolk; and other Noblemen, &c. have had grand shooting parties this month, at their several country seats. His Royal Highness the Duke of York [brother of George IV] has been one of the best shots at these parties. The following was the return of game killed at Wherstead:—On the first day (with five guns), 2 partridges, 151 pheasants, 6 woodcocks, 70 hares, and 36 rabbits—total, 265. On the second day (with 12 guns), 4 partridges, 433 pheasants, 4 woodcocks, 320 hares, and 58 rabbits—

total, 819—Grand total, 1804. The following is said to have been the number killed by each of the party on the Monday, including the wounded game, which was not picked up till the following day:—

Duke of York	128	Mr. Montague	70
D. of Wellington	120	Mr. Ponsonby	55
Lord of Granville	48	Mr. Arbuthnot	26
Hon. C. Greville	120	Sir R. Harland, Bt.	40
Hn. Mr. DeRoss	107	Rev. Mr. Capper	41
Hon. G. Anson	88	Total	921
Hon. G. Lamb	78		

Shooting

There was a shooting day on Wednesday, January 1, at Fryston, the residence of R. Milnes, Esq. The party consisted of Lord Pollington, Mr. Wyvill, the Hon. E. Petre, T. S. Duncombe, Esq.—Gossip, Esq. Sir

P. Musgrave, F. Lumley, Esq. and G. Bland, Esq. when 272 pheasants, 143 hares, 114 rabbits, and 2 woodcocks, were bagged.

Three Days Shooting.—The following is an accurate account of the game killed upon the Hon. Mr. Pelham's estate, at Manby, near Brigg, in Lincolnshire:—Dec. 5, 4 guns, 59 pheasants, 2 partridges, 2 woodcocks, 36 hares; total, 99—Dec. 6, 6 guns, 89 pheasants, 11 woodcocks, 66 hares, 8 rabbits; total, 174—Dec. 7, 6 guns, 109 pheasants, 9 woodcocks, 71 hares, 13 rabbits; total, 202.

A hen pheasant, ten cocks, and one pigeon, were actually shot a few days since with one charge only, by Mr. Holmes, jun. of North Farm, near Findon, Sussex.

Dreadful Accident on Chester Race Course

The sad catastrophe that befel WILLIAM DUNN, when riding Mr. Mytton's Aladdin colt, for the Produce Stakes at Chester, is one which, unfortunately is, and will ever be, in a great measure, inseparable from the lot of those who follow the occupation of a jockey. If, in the present instance, the unhappy man met with his death merely from Sir Watkin's filly not being able to keep on her legs, in consequence of a slip, which is common to all horses when extended, or turning a corner, in a race, nothing farther can be said on the subject, than to lament the untimely end of an excellent jockey, and a faithful servant, who has fallen a sacrifice to his duty to his master, as we would lament the fall of a soldier who had died in the service of his country. But if, on the other hand, as the *Chester Guardian* seems to imply, William Dunn lost his life owing to a defect in the course, *that defect ought not to have existed, had it been possible to have removed it!*

A fatality attends Chester racecourse; for scarcely a meeting passes but some accident takes place. Your readers must remember that Lord Stamford's rider was killed on the spot only three years ago: and had it not been that the poor man who has now lost his life upon it, eased his horse, and "let him in" (as they say), Harry Arthur would have been dashed to pieces against the post at the Castle-turn last year, which I myself witnessed. As it was, he was so much injured, as not to be able to ride for Sir Thomas Mostyn (his first master), for the rest of the week. This turn has been eased, but is still a very bad one; it is to the left-hand, very near home, and just where the strongest running is made. Some years ago, I witnessed such an accident at this turn as will never be witnessed again, by which a most valuable colt lost his life, and a Captain of Dragoons had such an escape for his, that seldom falls to the lot of any man. There is something sympathetic, as well as marvellous, in the circumstances attending it. A colt called *"Hair-breadth, by Escape,"* the property of Mr. Lockley, was winning his race cleverly; but in coming around this Castle-turn, he bolted—jumped over the cords—and knocked down Captain (now Sir John) Miller, of the Cornwall Fencible Cavalry, then quartered at Chester, who was riding on the course, in his uniform; and strange to say, the peak of his helmet, *whilst on his head,* entered the brain of *Hair-breadth, by Escape,* and killed him on the spot—whilst the only injury the Captain received, was a pair of black eyes, and I saw him at the ball in the evening.—Hair-breadth was a very promising colt, and the late Duke of Leeds had offered Mr. Lockley 400 gs. for him before starting.

Another most extraordinary circumstance connected with accidents on a race course, took place ten or twelve years since, at Knighton, in Wales. A gentleman was riding a very hard-pulling horse for the Hunter's Stakes, when one of his brothers went to a particular turn on the course to see how he got around it, being apprehensive for his safety. Just as the horses were coming up, a drunken fellow rode against him, and pushed him, horse and all, into the course, exactly before his brother, who tumbled over him, and all were down together. Another brother, who was on the course, and witnessed the accident, set spurs to his horse to get to their assistance, when he ran away with him, in the exact direction where his other two brothers lay, and tumbled over them, making three men, and three horses, all down at the same time; and the only bad consequences were, a few bruises, and one of the horses dislocating his shoulder.

One of the most distressing accidents which I ever witnessed on a race course, was the year before last, as Cheltenham, as it was occasioned by, apparently, wilful neglect of one of the course keepers. As the horses were coming in, a mare of Mr. R. Jones's was last; and before she had passed the rope, the fellow pulled it up, and gave her a tremendous fall. The boy who rode her pitched on his head, and his life was despaired of for several days,—nor will he ever recover it. This is one of the many instances of the necessity of employing persons, *in all situations about a race course,* who know something about racing, as, in

that case, they would always look out for a horse that was shut out, or beaten a long way from home; and there are always such persons to be found. Accidents of this nature tend materially to damp the pelasure of a meeting; and human life should not be put to the risk, when it can be avoided. No course that I was ever on is so well kept as Manchester. I have ridden over it amongst a hundred thousand spectators, and nothing can be better than the clear way for the race horses, and the good humour of the people. To return, however, to poor Dunn....

Dunn was a rider of the first class. His nerve was very good in a crowd, and he was particularly clever at a start. By some, he was accused of being a little foul in his riding against boys; but, in all situations in life, as well as on a race course, the old ones will have a turn of the young ones, when they can get it. In his race last year over Warwick, against Charming Molly, he certainly shewed the "old one." The mare's eyes being queer, she liked to go first; and Dunn, seeing the boy too quick for him at starting, cried out "No go," saying he had not got his reins right. On turning around again he clapped spurs to his horse—sent the dust into old Molly's eyes—and, by Stevens's account, who owned her—made the race safe. Stevens, however, will know better, another time, than to put up an exercise boy against a good jockey.

Although Dunn was a fine horseman, he had a curious, and rather unsightly way of holding his rein, which was—over-handed. He also sat very back on his horse, and had a long pull at his bridle. Nevertheless, he had, altogether, a very jockey-like appearance; and although I know nothing of his pedigree, he looked as though he were got by a gentleman. His race, however, is run; and I have reason to believe that his loss will be much felt by his master. Good, we are told, is often produced by evil. Let then the death of Will Dunn be borne in mind by all who have the management of racecourses, and *let it induce them to take possible care to preserve the lives of those who risk them for our pleasure, and our profit.*

NIMROD

Sporting Accidents

The town of Melton Mowbray was thrown into the greatest alarm on Friday, Dec. 27, by a report that Lord Robert Manners was drowned. It seems that his Lordship, with Mr. Richard and Mr. James Norman, went to a pond, distant about three miles from Melton, to skate; on rapidly sweeping by some ash trees, he was suddenly plunged into a very deep water. Lord Robert Manners is a strong muscular man, and with the confidence of a good swimmer he made several attempts to gain the surface of the ice, but unfortunately it only broke to sink him in each effort; he then extended wide his arms to keep himself up. The gentlemen, his companions in skating, much too young to render any assistance, were approaching him, and one was about to throw the end of his handkerchief, but his Lordship desired them not to come near him. Mr. Richard Norman then pulled off his skates, and ran to a house a quarter of a mile off—where, although the house (being occupied by two widow women) seldom has a man about it, he most providentially found a number of visitors, able young men and women. They all instantly rushed forth; but the mistress of the house called out, "Be sure and take every thing necessary with you! Don't have to come back again! Take a ladder, a rope, and the well-drag!" One person ran down to Lord Robert, to encourage him to hold up, with the information that help was at hand. His Lordship shook his head, saying, "It's too late." Instantly, however, the ladder was brought and passed to him: he grasped it, and by one last effort sprung up and was dragged out. Too feeble to walk, he was conveyed to the house, stripped, and put into bed. A messenger was immediately sent for medical aid, which he accidentally met within half a mile. To the medical attendant much danger still presented itself. The Noble Lord having been long in the water, and afterwards for some time exposed to very cold air, his Lordship's countenance had become black, his body was all over cold and damp, with feeble circulation, he was labouring most alarmingly for breath, and by times was hopelessly distressed; but after about a quarter of an hour the respiration again revived, and in about an hour his Lordship began to breathe freely, so that he could converse. Lord Robert Manners has presented 50 £ to the mistress of the house from which assistance was rendered, and 10 £ each to five other persons who were instrumental in extricating him from the water.

On Wednesday, January 1, as Mr. Shoulder, of Ambrosden, Oxon, gamekeeper to Sir Gregory Page Turner, Bart. was out rabbit-shooting, with one of his sons, in getting through a hedge, with his gun under his arm, the trigger most unhappily caught in one of the branches, which caused the gun instantly to go off, and the whole contents were lodged in his son's head, and killed him on the spot. The agonized feelings of the father may be more easily conceived than expressed.

Accident at the Seat of Lord Granville.—At Wherstead Lodge, in Suffolk, this month, the Noble Lord had a large party of friends to enjoy the sports of the field. On one day they were out scouring a wood. The morning was hazy, and the Duke of Wellington was so intent on his game that he lost sight of the party, and in firing his double-barrelled gun, he unfortunately lodged a part of the contents in the face of his Noble host; seven swan shot entered the cheeks and one the nose. His Grace, hearing an exclamation of "I am shot," threw down his piece and hurried to the spot, where he found his friend leaning against a tree, the face streaming with blood. One of the party gallopped off to Ipswich for medical aid, whilst the others carried the wounded Nobleman to the Lodge. A surgeon, in less than an hour, attended, extracted the shot, and pronounced the Noble patient to be not in any danger. His Lordship is now perfectly recovered.

The gamekeeper of R. O. Gascoigne, Esq. of Yorkshire, was severely wounded lately by the discharge of an assistant keeper's gun, and is since dead. He had the best medical advice that could be procured, and no expense was spared by his worthy employer to alleviate his sufferings. We understand he has left a pregnant widow and five young children.

On Due Discrimination between Barbarous and Fair Sporting

We most feelingly regret to have received accounts from various quarters, and from friends and subscribers, on whose information and veracity we can depend, of the great increase, within the last four or five years, of the SAVAGE and BARBAROUS SPORTS. We had flattered ourselves with the hope, that the increase of light and knowledge, and the gradual dispersion of prejudice among the upper ranks, and more especially the universal attention shewn of late to the education and instruction of the lower classes, could not fail to be attended with the most striking and important effects on the side of humanity, and in favour of that justice and mercy which every superior owes to those beneath him, and which, as rational human beings, we necessarily owe to the brute beasts of every description, which are sent by Providence for our use, and intrusted to our protection. Whatever wanton or interested profligacy may determine, or high-spirited thoughtlessness may dictate, it is a *sacred trust,* and the breach of it cannot be committed without great crime, great dishonour and infamy.

To the honour of our pugilistic class, perhaps, bull-baiting has not been, of late, so usually the entertainment, or afterpiece of a boxing match, as heretofore; but generally, the laudable attempts to put an end to those horrible cruelties, under the strange and unnatural idea of diversion, exercised upon those useful creatures which help to till our lands, supply us with food, and spend their lives in our service, have had little success, and the meritorious advocates of humanity have become discouraged, and almost hopeless. All those places in the country notorious for the barbarous diversion of bull-baiting, still appear to pursue the practice with an enthusiastic eagerness, more characteristic of Asiatic Turks or Tartars, than of the people so long shone upon by the glorious sun of intelligence and humanity.

According to our recent information, there are in the Metropolis, from half a dozen to half a score places, where miserable animals are kept for the purpose of being BAITED by fierce and savage dogs, at regular weekly meetings. These meetings are frequented by the most abandoned and profligate of the human race, the refuse and off-scourings of this vast city—pick-pockets and thieves of every description, with the idle, dissolute, and infamous of every class and service—low gamblers, and some, to their ineffable shame, of a higher description and education; jack-ass drivers, drovers, the scum and dregs of

Smithfield, nackers[25] or horse-boilers, said to be the most hardened, barbarous, and insensate miscreants, who, in this age of the world, contaminate and disgrace the surface of mother earth. Whole troops of this *canaille*, attended by their dogs—bull-dogs, terriers, and bull-terriers, are to be seen every *Sunday* morning, marching towards the fields northward of the city, where they amuse themselves with every species of cruelty, to the annoyance and abhorrence of all neighbours and passengers of a right feeling. The usual victims of barbarity, in the Metropolis, are *bears, bulls, monkeys, cats;* and even wretched *he-asses,* rendered savage by perpetual ill-usage and cruelty, are baited! And these horrors are in constant perpetration under the very noses of the police!![26]

With the above enormities it is perfectly congenial to class the late cruel attempt to drive our excellent horses, the flower and glory of the world, at the rate of twelve miles per hour, in the public stages; a velocity, the regular continuance of which is above the powers of animal flesh and blood—so the best practical judges had previously decided. We had notice of the natural consequences upon this insane and disgraceful attempt—broken legs, ruptured sinews, swooning in the collar, broken hearts! Were we not already superior to the whole world in our travelling speed; and was not the number of miserable cripples, its victims, daily seen in our streets, Repositories, at Smithfield, and in those real hells, the nackers' yards, altogether sufficient? Thanks to the interposition of the genius of cruelty itself, this precious scheme has been abandoned.

For ourselves, as publishers of a Sporting Magazine, we profess to patronize and recommend such sports only, as can be reconciled with justice, fairness, and a regard to the *essentials* of morality. We beg this may be considered our characteristic; and we never doubt that it will obtain us the patronage of the liberal, the warm-hearted, and the good, our great and constant object. We have approved of that *discrimination* in sporting, originally proposed by a well-known author, and agree with him, on the necessity of deciding and explaining, where *lawful sporting* ends, and where *barbarity* and *crime* begin. Thus, fair hunting, or other pursuits of wild animals, if attended with some temporary, but unavoidable cruelty, is a legitimate sport, and even natural and necessary occupation of man. Horse racing is, in principle, perfectly unobjectionable and useful, abuse and cruelty only being valid objections. On cock fighting, certainly less defensible than the former, thus much may be predicated on the favourable side—whatever inflictions the animals sustain, being the result of their own will and pleasure, and the steel wherewith they are armed is no instrument of cruelty, since it accelerates their release from suffering, performing the office of the knife, to which otherwise they are destined. Surely our lawful sports and amusements are sufficiently numerous, and hence we can have no apology for a continuance or recourse to barbarism and cruelty, which really do not befit modern light and civilization. It ought to be too late in the day, to hunt poor harmless domestic ducks to death with dogs, or to hang up poor geese by the legs upon a line, whilst grinning idiots on horseback torture out the lives of the fowls, by catching at their heads as they ride past, for the amusement of a surrounding crowd of empty-headed, callous-hearted, and open-mouthed asses in human shape! This latter infamy, we are sorry to be informed, prevails also on some parts of the Continent.

On Mr. Martin's Bill for Animal Protection and on the Subject Generally

In working this Bill[27] through the House, I had almost said *smuggling* it, a phrase sanctioned not only by the general and well known apathy there towards the subject, but by the equally well known and formerly well proven decided hostility of many persons of high consequence—Mr. Martin has earned immortal honour; with a distinction of the noblest kind, as having opened his heart and extended succour to beings endowed with feelings perfectly similar to our own, but void of all possible means of self defence. His reiterated personal, and practical exertions in attending to the execution of the law since its enactment, form a most unprecedented trait in the character of a member of the Legislature, and by the efficiency of so singular an example, have proved his enthusiastic ardour in a most just cause, and greatly enhanced his original degree of merit: and I freely pay my tribute of respect and applause to the unquestionable and superior desert of a public man, without regard to difference of political opinion, or bias, from some *trifling cause* of personal complaint....

Mr. Martin's Bill, it is true, might have been more explicit. *Animals* generally, might have been included, and the principle of the *jus animatium* might have been recognized, that is to say, the right of every thing possessing life and feeling, to mercy and fair treatment, the assertion and vindication of which, evidently and indubitably belong to every moral system of the social contract. Every sentient being is an object of the law's protection, or human justice is incomplete. My Lord Lauderdale,[28] it seems, determines not to legislate for morals. But such a resolve, applied to the Animal Bill, puts me in pain for his Lordship's politico-economic reputation, granting his logic, in that branch, not to be more sound, than in this of morals, as it regards beasts. Neither most certainly would I legislate for morals—I would not prescribe how often a man should kiss his wife, how much he should eat or drink, how much money or estate he should possess, how he should think or believe, or how he should treat or manage his beast—but in case of wanton cruelty to the latter, the line of mere moral demarcation is past, an act of aggression is committed, necessarily and properly within the cognizance and vengeance of the law....

The almost *altum silentium* [profound silence], under which the Bill past, was doubtless favourable to its success (thence no doubt the silence of certain honourable Members), as well as the lateness of the session, when probably, most of the *Wyndhamites*[29] and bull-hankers had retired, among whom we surely ought not to class the venerable keeper of the royal conscience.[30] A most respectable Morning Paper [the *Morning Post*], indeed that which has, for many years been looked up to as the visible head of English *liberalism,* has been in the periodical habit, from the commencement of the Animal Bill, of publishing nonsense verses or nonsense prose, in order to cast the dirt of ridicule upon it—but in this case, at any rate, the Editor has not discovered the test of truth. The same *bizarraric* has blemished the columns of one of our most enlightened and most popular weekly papers. In the leading article of this last, some weeks since, we observed a murmur at the supposed grievance, among others, that "a man could not spur his lazy donkey into action, without the fear of being summoned before a Magistrate." The Editor of a certain journal also, who no doubt, by virtue of his office, ought to be *au fait* with respect to the tactics of Smithfield; after a little varnish bestowed upon the atrocities committed twice a week, in that succedaneous hell, pronounces, as it were, *é*

cathedra, "the Bill can do no good." In conclusion, and by way of a consummation of hypocrisy and folly, the equal guilt of the higher orders with the lower, is adduced as an argument against any attempt at the correction of an acknowledged vice in both....

The egregious advocates on paper, and in general, for mercy to the brute creation, our *peers* in feeling—for if you goad them, will they not wince? if you teaze them will they not fret? if you torture them, will they not groan? if you deprive them, will they not sorrow? if you kindly treat them, will they not demonstrate pleasure and gratitude?—the above great humanists, I say then, seem ambitious of the character, once bestowed, right or wrong, on the Lord Chancellor Thurlow;[31] they oppose every thing, and propose nothing. Some little lurking prejudice or affection prevents them from *discriminating* between the *use* and the *abuse;* between the *unavoidable* rigours of the use, and the wanton cruelties of the abuse....

No legal remedy truly, must be applied, because royal, conquering, and aristocratic heroes and heroines, I had almost called them boobies and boobiesses—vain, ostentatious, unreflecting, and heartless, drive poor post horses to death, grammatically *by custom*—because the sports of the turf and field are yet, even under the improved humanity of modern days, too much tinctured and degraded with ancient barbarity: there is even a kind of jealousy and suspicion of latent *jacobinism* in the advocacy of the rights of animals, and the relative duties of men: this subject, like certain others, must not be probed to the bottom—*gardez vous, il ne faut pas approfondre,* for fear some selfish and paramount interest should be disturbed: you may write or spout as much and as oratorically as you will about it, goddess, and about it, but you must not descend below the surface, far less proceed to action. How then, are the aggressive acts of turpitude and cruelty towards beasts to be restrained, and which the persons whom I have now the honour to address, affect to wish put under restraint? Granting that the increasing light of the human mind will, in process of time, operate the desired effect, a concession which I make utterly void of conviction, why permit a longer existence of evil and of national disgrace, without the application of an obvious remedy? why has this infamy and wickedness been connived at, permitted, encouraged, so long? It is equally vain and groundless to say, either that the law cannot touch the case, and prove remedial, or that legislation is probable to have an improper and vexatious effect. If the infamous and unnatural pleasure of bullbaiting can still be enjoyed, it is a great defect in the late Bill; but if so, we may still hope the defect will be amended on some future occasion, that so foul a disgrace may no longer lower over the character of this country, as that our laws pander to the most vicious and impure inclinations of the human heart. God shield me! but how often have I longed to see a bait by some well-bred dogs; not, indeed, of innocent, perhaps harmless bulls, but of BULL-BAITERS, baited *in their turn*—nor could there possibly be a more just and equitable *talio* [retaliation]. . . . Should any township or parish still exist in this land of light and capacity for just morals, in which are not to be found men of sense and feeling enough, or of probity and courage enough, to unsheath the sword of the law against this moral pest; let us shake the dust from off our feet, and turn aside from that place—let it be thenceforth proscribed by the just and good, as the sink of infamy!

Vox Humanitatis

Part V
The Margins of Sports

May in London

The passing month is that which is most distinguished in the metropolis for the variety and gaiety of its amusements. Whoever has passed his days in distant retirement, and wishes to know what London can produce, must visit it in the month of May. Whoever would know the full tide of the happiness of town life, of all that fashion prescribes, and all that crowds follow, must come to London in May. London is the world, and May the sun that cheers, enlightens, and invigorates, all that can make life tolerable.—Sorrow is not banished by universal consent.—Time flies in a perpetual circle of delight, and the diversions of night and day are no longer acknowledged.

In May, the votaries of pleasure agree to assemble in general congress. Every town and every village send up their deputies and representatives, to assist in the councils of fashion, and to bring down the last intrigue, and the newest cap. On their return, they antimate rustic conversation by a detail of wonders, of plays and operas, concerts and exhibitions, routs and panoramas. They demand attention, and ensure submission, by the superiority of having seen and heard all that with which London gratifies the eye and ear. They shew, by the rapid circulation of a thousand private surmises, and a thousand confidential hints, how little can be learned from the printed reports of the papers, and how frequently a fashionable event is in danger of being mutilated by ignorance or suppressed from fear.

Then the parks on a May-Sunday! What a delightful *pele-mele!* To elbow all whom one wishes to know—to be admitted gratis to see *live* lords and ladies—and on *one's* return to be able to say that *one* actually saw all this with *one's* own eyes! What a triumph over rural ignorance! How little qualified are they to live in the world, and how shockingly unprepared to leave it must they be, who have not visited *London* in May—the *whole world* in May—*every body* in May!

Horse-Dealing in London
Or, An Expose of the Tricks and Technicalities
of the Metropolitan Jockies

"And that thou maie more livelier behoulde
"Eche private prancke." * * *
"A heape of hidden harmes I will unlapp."
                                    WENMAN

In these days of sporting and equestrian delights, when every man whose means will allow him, keeps a nag for his gratification, it is deemed equally unpardonable to impugn a gentleman's knowledge in horseflesh, as to cast an aspersion on his honour or courage. This being avowedly the case, we who have been admitted among the initiated, consider ourselves as conferring no trifling favour on our country friends in letting them into some of the secrets, and tipping them the proper signication, of a few of the cant terms, patronized by and inflicted upon the equestrians of the metropolis....

Dealers, in general, are too often branded with the odious stigma of rascality for the misdeeds of a few isolated individuals of the tribe. They suffer under a regular hereditary aspersion. There are certain designations which are entailed upon them in fee simple (perhaps) for ever. Prejudice wages eternal war with the trade. Their tricks are in every man's mouth, their conduct is eternally exposed to the keen scrutiny of the world, and every slight aperture in the web of their department is instantly magnified into an immense gap. We shall endeavour to set these things in their right light. Dealers are crafty, specious, and redolent of tricks, without a doubt, or a good proportion of them at least; but, after all that has been said, sung, and written against them, it is notorious as the light to "some few severals, of head-piece extraordinary," that every trade in the metropolis has its manœuvres, chincanery, management, and jockeyism, in an equal degree with horse dealing. The corn, coal, wine, land, money, house, and all other markets, are nearly upon a par in this respect. Every man knows something about a horse; his defects are not to be permanently glossed over: they may be concealed for a day, but the veil is soon rent, and the iniquity laid bare. Thus it is that a few of the most palpable and egregious mysteries of the jockies are detected, while those that are practised by the worthy members of many other trades and callings, which the community at large understand much less about, and have not such opportune means of unveiling, remain occult and undiscovered. Our object is, to let the world see a little more of the by-play of the inferior, or the more unprincipled gentlemen of the spur, and to rescue, in some measure the whole body of dealers from unmerited reproach. We shall commence our delightful task without any further prologue, by noticing one of the most usual achievements of the trade.

Bishopping, is filing the teeth and tusks of an aged horse to a moderate and juvenile length, and scooping a hollow in the mark tooth, which is afterwards darkened with a little caustic. Animals of twenty may be reduced to "second childhood," and made babies again by the aid of a skillful dentist, and it requires an accustomed eye to detect the forgery. When a young hand attempts this celebrated feat, and effects it unskillfully, the horse is regularly termed "a poor curate."

Diamonding, or *beaning*, is a method of making a horse that is lame on one leg appear to be passably upright. It is managed by inserting a sharp pebble *under the shoe of the sound foot*. Thus the horse is rendered equally lame on both feet, and consequently appears to be only a little *groggy*. If any suspicion is entertained that a horse has undergone the operation of beaning, it is advisable to have his shoes taken off, or if that proceeding will not be allowed, to thrust a knife between the shoe and the hoof, whereby the gravel or "diamond" may often be detected.

Setting the blowers, is manufacturing an apparently sound "pair of bellows," in a broken-winded animal. It is effected by putting the horse through a course of physic, and then increasing his exercise by degrees, feeding him on mashes and green meat, and allowing him no hay and very little water. Hog's lard and hellebore are plentifully administered, particularly on the morning of the day when the subject is intended to be submitted for sale. By these means the rankest *piper* may be lulled for a time. The method to discover if this trick has been played, is to pay great attention to the horse's mouth, which will be found greasy and disgusting, and his breath particularly offensive. Animals of the first courage and speed are often *touched in the pipes*, so that it is no subject of wonder that great pains are taken and considerable time employed to give them the appearance of soundness, for the purpose of deluding gentle people, who are "a little bit underdone." Horses that are in the different stages of bad wind, are designated as *high blowers, flank flappers, rum pipers, bouncing roarers,* and *rank bulls*.

Driving a skrew, is palming an unsound horse on a *flat*, for an immaculate animal. There is one indispensable circumstance in driving a skrew, which is, that the purchaser pays a good price for his bargain, otherwise the deal is not dignified with that title. Those *half-and-half* blades who sport a showy but worthless tit in their vehicles, are also termed *skrew-drivers* by the equestrian wags who exercise their wit with infinite relish on the *timber-legged toddlers* of Rotten-row and the Ring.

Nailing, in the common acceptation of the term, is equivalent to *driving a skrew, flooring a Johnny, hooking a gudgeon,* or *muffing a soft one.* Sometimes an obscure rascal offers a couple of high-flyers at a private stable in some unfrequented lane, with a reference to himself as Captain Any-body, or Mr. What-you-will, at a neighbouring coffee-house, and by dint of extreme swaggering and fine words, contrives to tickle some trout out of his *spanish*. In a few days the horses are of course discovered to be unquestionable skrews. The forlorn purchaser hurries away to the Captain, who very honourably offers to take them back if they don't suit; but being rather short of cash at the moment, tenders his bill, or, to use the flash term, "*flies a kite*" at a month, for the amount, sells the horses again, and immediately bolts. This is very appropriately called "*clenching a nail.*"

Corking the tallow, is a trick which is sometimes practised by the most despicable of the wretches who infest the market at Smithfield, to stop the emission, of *pus* from the nostrils of a *snitch,* or glandered horse. It is done by flowing some styptic powder up the nose; and there are villains in existence who will not scruple to lead an animal, in the last stage of glanders, among a set of sound horses, for the sake of realizing a few paltry shillings, after having stayed the external running, or, as they jocularly term the operation, "corked the tallow."

Puffing the glims, is the art of filling up the unsightly cavities above the eyes of an aged horse. A pin, or the point of a lancet, is inserted in the skin, and the breath blown through the aperture, until the animal's temples are as smooth as a foal's. Young horses are often sunk above the eyes, nevertheless "*puffing the glims*" is a very effectual operation, for the hollows considerably add to the other indications of age in the head of a horse, and when dexterously filled up, corroborate the testimony of a *bishopped* tooth.

Figging, is a way of inducing a nag to carry his tail cleverly, by a plentiful application of chewed ginger. This device does wonders, inasmuch as the unusually erect and cockish bearing of the tail, added to the electrical effect produced by the sly whisks of the *long-tailed poney* or dealer's showing whip, and the jerks of the twisted snaffle, with which horses are generally led out, give an appearance of showiness, spirit, and style, to the greatest slugs in existence.

Crabbing, is pointing out the defects of a horse when he is offered for sale at the hammer, or otherwise, so as to prevent a sale or deal being effected. Crabbing is sometimes, but rarely, practised on a fellow tradesman's horse, but often had recourse to when a covey of jockies are hankering after "real property," or a gentleman's cattle, in order to diminish their value in the estimation of the owner, or any bystander who is likely to become a rival bidder.

A quid, is a horse who chews his food, and throws it out of his mouth again. This is rarely the case. But the term "quid" is also applied to bad feeders, and to those horses who, from any cause whatever, are disabled or impeded from masticating or swallowing their food.

A woodpecker, or what is sometimes called a *crib-biter,* is a horse who takes the edge of the manger, or rack-stave, between his teeth, and sucks in the wind, so as to make a short grunting sort of a noise. Such horses are seldom in good condition, although we have met with a few inveterate woodpeckers with plenty of carcase and good sound hard flesh upon them. A long run at grass has been said to effect a cure, but it must be in cases only where the animal is young in the vice; for it is well known that a thorough old *timber-sucker* will cross a field of several acres, to obtain a nab at a post or gate-rail. We have seen some horses so addicted to crib-biting, as to suck at the manger while in the act of feeding. Aloes, train oil, dung, and many other things, we have known to be applied to the wood, without producing any ultimate effect: the horses' extreme *loathing* decreased in an incredible degree; within a few hours they became reconciled to the disgusting taste and smell, and recurred to the habit of pecking and sucking as stoutly as ever. The strap is the only preventive; but even that is but temporary, for the moment it is unbuckled, the animal nabs the manger again. The jockey suffers the crib-biter to indulge in his deeply-rooted habit, or straps him up until he intends to offer him for sale; when, if it be necessary to shew him in the stable, he either constantly keeps him on the fret, by the exhibition of his whip, or *doctors the manger* with aloes, which (if the beast is not accustomed to it) prevents him from shewing his vice for a short time, although, as we have just observed, the plan produces no ultimate reformation. Nevertheless, the jockey's purpose is often effected, and the gulled purchaser wonders at the strange appetite the horse manifests for timber, when he takes him to his private stable, and suffers him to stand quiet and undisturbed.

Swaddies, are horses picked out of the artillery or cavalry; and, being generally the refuse or lumber of the regiment, are, for the most part, of little value, although they often fetch enormous prices. The Repositories were deluged with them some time ago, but the flux has now considerably abated. They are notorious for their dangerous tricks and vices, and the knowing ones are particularly cautious now-a-days how they lay out their money upon horses which are even suspected of having been *swads.*

A feather, is an incipient cataract, which may easily be discovered by inspecting the eye of a horse when he is standing with his head outwards at the doorway of the stable. A *jack* is a young spavin. Splents, ringbones, thorough-pins, spavins, speedy-cuts, curbs, corns, thrushes, sandcracks, &c., &c. are generally called by their proper names; they are sufficiently apparent, without guide or instructions, to any one who has a *mediocre* eye, and is tolerably acquainted with the external appearance of the horse.

. . .

A *German,* a *bobby,* or a *robert,* is a horse who has received a grievous injury in the back, which renders him altogether incapable of work, although, to an inexperienced eye, he may appear to go sound. Judges of horseflesh describe them as having "a queerish sort of rum joint like in the loins." If this technical definition be well hoarded up in the memory, and well-remembered in the moment of selection, by the juvenile purchaser, he will be in no great danger of buying a *bobby.*

An astronomer, is a horse that is eternally poling his nose out, and looking sillily up to the sky. Such a habit is equivalent to the vituperation of a Xantippe, and would ruffle the temper of any man, who was a point less philosophical than the placid Socrates. There is no remedy for this vice but a martingal[e], than which none of the trappings of "the goodly steed" are more exceptionable. It therefore behoveth every man to beware of getting *an astronomer* into his stall.

A miller, is a horse who "mills," or "lets go" with his hind legs. Mares are more apt to mill than geldings; indeed they can never be depended on. Many mares, after having been driven for months, nay years, have been known to kick furiously in harness without any apparent, or at least efficient cause, and never give in while there was a spar dangling at their heels, or until they were wholly incapacitated from further exertion. A regular miller may often be detected by scars on the hind legs, or *caps* on the hocks, although it is by no means a consequence that a horse should be set down as addicted to milling, from the unsupported circumstance of his exhibiting a capped hock. It should be esteemed a subject of suspicion, but not absolutely conclusive of the question.

A methodist or *devotee,* is a horse who is intolerably fond of kneeling. There is not a more dangerous beast among the reclaimed quadrupeds than an incorrigible *methodist.* To the driver he is particularly dangerous. When he attempts to save the creature from coming down, if the latter tumbles in spite of his efforts, it is two to one that he is pulled out with a most appalling jerk. Horses that appear greatly alarmed, toss their heads up and break into a canter, when they stumble and recover themselves, may, without a moment's hesitation, be noted down as methodists from time immemorial, that have been repeatedly punished for their tripping and tumbling.

A lawyer, is one who likes to be well paid for his work—a hard-skinned, insensible slug, callous to the eternal hints of the ineffectual thong, capable of exertion, but unwilling to progress at any pace exceeding a two-mile an hour toddle—a high feeder, who delights in nothing so much as rioting on the good things which are applicable to his rapacious stomach—a wicked, mischievous brute, active enough in a squabble, but miserably elephantine and unwieldy in actual business—a pretender, that mends his pace for a moment when he is goaded, and instantly relapses into his customary crawl again. He will not hurry a foot faster, although your best interests depend on his speed. He affects zeal and mimics activity, but the miserable simpleton who trusts to him, is inevitably doomed to go through the world at a lingering, unprofitable, snail's amble.

A flat-catcher, is a fine showy animal, but intrinsically worthless, except to serve the purpose of those persons who purchase none but horses of this description, which they get at a low price, and vend again, at an egregious profit, to some of the "cart-load of *Johnny Raws* that are once a-week tilted on the flags at Charing Cross." The figure of a flat-catcher is generally striking: he is in high condition, with great mettle, and showy elevated action; but after half an hour's smart trot over the rough stones of Gray's Inn-lane, and up Pentonville Hill, if he is put in the stable until he grow cool again, and then led out for inspection, he will invariably appear to be "all to pieces," and not "worth a ducat." There are many flat-catchers that have been bought and sold two or three dozen times about the Metropolis in the course of a few months, and repeatedly "turned themselves over," or fetched double the money they cost the jockey vendor.

Now, reader, what say you? Are these things notable? Are they entertaining, redolent of edification, things novel and unknown?* Are they passably rich, marrowy, and not utterly unworthy of thy attentive perusal? Art thou tired of our company? We hope, we opine not; and shall, therefore proceed another short stage, and then put up for a time. The appellations of the jockies shall be our theme for a moderate space, and we shall then wind up our dissertation with a few observations to which we solicit a little sober attention.

Guinea-pigs, or *jackalls*, are inferior members of the trade, who look out for purchasers, and bring them to the regular dealers; for which services they are commonly remunerated with a guinea, or more, according to the fish they bring to the net, and the magnitude or profit of the deal. Guinea-pigs have also another occupation: they are employed by dealers to hunt about for tradesmen and gentlemen who have horses to dispose of, and, by contriving to get the parties together so as to bring about a sale or "*a swop*," are entitled to *tip* from both.

Chaunters are poor undone devils, or impudent swindling varlets, who "*floor*" a customer in the way we have before particularized, under the head "*nailing*." And here it is material to observe, that although a fellow of the above genus occasionally "*tips a stave*" in a paper, real, good, sound cattle are daily advertized by reputable dealers who have just received lots of horses from the country fairs, the conductors of Repositories who have a string of *machiners* to dispose of, and proprietors of well-known commission stables, into whose hands gentlemen's cattle and carriages are continually placed, for the purpose of sale. A newspaper is the only vehicle for information in these circumstances; but, like every other good practice, it is sometimes infringed upon, and warped to the advantage of a knave. When a gentleman, who is a stranger in town, goes to see a horse which has been advertised, he has only to look about for a moment, and mark the appearance and situation of the place to which he is invited. A regular, established, respectable-looking yard, *and the appearance of its proprietor as the agent of*

---

*We speak here to our provincial lectors. Gentlemen who have been accustomed to the sporting circles of London, are doubtless equally awake (by hearsay at least) to some of the practices we have detailed, as ourself.

the seller, are, in most cases, sufficient testimonials in favour of the property advertised, to induce him to purchase, if the price, figure, and speed of the animal suit the wants or inclinations of the visitor.

A single stable, in a bye street, with a fellow in the garb of a gentleman, and a groom in livery in attendance, are subjects of suspicion; and it rarely happens that a person who deals with these, the genuine chaunters, does not find himself most miserably nailed.

Copers are petty dealers, who never possess above a brace of horses, which are generally called *skrews*. They *hawk* them about to different parts of the Metropolis, and unblushingly practise the same dainty devices as their brothers in iniquity, the *chaunters, nailers,* and *clenchers.*

Poundage coves, or *men of feeling,* are persons of straw, who disguise themselves as gentlemen, and assist the copers by backing their skrews. They represent themselves as the proprietors of the animals offered for sale; and although they know them to be broken-down jades, recently patched up to deceive the indiscreet, warrant them sound, and abide by the consequences. For these services, they are remunerated by *having a feeling* in the purchase money, or a *poundage* on the amount. This order of bucks is not very numerous, and we are happy to say that they have considerably decreased of late.

Jockey gentlemen are the most dangerous of the whole tribe. We do not scruple to assert that there is more jockeyship, in its true sense, practised by the world at large, than by the members of the trade. A man is thrown off his guard when he deals with a gentleman, who, we are sorry to say, often makes up in misrepresentation what he lacks in practical deceit, and considers a neat and dexterous feat of jockeyship as a feather in his cap. Many old hands make it a rule of their conduct never to purchase horse-flesh of "a very particular friend." This, perhaps, is going a little too far, but the principle is good in the main. We feel it to be a duty incumbent on us, in this place, to notice the very questionable method which some gentlemen adopt of netting a pitiful hundred or two, at the expence of their less acute countrymen. They purchase a few broken-down hunters, and, after giving them a run at grass, mix them up with a small proportion of genuine cattle, and offer them for sale, with high-sounding names and forged pedigrees, as a part of their stud, which, through some fortuitous circumstance, they are reluctantly compelled to drop. It is no uncommon thing for good hunters to be sold without warranties, so that suspicion is seldom aroused—the *cat's meat* fetches a respectable price, and the jockey gentleman runs no risk of being obliged to refund.

Leggers-in. Under this denomination may be classed all the principal dealers who frequent the Repositories. The practice which has given birth to this appellation is this:—When a promising horse is submitted for sale by auction, dealers who wish to purchase him covey together in a corner, and, after settling the utmost extent of the money it is advisable to offer, commission one from among them to step forward and bid to that amount, while the rest all stand mute. When the lot is knocked down, the *leggers-in* form a circle, and one offers a shilling to each of the others, provided he may be allowed to take the horse at the auction price. The next person may accept the shilling (or whatever happens to be bid by the dealer preceding him), and stand out, or make an advance, and so on round the circle, until sometimes the money given away in this manner amounts to a guinea or two each. This is a most advantageous plan for the trade; and few dealers of note leave a Repository, without earning something considerable by *legging-in*. Many persons purchase horses at Repositories after they have been knocked down to a dealer, by giving him a trifling advance on the amount of the auction money. The dealer, in such cases, oftentimes takes the responsibility of the warranty on himself, which is a most material object, inasmuch as any warranted horse that is purchased at the hammer must be returned, if unsound, in the afternoon of the day ensuing the sale. A horse which is warranted by a dealer may, of course, be returned, if decidedly unsound, within any reasonable time after he is purchased.

We shall now conclude our protracted *exposé* of the tricks of the jockies, both high and low, with a few words of advice to purchasers. If either of our readers is, or hereafter may be, in want of a horse, let him prefer the dealer of respectability (smile not, my masters, there are many such in London, notwithstanding the truths we have told) to the itinerant *coper*, or *jockey gentleman*. There are also several commission stables in our *public streets*, which deservedly enjoy repute. We have gentlemen jockies too, whom perhaps it might be deemed invidious to particularize, and we shall therefore refrain from nominating individuals. The secrets we have divulged will convince every body that there are pernicious dregs in the trade, but the evil is in some measure balanced by the body of respectable persons who thrive and live in good estimation as horse dealers. To put things at the worst, if a man purchases a horse with a warranty, of a regularly established dealer, he can at any time compel him to act fairly, even if he should so far forget his own interest as to be otherwise inclined. A vagabond's warranty and word are equally worthless, yet by some strange infatuation gentlemen often deal with a set of well-dressed, plausible rascals, without "a local habitation or a name," rather than the fixed and well-known tradesman, whose livelihood depends upon his credit with his local connexions, and his dwelling in the centre of his patrons and customers. He will never decamp or act dishonestly for the value of a horse, even if it were merely for his own advantage—his future prospects entirely depend on his present behaviour, and he will seldom shew the least symptom of reluctance to submit a horse which he avows to be sound, to the inspection of a veterinary practitioner, on the part of the purchaser.*

C.

*The usual fee to a veterinary surgeon for examining a horse, is half-a-guinea; and it is often agreed by and between the dealer and vendee, that if the animal is returned as unsound, the former shall pay the inspector's fee.

Poachers

A desperate affray took place in the coverts of Sir Henry Bunbury, Bart. at Mildenhall, on Saturday night, Nov. 23. The gamekeepers being alarmed by the discharge of guns, went out in a party of seven, and were attacked by a body of 15 or 20 poachers, who beat them very severely, and fired upon them with the muzzles of the guns so close as to set fire to the clothes of two of them; but fortunately none of them were dangerously injured, though one was shot in the arm, another in the hand, and a third was also wounded. Two of the keepers fired in their defence, and one of the depredators fell to the ground, where he lay groaning loudly, till the weaker party were forced to fly for assistance, and on their return, the villains were gone, and had carried off their wounded companion, who had evidently bled most profusely.

On the 16th instant, Mr. W. Toomer, one of the New Forest keepers, accompanied by his assistant, had a serious brush with four deer stealers, and the assistant was severely hurt by blows on the head.

On the 30th October, John Watts, Earl Craven's keeper, at Combe Abbey, was nearly killed in an affray with two desperate poachers, named Smith and Porters, who have since been taken in London.

Some informers have lately been busily employed in Sussex, laying informations against those who sport without a certificate.

A Specimen of Some Modern Gamekeepers

Honourable mention having been made some months since in the *Sporting Magazine* of John Jenkins, a gamekeeper of the old school, singularly qualified for the office, and inflexibly true to his trust, I have to solicit your insertion in your next number, Mr. Editor, of what goes to the composition of many a gamekeeper of the present day.

AN OBSERVER

A young fellow, of an enterprising spirit, the son of some farmer whose returns have enabled him but ill to requite those who laboured for him, disgusted with the poverty of the prospect at home, longs to be more acquainted with what he has but indistinctly heard of, and *"bonà fide"* to see the world. In addition to this impatience for new scenes, certain other motives influence, and in a manner urge him at times, to the prosecution of his designs. He may have contracted debts, which, however apparently insignificant, it may not be in his power to liquidate. He may have been detected in nocturnal spoliation of game on the neighbouring manors (no uncommon "*freak,*" as they call it, among some of the junior yeomanry). He may have committed himself beyond parochial sufferance by having had a multiplicity of sweethearts, and having given to each of them a similar proof of his regard. Without much ado, therefore, he flies his country, and proceeds for the grand mart direct, where, after straining his eyes in amazement at the glare and splendour of the metropolis, and after wearing out his welcome at the house of some fiftieth cousin, he finds himself in a dilemma he little dreamed of before he quitted the country. Projects on projects in consequence fill his head; in the revolution of which, he longs to gratify a secret amibtion, which 'whilom' fired his mind whilst running his eye along the barrel of his gun as a "boy-bird-keeper on his native plains." In his suspense, he throws his agricultural knowledge into the scale, which so preponderates as to make his scruples kick the beam. And now he provides himself with a fustian jacket, and the usual requisites to a fowling costume. Thus equipped, he beats the rounds from register office to register office, till, as a '*dernier resort,*' he ventures his last few shillings, and makes known his wants in some widely circulating paper, by an advertisement to nearly the following effect:—

> Wants a place as bailiff and gamekeeper, a stout healthy young man from the country—as bred in the farming line, is well

acquainted with ploughing, sowing, drilling, hoeing, reaping, mowing, sheafing, stitching, hedging, ditching, thrashing, plashing, breeding, feeding, and whatever is required in husbandry both old and new—is an excellent shot—understands the management and breaking of sporting dogs—wages not so much an object as a permanent situation.

We will now suppose him in the service of some nobleman or opulent gentleman, if not in consequence of this flashy advertisement, at least in consequence of such appropriate answers as he gave to the interrogatories put to him prior to his initiation; and it seldom happens but that any one similarly situated feels the importance of the change. A perfect revolution, therefore, is commonly effected in the farming interest of such establishment, to the exclusion of old customs, old servants, old everything, and to the introduction of what is reconcileable to the master only from the promise of incalculable improvement and benefit in reversion. To the preservation of the game, and to the punishment of trespassers, the same principles and motives operate on the master and man, with this difference however very commonly, that the man assumes and exercises more power than he can justify, and that his invariable attention to what is conducive to his pleasure, takes from the requisite attendance on his other duties. And what is the result of this, as some may call it, elaborate account of things? why, that the estate, once a noble estate, possibly in the lapse of three or four years is reduced to less than one half of its former capacity of production, and in the room of that good understanding between all ranks, which is the cement of society, implacable animosities are raised between the extensive land owner and the surrounding neighbourhood.

Part VI

The Passing of Youth

Death of the Dowager Marchioness of Salisbury

A much greater sensation has been occasioned by the manner in which the late Dowager Marchioness of Salisbury came by her death, than if her decease has followed the common course of nature; for she was full of years, and her earthly pilgrimage had extended far beyond the period allotted to man: and though regret might have mingled with the announcement that she had been "gathered to her fathers," we should have been spared the pain of recording the horrible catastrophe which put a period to her existence.

In pursuance of her usual custom of passing the Christmas with her son, the Marchioness left town on the 26th of November for Hatfield House, the magnificent mansion of the Marquis of Salisbury, and took possession of the suite of apartments in the West wing which she had occupied, as a temporary summer and winter residence, ever since the death of her husband, the late Marquis. Although Her Ladyship was labouring under some of those concomitants even of a green old age, she was hale and vigorous considering, her advanced period of life—(she was in her 86th year)—and on her late visit to the scene of her early pleasures she exhibited a flow of spirits which surprised those who were best acquainted with her usual cheerfulness. It appears that on the afternoon of Friday the 27th, the day after her arrival, she retired a short time before dinner to her dressing-room to write a note, and her attendant left her with three lighted candles on the table. Whether the flame came in contact with her cap, or whether a spark from the fire ignited her dress, cannot be ascertained, as nobody saw her alive after her attendant left her. The Marquis, on the alarm being given, made the most strenuous efforts to rescue her from her awful situation, but, on attempting to enter the room, he was driven back by the dense smoke and flame which issued from the burning chamber. Every exertion to save her was in vain: she perished in the fiery furnace, and the venerable Lady found a tomb amid the mouldering ruins of the palace over which she had presided for more than half a century. The whole of the West wing was totally destroyed, and in a few hours nothing but a blackened shell remained to tell what it once had been. The fire was confined to that part of the mansion, having happily, and by uncommon exertions, been subdued by twelve o'clock the same night.

The Marchioness was in early life a devotee at the shrine of Diana,

and if she was not the founder of the Hatfield Hunt, she presided for a long series of years over the destinies of that Pack, now under the management of Mr. Delme Radcliffe, under the appellation of the Hertfordshire Hounds: and this she continued up to her 70th year; when, with a spirit unsubdued by advanced life, she was heard to say, if she could not hunt a pack of fox-hounds, she was still able to follow the harriers. Her Ladyship's ardour in the chase was excessive; and a friend who sits at our elbow assures us that he was a constant attendant of the Hunt for eighteen successive years, during which she was seldom absent a day from the covert side. She was an elegant and accomplished horsewoman, and rode with as much intrepidity as judgment: no day was too long for her, and she was ever anxious to give good sport to the field, which was generally well attended. Her affability to all was proverbial; and, in short, as our friend says, "she *was* a Lady" in every sense of the word; and, during her reign, Hatfield House was remarkable for its character of hospitality, maintained with the greatest splendour. The family were honored with the visits of George III and Queen Charlotte, at the time when the late Marquis of Salisbury was Lord Chamberlain to His Majesty, with whom he was a great favorite.

To the last Her Ladyship scarcely ever omitted her daily ride into the Park on horseback, except when the weather would not permit, and then she went to the King's Riding House at Pimlico for an hour: and so highly did Her Ladyship stand in the estimation of the late King (George IV), that he caused an opening to be made into the interior of the Green Park, exactly facing her garden-gate, that she might have the exclusive privilege of enjoying her favorite exercise there undisturbed.

Hunting, however, was not the only sport to which the deceased Marchioness was attached, Archery and Coursing having been equally patronised by Her Ladyship. The very first volume of our work (in 1792) is embellished with a descriptive view of Archery at Hatfield Park by the Marchioness [see page 195], engraved by Cook from a painting by Corbold—that amusement having then been brought into fashion by some of the most illustrious in the land, at the head of whom Her Ladyship stood pre-eminent. In our 27th volume also (in 1805) is an Engraving, by Scott from the Younger Sartorius, of "Coursing at Hatfield" [see page 6], that delightful domain being thrown open to the public once a week during the season, beginning in November and ending in January. There was also "Bryant's Day," as it was called, Mr. B. being then the landlord of the Salisbury Arms Inn at Hatfield, and having been complimented by the Marchioness with one separate and distinct day of coursing, in order to invite his friends to the sport, and afterwards to dine at his house.

From the tottering state of the walls of his magnificent mansion the workmen could not safely remove the ruins in the interior till upwards of a week after the appalling event, and on the 13th of December some portions of the body were discovered—sufficient, however, to identify Her Ladyship—which were collected and deposited in a shell previously prepared for their reception. A Coroner's inquest was necessarily held, and a verdict of "Accidental Death" recorded. The funeral was strictly private, and her remains were deposited by the side of the late Marquis in the family vault of the Cecils in Hatfield Church, followed to the last receptacle of perishing mortality by the regrets of all ranks, and the lamentations of the poor to whom she was a liberal benefactor. . . .

Conclusion

Lady Salisbury's death in 1835 not only marked the end of a spectacular sporting life but symbolized the end of the youth of English sporting life in general—the end of an era rather than the death of sports. Her life of eighty-five years almost exactly spanned the first period in the history of modern sports. She saw fox-hunting take on a new form and character, and that was the sport with which she became identified. She also saw Thoroughbred racing, the team sport of cricket, and the cruel sport of pugilism become disciplined by authoritative rules as popular national sports. She died in the midst of the great age of coaching, and it survived her by only a decade. An equestrienne, the marchioness's life almost exactly coincided with the glorious age of equestrianism.

Lady Salisbury died unaware that her world was ending. Looking backwards we can find other symbols that it was. John Mytton, the notorious sporting "eccentric," as he was known in the prints, well known in the chase and on the turf, died a year before Lady Salisbury. In the year following her death, McAdam, the road engineer whose work contributed so much to the glory of the passing coaching age, and Mendoza, who helped make a "sweet science" of boxing, both died. In 1836 Surtees, or Nim South, gave up sporting journalism for the life of a fox-hunting country gentleman in County Durham. He continued to write his immortal sporting pieces and books; his recently created fictional cockney fox hunter, John Jorrocks, would delight the reading public for some years to come. Another famous sportsman would die in 1843. This was Nimrod, who glorified in his writings the chase, the turf, and the road. Pierce Egan had passed his meridian by the late 1820s, when his favorite sport of boxing entered into a period of decline that would last for a generation. Just as Nimrod's prominence overlapped Egan's, so Nimrod's equestrian sports were without rival for preeminence after boxing began to decline and before mass spectator team sports bloomed.

Another chronological coincidence was that boxing's decline overlapped the growing influence of Evangelicals and middle-class Nonconformists, particularly Methodists, upon the national conscience. The decline of pugilism was in part owing to a growing meliorative influence, often religious in origin, upon English life, which contributed to the strengthening moral fervor that abhorred the inhumanity

of man to man and to animals. The cruel or bloody sports were increasingly under attack in the second quarter of the nineteenth century by people whom Egan called Puritans. Ultimately the bloody animal sports fell under statutory ban. Competitive sports such as cricket or pedestrianism were of a different character, as was horse racing, and there was no systematic attack upon them, or upon fox-hunting or steeplechasing, even though such sports occasioned accidents and sometimes death.

The youth of sports ended not simply because the persons associated with it were passing from the scene, some by death and others by retirement from active participation. Deeper, more subtle changes were taking place in England's social and political life, and these changes affected and altered the character of sports. Some of them had been at work for decades, but less vigorously. By the end of the Napoleonic Wars they were more visible as the nation settled into peacetime ways, and as the cumulative effects of earlier changes, accelerated during the wars, were felt. The steam engine as a source of power was long known. Its direct consequences were power-driven machinery, factories and mills, and urban communities growing up around them, changing the face of England. The application of steam power to transportation produced the railroad. By the 1830s the building of a railway network throughout the nation was well begun.

The effect of all these changes upon sporting life was predictable long before it was so obvious that few could fail to recognize it. Yet people were slow or reluctant to think from obvious cause to forseeable result. Among sporting journalists, for example, only Surtees seemed concerned with the potential of the railroad's cutting through the countryside to damage or, he feared, even destroy the equestrian sporting life he loved. Surtees was too gloomy in thinking about the future of fox-hunting in the new environment. That rural sport accommodated itself to the physical changes brought by railroad rights of way. In the end, all sports benefitted from the increased mobility of people. When William Hazlitt went from London to the boxing match between Hickman and Neate near Newbury in 1821, he had to spend a day behind the horses going out, the night before and the night after the match in Newbury, and another day on the road back to London. With the coming of the railroad, a racing fan could travel from Paddington Station to Newbury, taking lunch on the train, and return after the races in time for dinner in London.

Steam travel also changed the sporting life in indirect but profound ways. It enabled industrial towns to grow rapidly and to continue to grow as industry expanded in response to the growth of domestic and worldwide markets brought closer by steam transport. London, with a population of one million in 1801, doubled in population by mid-century and doubled again in the last half of the century. The great English cities—Birmingham, Liverpool, Manchester, Leeds, Bristol, Sheffield, to name only the better known—and many smaller ones that had grown out of former rural villages or trading centers, were giving to the nation an urban character. The census of 1851 revealed the new social truth that half the population was urban; by 1901 it was 75 percent urban, and some rural counties had lost population. The landed interest, previously England's greatest single national interest, was losing its front rank in the nation's economic life, and was already perceptibly less preeminent in social and political life.

The Great Exhibition of 1851 in the Crystal Palace in Hyde Park forecast the future while honoring the present machine age and the past technical achievements which had made it possible. Victorian England was patting herself on the back for her material supremacy; the exhibitions featured technology, machines, and inventions; the arts and culture hardly counted, except for the industrial arts. And the railroads brought millions of provincials into London to share in the public pride of a self-confident, urbanized, industrialized England.

Of course, countless villages and small towns remained, and still exist. But the old village life was losing some of its particular manifestations. Among these were ritualistic, traditional village activities and, more to the point here, village or rural sports and recreations. Books about these had to be historical, not descriptions of the current scene. If village cricket remains on Saturday or Sunday afternoons, it is nevertheless enveloped in nostalgia; the players have already devoured the sports pages telling of big-time matches, county cricket, or the international test matches. The same is true of soccer and rugby. When villages try to continue or revive traditional sports and recreations, nostalgia and self-consciousness hang heavy over the scene.

If the rural sporting ethos was changing into attentiveness to national and professional sports in the early nineteenth century, this was only the other side of the coin from the new urban sporting ethos. As the urban population burgeoned, the recreations of the urban population—factory, mill, and office workers—demanded attention. Free Saturday afternoons had to be occupied and sports adapted to the new opportunities and the new needs. Public transportation was available to bring people to sporting events, not only the railroads to move urban people and rural sports fans to the new mass spectator events, but inner-city transport to carry urban people across the city in trains and later motorized busses, and in London the underground system.

Conclusion 205

Thus, the age of equestrian sporting preeminence ended during the age of steam even before the automobile and the bus arrived. The new mass spectator sports, organized just after the mid-nineteenth century, were urban sports, not village sports, held in great arenas, the homes of professional teams. Allegiances were to these, and village sports were overshadowed to the point of obscurity. At Wembley Stadium in London, the Cup Finals have become the "Coop" Finals to which thousands come by train or bus from Lancashire or Yorkshire to cheer their heroes and drink the London pubs dry while they fill the air with sporting songs and northern speech.

Lady Salisbury, John Mytton, Pierce Egan, Nimrod, or Surtees could have no vision of these vast changes. Pugilism, the equestrian sports, the village and rural sports—these were their sporting life. The closest thing to a mass spectator sport their age knew was a boxing match to which crowds traveled by foot, on horseback, or in a variety of horse-drawn vehicles, and then they went out into the open fields away from the cities, always apprehensive that some rural magistrate might disperse the unlawful assemblage. They didn't even deign to notice, nor did anyone else in their time, the polite sports of golf and tennis. Today the Fancy might be in the stands at Wimbledon or among the galleries at St. Andrews, perhaps reflecting upon the changes that time brings.

In our mature and aging years we look upon our happy youth and think things were better then. And so it is with sports. The youth of sports had about it a light-heartedness and spontaneity, a freshness, an absence of over-regulation, that appeal to our jaded minds and tired eyes.

Sources of Selections

All selections are from *The Sporting Magazine*. For the history of this periodical, see the Introduction.

THE SPORTING SCENE

Sporting Intelligence. 60 (Apr. 1822): 42-55.

THE EQUESTRIAN SPORTS

Riding to Hounds. 61 (Jan. 1823): 178-84.
On the Letters of Nimrod. 61 (Mar. 1823): 297-98.
Nim South's Southern Tour. 76 (June 1830): 98-109; (July 1830), pp. 197-208; (Aug. 1830), pp. 292-304.
Fox-Hunting—Leicestershire. 59 (Jan. 1822): 177-83.
Oxfordshire—Sir Thomas Mostyn's Country. 59 (Mar. 1822): 255-59.
Sporting Trifles. 7 (Jan. 1796): 176.
His Majesty's Stag-Hounds. 61 (Nov. 1822): 88-89.
Lord Derby's Stag-Hounds. 60 (Apr. 1822): 40-41.
A Brief Review of the Racing Season of 1828. 73 (Dec. 1828): 74-80.
Eclipse. 61 (Feb. 1823): 237-38.
Guy Stakes at Warwick. 77 (Mar. 1831): 302-03.

A MISCELLANY OF SPORTS

Pedestrianism, with a Sketch of the Life of Mr. Forster Powell. 1 (Oct. 1792): 7-11.
Pedestrianism. 61 (Oct. 1822): 50-51.
The Game at Golf. 72 (Aug. 1828): 291-93; 73 (Dec. 1828): 134-35.
Skating. 61 (Jan. 1823): 230-31.
Fish and Fishing. 61 (Dec. 1822): 153-56.
Billiards—The Dutch Baron. 14 (Apr. 1799): 3-5.
Pistol and Rifle Shooting. 72 (Aug. 1828): 303-05.
Archery. 68 (Sept. 1826): 378-79.
Royal Kentish Bowmen. 20 (Aug. 1802): 254-55.
A Town Besieged in Time of Peace. 75 (Apr. 1830): 369-71.
The Laws of Cricket. 2 (June 1793): 134-36.

Amazonian Cricket Match. 39 (Oct. 1811): 3-4.
On Throwing the Cricket Ball. 61 (Jan. 1823): 208-09, 226.
Cricket. 68 (Sept. 1826): 376-78.

THE BLOODY SPORTS

Billy the Rat-Killer. 61 (Oct. 1822): 50; (Nov. 1822): 103.
Bull-Baiting at Bristol. 59 (Mar. 1822): 271-75.
Vindication of Cocking. 61 (Mar. 1823): 298-99.
Fight between Crib and Molineux. 37 (Dec. 1810): 97-102.
A Fresh Challenge. 37 (Dec. 1810): 102
The [Second] Battle between Crib and Molineux. 39 (Oct. 1811): 20-24.
Sparring. 39 (Dec. 1811): 139.
Pugilism—Between Owen and Mendoza. 56 (July 1820): 174-77.
Wrestling. 68 (Sept. 1826): 379.
Shooting Parties. 63 (Jan. 1824): 227.
Shooting. 61 (Jan. 1823): 226.
Dreadful Accident on Chester Race Course. 60 (May 1822): 97-99.
Sporting Accidents. 61 (Jan. 1823): 226-27.
On Due Discrimination between Barbarous and Fair Sporting. 60 (Apr. 1822): 38-40.
On Mr. Martin's Bill for Animal Protection. 61 (Oct. 1822): 28-31.

THE MARGINS OF SPORTS

May in London. 32 (May 1808): 86-87.
Horse-Dealing in London. 60 (May 1822): 69-74; (June 1822): 117-20.
Poachers. 61 (Nov. 1822): 103.
A Specimen of Some Modern Gamekeepers. 61 (Nov. 1822): 65-66.

THE PASSING OF YOUTH

Death of the Dowager Marchioness of Salisbury. 87 (Jan. 1836): 258-61.

A Note on the Illustrations

Just as the rising enthusiasm for sports in late eighteenth-century England generated sports journalism, so too it produced a crowd of genre painters, artists who portrayed the sporting life of their time. Their work became widely known and readily available, even to persons of modest means, through the medium of line engraving, as individual prints suitable for framing and as illustrations in books and periodicals. Athletes, sporting scenes (especially hunting), and animals (horses and dogs, in particular) were the favored subjects.

These subjects had occasionally interested painters and sculptors as far back as ancient times, but through the centuries the tense and brutal realism of "The Discus Thrower" or "The Boxer" had become conventionalized and formalized. It was primarily George T. Stubbs (1724-1806) who broke with the mannerism of traditional sporting art. Informed by study of animal anatomy, Stubbs inaugurated a new era of realism in sporting art, and others followed him, encouraged by the growing public interest in the genre. When Stubbs died, John N. Sartorius (the Younger, 1759-1828) was flourishing, Henry Alken, Sr. (1785-1851) was a young painter, and John F. Herring (1795-1865) and F. C. Turner (1795-1846) were but lads. These outstanding sporting artists, along with many who were less well known, made sporting paintings and prints perhaps the most widely known of the fine arts of their period.

If the leading characteristic of English sporting art was realism in the depiction of humans and animals, there was also an element of romanticism, for sporting scenes were often laid amidst or against the background of romantic landscapes. It seems appropriate that in the greatest age of English sporting art, Constable and Landseer were also flourishing.

The Sporting Magazine thrived in this same period, its pages reflecting not only the sporting life but also the sporting art of the times. Each issue contained a frontispiece and numerous other engravings taken from the work of leading sporting artists. Portraits of horses were most numerous, but dogs, game birds and fish, well known sportsmen, and sporting scenes from exotic lands were frequent subjects. Even animals and scenes from mythology and literature appeared from time to time. Occasional reviews of sporting art exhibits also appeared.

A Note on the Illustrations 209

All the illustrations in this book are taken from *The Sporting Magazine*. They do not always accompany the article with which they originally appeared, however. I hope readers will forgive this liberty. In the following list, artists' and engravers' names are given when they could be determined.

SOURCES

Jacket: "View of Thornville Park." 29 (Nov. 1806): 89.
Frontispiece: "A Fox-Hunting Breakfast." Painting by Samuel Howitt; engraving by J. Scott. 11 (Oct./Mar. 1796-1797): frontispiece.
p. viii: Title page of Volume 1 (Oct. 1792-Mar. 1793). Engraving by Cook.
p. 6: "Coursing at Hatfield." Painting by the Younger Sartorius; engraving by Scott. 27 (Dec. 1805): 107.
p. 11: "The Way we should go." Painting by B. Herring; engraving by W. Backshell. 123 (May 1854): 426.
p. 12: "Skittles." Samuel Howitt. 18 (June 1801): 137.
p. 14: "Cudgel-Playing." Samuel Howitt. 15 (Oct. 1799): 41.
p. 21: John Wheble. Drawing by J. Jackson; engraving by Fry. 58 (May 1821): 61.
p. 27: "Partridge-Shooting." Painting by Corbould; engraving by Cook. 2 (Aug. 1793): 299.
p. 31: "Death of the Fox." Painting by Sawrey Gilpin; engraving by T. Cook. 2 (May 1793): 92.
p. 38: "The Chaise Match, Run at Newmarket Heath, on Wednesday the 29th of August, 1750." Drawing by James Seymour; engraving by J. Scott. 18 (June 1801): 115.
p. 40: "Steeple Chase in Beds." Sketch by J. A. Mitchell. 76 (May 1830): 48.
p. 42: "Maniac." Painting by G. H. Laporte; engraving by J. Scott. 67 (Jan. 1826): 116.
p. 44: "Pigeon Shooting at the Warren House, Billingbear, Berks." Painting by Corbould; engraving by Cook. 1 (Feb. 1793): 251.
p. 47: "Poacher Detected." From a sketch by Abraham Cooper. 64 (Apr. 1824): 40.
p. 51: "The Whipper-In." Painting by Abraham Cooper; engraving by J. R. Scott. 76 (July 1830): 196.
p. 56: "A Thorough-bred One Falling at His Fence." Painting by G. H. Laporte; engraving by I. Romney. 79 (Dec. 1831): 160.
p. 59: Painting by F. C. Turner; engraving by J. Engleheart. 85 (Nov. 1834-Apr. 1835): title page.

p. 63: "Horse & Rider, Both Shy." Painting by Thomas Woodward; engraving by J. Webb. 68 (June 1826): 172.

p. 68: "Stag at Bay." Engraving by Cook. 3 (Oct. 1793): 3.

p. 72: "Hoik In, There!" Painting by Henry Alken; engraving by J. H. Engleheart. 122 (Nov. 1853): 360.

p. 75: "Death of the Fox." Samuel Howitt. 39 (Feb. 1812): 233.

p. 80: "Who-Whoop." Painting by F. C. Turner; engraving by I. Romney. 79 (Feb. 1832): 260.

p. 85: "His Majesty [George III] going out with his Stag Hounds on Windsor Forest." Painting by Stothard; engraving by Cook. 1 (Oct. 1792–Mar. 1793): frontispiece.

p. 87: Engraving by J. Scott. 62 (Apr.–Sept. 1823): title page.

p. 89: "Dead Heat Between Lanercost & Bee's Wing." Painting by R. Harrington; engraving by J. Engleheart. 99 (Apr. 1842): 428.

p. 91: "The Oatland Stakes at Ascot, June 1791." Painting by Corbould; engraving by Cook. 2 (Apr. 1793): 52.

p. 94: "Eclipse, with his Jockey, Jack Oakley, going over the Beacon Course." Painting by J. N. Sartorius the Elder; engraving by J. Webb. 66 (June 1825): 140.

p. 97: "The Recluse Angler." Self-portrait by Eckstein; engraving by William Nicholls. 29 (Jan. 1807): 167.

p. 102: "Female Running Match" ("Rural Sports"). Samuel Howitt. 16 (Sept. 1800): 252.

p. 108: "Skaiting [sic] at Hyde Park." 21 (Mar. 1803): 336.

p. 110: "Perch Fishing Party." 24 (May 1804): 93.

p. 112: "Sussex Carp." Painting by Abraham Cooper; engraving by W. Raddon. 68 (June 1826): 180.

p. 114: "Billiards." Painting by R. W. Satchwell; engraving by J. Scott. 13 (Nov. 1798): 63.

p. 116: "Woodcock Shooting." Painting by Abraham Cooper; engraving by Webb. 64 (Sept. 1824): 319.

p. 118: "Fairlop Oak with a Meeting of the Hainault Forresters." Engraving by T. Cook. 3 (Jan. 1794): 167.

p. 128: "Grand Cricket Match, played in Lord's Ground, Mary-le-bone, on June 20 & following day between the Earl's of Winchelsea & Darnley for 1000 Guineas." Engraving by Cook. 2 (June 1793): 134.

p. 132: Designed and etched by Wm. Smith. 80 (May–Sept. 1832): title page.

p. 135: "Game Cocks." Painting by the Younger Marshall; engraving by I. Romney. 79 (Dec. 1831): 68.

p. 139: "Lord Camelford's Dog, Trusty, 'a celebrated fighting dog.'"

Painting by H. B. Chalon; engraving by H. R. Cook. 29 (Dec. 1806): 103.

p. 143: "Cock Pit Royal, 1796." Samuel Howitt. 9 (Dec. 1796): 158.

p. 148: [Tom] Molineux and [Tom] Cribb. Drawn by J. Emery. 37 (Jan. 1811): 141; (Mar. 1811): 281.

p. 162: "Cornish Wrestling." 15 (Feb. 1800): 264.

p. 165: "Evening, or the Sportsman's Return." Painting by George Morland; engraving by W. Nichol. 29 (Nov. 1806): 51.

p. 168: "Hornpipe leaping over Pepperpot his Rider and the Farmer's Son at Lincoln Races, Friday the 8th Septr. 1797." Painting by Samuel Howitt; engraving by J. Scott. 11 (Nov. 1797): 94.

p. 172: "Bear Baiting." 5 (Jan. 1795): 204.

p. 175: "Gin and Bitters." Painting by James Bateman; engraving by H. Beckwith. 99 (Jan. 1842): 249.

p. 179: "Smithfield Market." Painting by Pye. 20 (Apr.–Sept. 1802): frontispiece.

p. 186: "The Spicey Screw." Painting by F. C. Turner; engraving by J. H. Engleheart. 95 (Feb. 1840): 324.

p. 192: "The Poacher." Painting by W. Kidd; engraving by T. Westley. 92 (Aug. 1838): 281.

p. 195: "Archery at Hatfield by the Marchioness of Salisbury & &." Painting by Corbould; engraving by Cook. 1 (Oct. 1792): 54.

p. 198: "The Accomplished Sportswoman." Engraving by Cook. 4 (June 1794): 154.

p. 202: "Hold Hard, There!" Painting by Henry Alken; engraving by J. H. Engleheart. 126 (Nov. 1855): 380.

p. 205: Designed and engraved by J. Scott. 16 (Apr.–Nov. 1800): title page.

p. 216: Engraving by J. Scott. 11 (Oct. 1796–Mar. 1797): title page.

Notes

INTRODUCTION

1. Pierce Egan the elder (1772-1849) may have been chronologically the first of the modern type of sporting journalists. He was mainly interested in London sports, especially boxing, though, like Badcock, he knew something of equestrian sports. Like Damon Runyon a century later, Egan was deeply interested in the people who made up the sporting world. Jonathan Badcock, a contemporary, was as knowledgeable of sports as Egan, and was a bitter rival for public attention, but was not so engaging a person.

2. Pierce Egan, *Boxiana* (London, 1818), 1: 10-11. Jonathan Badcock, *Sketches from the Fancy: Or True Sportsman's Guide* [1826] (Barre, Mass.: Imprint Society, 1972), pp. 7, 10, 12.

3. Egan, *Boxiana*, 2: 13. The London *Times*, which devoted many columns to the imperial and royal visit, did not mention this event. The *Times* did not yet have a regular sports column, let alone a sports page.

4. In 1829 Egan named twenty-nine boxers who kept taverns, most of them in London. *New Series of Boxiana* 2 (1829): 722. (When combined with the three volumes of *Boxiana*, this is number 5 in the set.) On Jackson's retirement, see J. C. Reid, *Bucks and Bruisers: Pierce Egan and Regency England* (London, 1971), p. 136.

5. Polo was a later import from India; the first match of record in England was in 1871.

6. Quoted in Samuel Smiles, *George Moore, Merchant and Philanthropist* 2nd ed. (London, 1878), p. 28, n. 1.

7. Reid, *Bucks and Bruisers*, p. 39.

8. Egan, *Boxiana*, 5: iv.

9. Dennis Prestidge, *Tom Cribb at Thistleton Gap* (Melton Mowbray, England, 1971); Reid, *Bucks and Bruisers*, p. 13; Egan *Boxiana*, 1: 401-20; London *Times*, September 28 and 30, 1811.

10. All of Hazlitt's pieces in *The New Monthly* were so signed. It does not indicate that he was ashamed of his authorship of these sporting pieces. For the provenance of the article, see Stewart C. Wilcox, *Hazlitt in the Workshop: The Manuscript of "The Fight"* (Baltimore, 1943).

11. There is a complete run of *The Sporting Magazine* in the excellent turf library at Keeneland Race Course, Lexington, Kentucky. The run comprises 156 volumes: October 1792 through December 1870. I am grateful to the Keeneland Association for providing access to their library, and to Mrs. Amelia Buckley, former librarian, and Ms. Doris Waren, now librarian, for making it so easy and pelasant to work in the Keeneland Library. In my list of happy libraries, it stands ahead of the runner-up, the Kew Gardens Library in London, England.

Another volume is in the set at Keeneland, *Index of Engravings with the Names of the Artists in the Sporting Magazine* (London, 1892). The *Index* contains as introduction a history of *The Sporting Magazine* written by Francis Charles Lawley (1825-1901), an Oxford graduate and a Fellow of All Souls who sat in the House of Commons and was private secretary to Gladstone. Later he became a journalist and reported on the American Civil War for the London *Times*. Returning to England, he wrote on sports for the *Daily Telegraph*.

Another complete run of *The Sporting Magazine* is in the Margaret I. King Library of the University of Kentucky, a bequest of the late William Arnold Hanger. This set, now available for use by researchers, had not been catalogued when I began my research.

12. *Index of Engravings*, p. 10.
13. Ibid., pp. 7-11; see also the obituary in *The Sporting Magazine* 58 (May 1821): 61-64; Donald C. Bryant, "A Note on Burke's Parliamentary Character, 1774," *Burke Newsletter* 5, no. 1 (Fall 1963): 237; Robert R. Rea, *The English Press in Politics, 1760-1774* (Lincoln, Neb., 1936), pp. 168, 202-10; and H. R. Fox Bourne, *English News Papers* (London, 1887), 1: 198-201.
14. *Sporting Magazine* 1 (1792): iv. Whebles's claim was not an empty boast. He was a pioneer in a new field of journalism.
15. Ibid., 59 (1822): 198, 177-78.
16. E. W. Bovill, *The England of Nimrod and Surtees, 1815-1854* (London, 1959), pp. 14-23 and *passim; Dictionary of National Biography, Supplement*, 1: 53; *Index of Engravings*, pp. 11-18.
17. R. S. Surtees, *Handley Cross* (London, 1951 [1845]), pp. 428-29.
18. Bovill, *England of Nimrod*, pp. 23-27 and *passim; Dictionary of National Biography* 55: 174.

THE SPORTING SCENE

1. McAdam (1756-1836), the famous road engineer from whose name the word macadamize derives.
2. Named for Robert Barclay Allardice (1779-1854), usually called Captain Barclay. He accomplished the feat, which consisted of walking one mile in each of one thousand consecutive hours. Barclay was considered an expert on the subject of physical conditioning of athletes.

THE EQUESTRIAN SPORTS

1. Here is the anticipation of the writer's fully developed fictional character, John Jorrocks.
2. Hugo Meynell of Quorndon Hall, Leicestershire, who hunted the Quorn country from 1753 to 1800, established the fame of the Quorn hunt. Perhaps his is the greatest name in the history of fox hunting, for he gave form to the sport.
3. Bart., M. P., 1776-1831. Not a "backwoodsman" like John Peel, Sir Thomas belonged to the upper gentry, though in the House of Commons he was a backbencher. He sat for the county of Flint, as his ancestors had done for generations. He maintained a pack of fox-hounds in Oxfordshire for many years, and a house in St. Jameses, London, where he died.
4. Née Lady Emily Mary Hill, daughter of the Irish Earl of Downshire. See her obituary in *The Sporting Magazine*, pp. 197-200, above.
5. Later George IV, 1820-1830. On the race course as in the field, the prince's reputation as a sportsman was stained.
6. Duke of Cumberland (1721-1765), third son of George II.
7. Nimrod's *The Life of John Mytton* (London, 1835), not one of his better works, describes the remarkable career of this amazing fox-hunter, who died in 1834. The turf was only Mytton's secondary interest. *The Sporting Magazine* printed an unusually long obituary, or memoir, of him; see vol. 84 (May 1834): 3-8

A MISCELLANY OF SPORTS

1. The correct spelling of Powell's first name is Foster, as later in this article. His dates were 1734-1793. As so often in the walking or running sports, records were made only to be broken. Thus Captain Barclay, in the next generation, outdid Powell.
2. If he travelled one hundred yards for each stone, he would have covered 5.68 miles.
3. That is, one mile in each of 1,000 successive half hours.
4. As of June 1979, the world record for the 3,000-metre race was 4:04.06. The

distance is 218.64 metres less than two miles. (The 3,000-metre event was not held during the 1980 Winter Olympics.) Considering training, skates, and the condition of the ice, the 1823 skater could be proud of himself.

5. Cotton (1630–1686), poet, sportsman, and friend of Walton, wrote the section on fly-fishing which was added to the fifth edition (1676) of Walton's *The Compleat Angler*.

6. John Gay (1685–1732), known primarily as author of *The Beggar's Opera*, also wrote a poem, "Rural Sports," on hunting and fishing.

7. Although this article is unsigned, a slightly altered version of it, with the past tense replacing the present tense, appeared in Pierce Egan's *Sporting Anecdotes, Original and Selected*, 2nd ed. (London, 1807), pp. 135–37. Thus the account appeared first in *The Sporting Magazine*, and the use there of the present tense substantiates its priority. In a letter to the Prime Minister, Sir Robert Peel, dated December 5, 1842, in which Egan begged for a government pension, he appended a list of his writings, and added, "I have also sent numerous Contributions to Magazines &c." Reid, *Bucks and Bruisers*, pp. 185–56, 231.

8. The bail is the bar laid across the tops of the stumps. A wicket consists of three stumps surmounted by two bails meeting at the middle stump.

9. Analogous to the line of the batter's box closest to the pitcher's mound in American baseball. The bowling crease and the return crease define the area of what in baseball is the pitcher's mound. Literally, a crease is a line. The batter must have one foot behind the popping crease.

10. A notch is the same as a run in baseball.

11. This is the rule discussed in George MacDonald Fraser, *Flashman's Lady* (New York, 1978), p. 9. Flashman wanted to retain the rule unchanged.

12. This account, somewhat altered, appeared in *Pierce Egan's Book of Sports and Mirror of Life* (London, 1847), p. 349. The first edition was 1832. If Egan contributed the original account to *The Sporting Magazine*, then he was simply reprinting his own article in the *Book of Sports*.

13. *The Sporting Magazine* was one up on the *Guinness Book of World Records* (New York, 1980), which does not yet list records for throwing a baseball or a cricket ball.

14. After a requisite number of balls have been bowled, a new over begins with bowling in the opposite direction by a different bowler.

THE BLOODY SPORTS

1. Whether this was Billy's record is not known. The record listed in *Guinness*, p. 80, is 500 rats killed by "Jenny Lind," a bull terrier, in an hour and thirty minutes in Liverpool, England, in 1853, but under what conditions is not stated. Jenny's average was 100 rats in eighteen minutes; whether Billy could have kept up his speed for another 400 rats is matter for speculation. Had he been able to, he would have needed just thirty-six minutes, two and one-half seconds to kill 500 rats.

2. Boxing matches, spontaneous or prearranged, usually accompanied bull or badger baiting. Bristol was notable for producing many good boxers.

3. The steel spur, hollowed to fit over the natural spur, and strapped on the cock's leg, is a fearsome weapon, sharp as a needle.

4. Big Ben Brain and Tom Johnson belonged to the generation of boxers in their prime in the 1780s, when Johnson held the title of champion.

5. The preferred spellings today are Cribb and Molyneux. Tom Cribb (1781–1849) reigned as champion of England from 1809 to 1822. This fight in 1810 was in defense of his title. His second fight with Molyneux the following year was his last fight, yet he was recognized as champion for eleven more years before he resigned the title. According to legend, Tom Molyneux was a Virginia slave who took his master's name and who won his freedom in 1804 by winning a fight in which his master had bet heavily on him. For the next five years, in New York mainly, he boxed under the tutelage and management of an English sailor, himself a boxer, who had deserted ship and stayed in America. The sailor encouraged him to go to London. His written record begins there in 1809,

when he sought out Bill Richmond, a tavern keeper who was the first American black to win fame in the English ring, though he never attained the championship. Cribb beat him in 1805. Richmond took Molyneux under his sponsorship and tutelage. After winning two fights, Molyneux obtained recognition and Cribb had finally to accept his challenge. This was that famous fight, marred because to some it appeared that Cribb had received the benefit of what today would be considered a long count, after which he was able to continue. The two accounts in *The Sporting Magazine*, of which this is one, do not tell of this incident.

6. Again the spelling seems to be a matter of choice, though moderns, copying one another or the *Dictionary of National Biography*, prefer Gully (1783-1863). He fought only three times in his career, yet earned recognition as champion. He declined the title. He had perhaps the most unusual career in the history of boxing. He was discovered in a debtor's prison by Henry Pearce (1777-1809), known as the "Game Chicken," who beat him in a spectacular fight in October 1805. This was Gully's first fight, yet he stood up to Pearce, the man who two months later would take the title from the champion and after that victory would fight no more. Retiring from boxing in 1807 after two victories in that year, Gully made room for himself at the top in the business world as a coal-mine owner. He sat in the House of Commons for five years in the 1830s. As an owner of a racing stable, he won, among other classic races, the Derby, three times.

7. "Gentleman" John Jackson (1769-1845) won the title in 1795 from Daniel Mendoza (see notes 19 and 21, below). Immediately thereafter he quit the ring and set himself up as a boxing instructor to young gentlemen. Lord Byron in his *Hints from Horace* wrote that men "must go to Jackson ere they dare to box." Boxers, either active or retired, served as seconds or referees in boxing matches.

8. Under the prevailing Broughton rules, and until the Marquis of Queensberry rules, grappling was permitted. Rounds were of uneven length, ending when a contestant was knocked down, fell, or was thrown down. The interval between rounds was thirty seconds. Except for sparring exhibitions, bare knuckles prevailed until the Queensberry rules prescribed padded gloves.

9. John Liston, d. 1846, a popular actor.

10. Cribb's personal affairs precluded the May bout, and it was finally arranged for September 28, 1811.

11. Ward and Gibbons, like the other two, were past their prime as front-rank boxers.

12. He was actually five feet nine inches tall.

13. On later examination, the surgeon announced that Molyneux was in "a very dangerous state," with a fractured jaw and two broken ribs. See *Sporting Magazine* 39 (Oct. 1811): 19.

14. A tough neighborhood just off Charing Cross Road.

15. Cribb was a coal merchant.

16. See "A Miscellany of Sports," note 1, above.

17. The Fives Court (fives was a type of handball) in St. Martin's Street, Leicester Fields, London, was a yard, enclosed by houses and walls, where a boxing stage was erected for exhibitions. The boxers wore gloves. Admission was three shillings per head and the take went as a purse to the announced beneficiary, often a boxer lately defeated or in need, for whom the exhibition was held. The fraternity of boxers gave their efforts generously, and used the exhibitions as opportunities to display their skills. The size of the crowd depended on the popularity of the beneficiary or the depth of sympathy for him.

18. James Power (1790-1813), a skillful boxer in demand for sparring exhibitions. Too light to be a serious contender for the first rank among boxers, he damaged his health by high living and died of consumption.

19. Daniel Mendoza (1764-1836), a native of London's East End, was famous as a "scientific" boxer. He was recognized as champion from 1791 to 1795. After losing the title to "Gentleman" Jackson, he conducted a boxing school, like his conqueror, and moved in respectable circles in London, always prominent among the sporting crowd

amidst the ups and downs of his fortunes. Tom Owen (b. 1768), the Fighting Oilman, never attained the championship, but he was a prominent contender and beat some good men. He claimed the title in 1796 after beating William Hooper, the Tinman, but the claim was not recognized. He fought more frequently than most ranking boxers. Perhaps his chief claim to fame was his invention of the dumbbell.

20. The Puglistic Society, when organized six years earlier, tried to serve boxing as the Marylebone Cricket Club served cricket. One of the organizers was "Gentleman" John Jackson, in whose rooms in Bond Street the founders gathered.

21. Mendoza was discovered, so to speak, by "Gentleman" Richard Humphries. Bad feeling arose between them, to the discredit of Humphries more than Mendoza, and it stained their boxing matches.

22. "Tossing his hat in the ring" was a defiant ceremony performed by a boxer before entering the ring. Politicians accouncing their candidacies to an expectant (or bored) public only imitate, figuratively speaking, boxers of the bare-knuckle era. All of the seconds mentioned here had been well known as pugilists.

23. The scratch was a mark in the center of the ring. If a boxer could not make it to the mark unaided, he was declared beaten, or "not up to scratch."

24. So long as Owen did not strike, bite, gouge, or kick Mendoza in this situation, he was within the rules.

25. Sometimes spelled knacker: a person who bought worn-out horses and slaughtered them for their commercial products, such as glue.

26. Such as were the police at this time, before the establishment of the metropolitan police a few years later.

27. 3 Geo. IV, c. 71.

28. The eighth earl (1759-1839). A liberal when young, he was much less the reformer in his late years.

29. Sir George O'Brien Wyndham, third Earl of Egremont (1751-1837), was a noted stock breeder. The wording exaggerates his parliamentary influence.

30. As Lord Chancellor, the first Earl of Eldon (1751-1828) was the "keeper of the king's conscience," a reference to the time before the Reformation when every Lord Chancellor was an ecclesiastic. Lord Eldon, who opposed the bill, had no interest in this kind of measure, but the time had long since passed when a Lord Chancellor felt obliged to act as he thought the king's conscience would direct.

31. As Lord Chancellor from 1778 to 1792, Edward, first Baron Thurlow (1731-1806), upheld the legislative supremacy of the Imperial Parliament over the American colonies and opposed reforms in the administration of Ireland. In general he held to a high view of the royal prerogative at a time when some remaining prerogative powers were being challenged. Thus he was generally in the position of opposing change.

www.ingramcontent.com/pod-product-compliance
Lightning Source LLC
Chambersburg PA
CBHW022059160426
43198CB00008B/281